F

A FIRESIDE BOOK

PUBLISHED BY SIMON & SCHUSTER INC.

NEW YORK • LONDON • TORONTO • SYDNEY • TOKYO

HEAVEN IS A PLAYGROUND

RICK TELANDER

Simon & Schuster Building
Rockefeller Center
1230 Avenue of the Americas
New York, New York 10020

FIRESIDE and colophon are registered trademarks
of Simon & Schuster Inc.

Designed by SNAP · HAUS GRAPHICS
Manufactured in the United States of America

1 3 5 7 9 10 8 6 4 2   Pbk.

Library of Congress Cataloging in Publication Data

Telander, Rick.
Heaven is a playground.

A Fireside Sports Classic
A Fireside Book.
1. Basketball—New York (N.Y.) 2. Afro-American
basketball players—New York (N.Y.)—Case studies.
3. Playgrounds—New York (N.Y.) I. Title. III. Series.
GV885.73.N4T44 1988   796.32'3'09747   88-4600

ISBN 0-671-66650-9 Pbk.

To Robert Van Sant, an inspiration

"It is not only possible to say a great deal in praise of play; it is really possible to say the highest things in praise of it. It might reasonably be maintained that the true object of all human life is play. Earth is a taskgarden; heaven is a playground."

—G.K. Chesterton

CONTENTS

INTRODUCTION

"The only thing in this country that blacks really dominate, except poverty," says coach Al McGuire of Marquette, "is basketball."

We all know it by now. Basketball is *the* black man's game. Twenty-seven of the thirty-four college consensus All-Americans since 1971 have been black. Fourteen of the last fifteen Most Valuable Players in the NBA have been black. Lenny Wilkens, former coach of the Portland Trailblazers, even admits that the old and infamous "quota system" has been forced to work in reverse in the NBA. "The unwritten rule now is that there should be a minimum of three white players on each team," he says.

With black dominance has come speculation on the role of environment in the game—specifically, do city slums make good basketball players or do blacks have an innate talent for the game? Writer Pete Axthelm points out that when Irish and Jewish boys controlled the New York City playgrounds, they controlled the sport at its highest levels, too. But no ethnic or racial group has ever held the overwhelming superiority that blacks now do. One might ask why Puerto Ricans and other Latins, likewise exiled to urban American slums, have yet to produce any substantial stars.

Recent studies have indicated that perhaps basketball is the blacks' game simply because it best fits their physical attributes. Anthropology professor Dr. Edward E. Hunt, Jr., has pointed out that because blacks have more tendon and less muscle than whites, as well as variances in the structure of the heel, they are blessed with "tremendous leverage for jumping." Differences between black and white athletes in the proportionate length of arms and legs, the density of bones, the size of hips, and the amount of subcutaneous fat also account for an overall black advantage, he claims. In another study, *The Physique of the Olympic Athlete*, Dr. J. M. Tanner reports that there are many "racial differences" between black and white athletes and that ". . . we must not lump these different populations together."

The black athletes themselves are aware of special abilities. Says running back Calvin Hill, of the Washington Redskins: "I have a theory about why so many pro stars are black. I think it all boils down to the survival of the fittest. Think of what the African slaves were forced to endure in this country merely to survive. Well, black athletes are their descendants." Or as Lee Evans, former Olympic and 400-meter world record holder, states concerning athletic supremacy: "We were bred for it."

Obviously black superiority in basketball rises from a combination of many factors. But one would not be far wrong in saying that in the cities, environment and black potential have merged to form unusually fertile ground. Indeed, nowhere does the game of basketball thrive as it does in the ghetto. And in that regard, few cities have ghettos as thriving as Brooklyn's.

When I left Chicago in late May of 1974 to spend the summer in the Flatbush section of New York City's most populous borough (a sign near Gravesend Bay proclaims Brooklyn as the fourth-largest city in the United States) I felt badly out of place. Raised in the Midwest, I had much the same vision of Brooklyn that I imagine most foreigners have: a bleak urban backdrop peopled with ethnics jabbering in brassy, accusatory Brooklynese (wasn't everything on Toidy-Toid Street?), hoodlums leaning against poles on street corners picking their teeth with switchblades, thieves and murderers lining the profound ghetto sections like ants on a dump. Lurking bluntly in the front of my mind was a short scene from the old war flick *Guadalcanal Diary*. In the movie, an officer asks Brooklyn G.I. William Bendix if the blackjack he's slapping around is official army issue. "Naw," Bendix replies, "dis is Flatbush issue."

But if I felt awkward at first, I was comforted to learn Brooklyn is a provincial hinterland even to those nearby. In midtown Manhattan I often ran into New York City natives who had never made the passage to their neighboring borough. When asked why not, they invariably asked, "What for?" The truth, one finds, is that Brooklyn is much as one expects and yet quite different—with millionaires' homes, parks, and libraries— a place that historically has caught more than its share of abuse.

Before this trip I had been to Brooklyn only once, on a story assignment for *Sports Illustrated* during the summer of 1973. For part of the piece, which was about collegiate stars who return to their old playgrounds, I tried to locate Austin Peay State University's superscorer, James "Fly" Williams. The search was fruitless—Fly was of the ranks of slippery, ephemeral city dwellers who leave no tracks, a man who appeared and vanished without pattern.

Finally, a high-school coach in Long Island suggested I try locating a Mr. Rodney Parker. Who, I asked, was Rodney Parker? Basically he was a thirty-six-year-old black, self-educated ticket scalper-street hustler who spent most of his time scouting young playground stars. It was Parker who got Williams straightened out and selected Austin Peay as the school for him. Why did he do these things? A lot of reasons and no reasons. Nobody seemed to know.

On the phone Parker had been friendly and blunt. "How many players you want? Fifteen? Twenty? You want the Fly, is that it? O.K. Tomorrow at noon at Foster Park. They'll be there."

And the next day they were there, perhaps a dozen players, Fly in the forefront like a peacock among pigeons. One of the youths in the group, Anthony Harris, a huge teenager under Parker's guidance, had tried to explain what he knew about Rodney. "See, it's just that he helps a lot of us—particularly the ones that are in trouble—and we listen to him. He gets us into prep schools to fix our grades up, he tells us when streets games are happening, he buys us soda, and he never asks for nothing. I used to think, 'What's in it for him?' and when I'd asked him he'd just smile and say, 'Be cool. Be cool.' I call him 'the Mystery Man.'"

About himself Parker was alternately vague and provocative. "I like the ink is all,' he'd say. And later, "I'm a story in myself."

In the park there were things happening around me, a ceaseless flow of energy I sensed as much as saw; I could feel stories everywhere. Though I stayed in Brooklyn for only a short while, I found the scene continually running through my head once I had left. Tantalized, I wanted more than I had gotten. This book is the result of my return trip—a summer-long experience in which I hung out, like my subjects, at "home base," the small square of asphalt known as Foster Park. Until I got my bearings, Rodney Parker was my guide. The ballplayers, by and large, were my companions.

Everything that goes on in the book is true; I saw most of it firsthand, and what I didn't observe I got from my system of informants, a loose network of cooperative six-year-olds and numbers runners and most anybody else prone to friendliness and hanging out in parks with his eyes open.

I have tried not to evaluate the events overly much, just as I tried my best during the summer to stay out of the way, to let things happen in natural fashion. I dressed pretty much as everyone else did (shorts, sneakers, later on a golf hat and an ABA wristband) and I played ball, ate, drank, and laughed much as they did. Certainly I was visible, but I feel I overtly affected very little. For instance, I had to ask questions, and I carried a tape recorder. But the recorder was also an AM-FM radio and if a situation grew too uneasy, with a flip of a switch I could fill the air with high-velocity funk.

There were times, I'll readily admit, when I was scared. Journeys into Bedford-Stuyvesant, trips through Harlem, games at foreign parks where evil seemed to hang like vapor in the air—all made me wonder about the merits of close-range journalism. But I seldom went alone, or if I did, the smiling face of Nate Archibald on my T-shirt commanded an element of respect. Small boys and older ones alike would recognize the

NBA star and holler "Right," or "Do it, Skate," occasionally snapping into exaggerated military salutes as I walked by.

Many times I saw things in the ghetto I either could not understand or could think of no justification for. At those instances I felt a kinship with war photographers, men who capture suffering on film and yet do nothing to alleviate the immediate condition. But I found that it is virtually impossible to remain uninvolved; by the end of the summer I was reluctantly organizing games, coaching, planning field trips, lending money, offering advice and leadership to boys who often literally begged for assistance.

The only injuries I picked up during my stay were shinsplints and a flareup of tendinitis in my knees. Fourteen-year-old Albert King once slam-dunked the ball over the top of me, nearly tearing the thumb off my writing hand, but the joint gradually healed and my left-handed dribble improved in the interim.

To be sure, I was a white among blacks and there were some difficulties, but I think we never doubted each other's purpose or sincerity about the game. If there was ever a need for a touchstone, a plank to lash our vastly different situations to, we simply retreated to basketball.

I think it was notable that one of the few things my presence affected was not player interaction or spontaneity, but response to achievement. After executing a stylish move to the basket, a player frequently would search me out on the sidelines and shout, "Put that mother in the book!"

Some of them I did. Others I didn't. A lot of things I know I missed. But then I was only in Brooklyn for a summer and Rodney Parker says you could live there a lifetime and never get it all.

MAY

1

Coming around the corner of Foster and Nostrand at dusk, I see a ten-foot fence and the vague movements of people. Men sit on car hoods and trunks, gesturing, passing brown paper bags, laughing. Stains on the sidewalk sparkle dully like tiny oil slicks in a gray ocean. Garbage clogs the gutters. At the main entrance to Foster Park, I step quickly to the side to dodge a pack of young boys doing wheelies through the gate. When I came out of the subway, I had asked directions from an elderly woman with a massive bosom like a bushel of leaves, and while she spoke I had involuntarily calculated the racial mix around me—ten percent white, ten percent Latin, eighty percent black. Now, as I walk into the park I am greeted by a lull in the noise, pulling back like musicians fading out to display the rhythm section at work: a million basketballs whack-whacking on pavement.

Rodney Parker is there on the first court, standing still thirty feet from the basket, slowly cocking the ball. He is wearing red sneakers, sweat pants, and a sun visor that splits his Afro like a line between two cumulus clouds. His tongue is pointed out the side of his mouth, and as he shoots, he tilts his entire body sideways like a golfer coaxing home a putt.

The ball arcs up and through the iron hoop and Rodney bursts into laughter. "Oh my God, what a shot! Pay up, Clarence. Who's next, who's got money!"

In 1966, Rodney, his wife, and two children moved from the

East New York district of Brooklyn to the Vanderveer Homes, the housing project that cups Foster Park like a palm on the north and east sides. At that time the area was a predominantly Jewish, Irish, and Italian neighborhood of tidy shops, taverns, and flower beds. The Parkers were among the very first blacks to move into the Vanderveer and Rodney, a basketball fanatic since childhood, became one of the first blacks to hang out at Foster Park.

Never one to maintain a low profile, Rodney was soon organizing games between the white neighborhood players and his black friends from East New York and Bedford-Stuyvesant. On weekends he would preside over these frequently wild contests, usually from his vantage point as fifth man on a team that might include several college stars and pros. He would be everywhere, screaming, refereeing, betting money on his thirty-foot shots, with two hundred, three hundred or more people whooping it up on the sidelines. For identification purposes some people began referring to the playground as "Rodney's Park."

Then as now, Rodney's occupation was that of ticket scalper, a free-lance bit of wheeling-dealing that took him to all the big sporting events in the New York area, and put him in contact with most of the sporting stars. He already knew several basketball heroes from his neighborhood, among them, pros Lenny Wilkens and Connie Hawkins, and with the connections he made through scalping, it wasn't long before Rodney was giving reports on Brooklyn players to coaches and scouts and anyone else who might be interested.

Rodney, whose education ended in ninth grade and whose basketball abilities were never better than average, derived a deep sense of personal worth from his hobby. "I can do things that nobody can," he liked to say. He helped boys get scholarships to college, he pushed them into prep schools, he got them reduced rates to basketball camps, he even arranged for two of the local white baseball players to get tryouts with the New York Mets. He became known around the park as somebody who could help out if you played ball and weren't getting anywhere on your own. Kids said that Rodney knew everybody in the world.

Now, seeing me by the fence, he comes over and demands that I play in a game immediately to help me get acquainted with "the guys." He charges into the middle of the players and throws commands left and right. This is the rabble—the young men who populate every New York City playground all summer long. Faceless, earnest, apathetic, talented, hoping, hopeless, these are the minor characters in every ghetto drama. They move, drifting in and out in response to Rodney's orders.

The ball bounces away from one of the players and is picked up by a small boy on the sidelines. He dribbles it with joy.

"Gimme that ball 'fore I inject this shoe five feet up your black ass and out your brain," hollers a somber-looking player named Calvin Franks.

The boy dribbles, wriggling his hips and taunting. Franks lunges at the youth who drops the ball and sprints through a hole in the fence into the street.

Franks retrieves the ball and begins talking to himself. "Calvin Franks has the ball, oh shit, is he bad. He takes the man to the base. . . . No, no, he shakes one! . . . two! . . . he's on wheels . . . the crowd stands to watch the All American . . ." Franks shoots and the ball rolls up and around the rim like a globe on its axis, then falls out. "He's fouled! Butchered! They gots to send him to the line . . ."

The sun is gone now, passed behind the buildings in a false, city sunset. Old women with stockings rolled to their ankles doze near the slides.

A boy locates his younger brother who had errands to do at home and pulls him from a card game. "I'll kick yo' ass!" he shouts, slapping his brother in the face. The youth runs out of the park, blood flowing from his nose. The friends at the game laugh and pick up the cards. Crashes of glass rise above the voices, forming a jagged tapestry interwoven with soul music and sirens.

I am placed on a team with four locals and the game begins. Rodney walks to the sidelines and starts coaching. He hollers at the players to pass the ball, not to be such stupid fools. Do they want to spend their whole useless lives as nobodies in the ghetto? Pass, defense. "You're hopeless! Fourteen-year-old Albert King could kill you all," he shouts.

"Rodney, my man, my man! This is pro material," screams Calvin Franks. "Kareem Jabbar come to Foster Park."

There are no lights in the park and vision is rapidly disappearing. The lights, I learned last summer, were removed several years ago to keep boys from playing basketball all night long.

"What? What's happenin' here?" says a young, stocky player named Pablo Billy, his eyes wide in mock surprise as he dribbles between his legs and passes behind his back.

"Boom! She go boom!" yells Franks.

"You done now, Skunk," answers Lloyd Hill, a skinny 6'3" forward with arms like vines and large yellowish eyes.

"Here come the street five! Jive alive. Loosey goosey."

"Look at him!" shrieks a player named Clarence, apparently referring to himself, as he spins out of a crowd. "His body just come like this."

The fouls become more violent now, with drive-in lay-ups being invitations for blood. I don't consider myself a bad basketball player, a short forward who at twenty-five could probably play on a few mediocre high school teams, but out here I pass the ball each time I get it, not wanting to make a fool of myself. Players are jumping over my head.

"Gonna shake it, bake it, and take it to the . . ." A youth named Eddie has his shot batted angrily out to half court. "Nullify that shit," says someone called "Muse" or "Music," I can't tell which.

The Vanderveer project rises on our left like a dark red embattlement against the sky, TV's flickering deep within like synchronized candles. The complex covers parts of four city blocks and houses nearly ten thousand people, a small American town. At one time—no more than ten years ago—the Vanderveer was totally white. Flatbush itself (a name coming from *Vlacke Bos* which is Dutch for wooded plain) was a haven for the working and middle-class whites who had fled Manhattan and inner Brooklyn, believing no city problems could reach this far.

By settling in the neighborhood, Rodney and the other first blacks started the chain reaction again. Within days, white residents began leaving. Apartment for Rent signs went up as fast as the rented vans carried families and belongings out further to Canarsie, Sheepshead Bay, or Long Island. The exodus continued in an unbroken stream until by 1970 the Vanderveer and surrounding area was less than half white. By 1974, whites had become a small minority and the Vanderveer Homes had turned entirely black, the number being split fairly evenly between West Indian immigrants and "native born." Soon, the real signs of decay began to appear—the broken glass, graffiti, garbage, and battered buildings that had been predicted by the doomsayers all along.

If, indeed, there was any plus side to the degeneration, it showed itself on the Foster Park courts where a new grade and style of basketball was developing. Premier leapers and ball-handlers appeared almost overnight. Patterned play and set shots dissolved to twisting dunks and flashy moves. Black players seemed to bring more of themselves to the playground—rather than follow proven structures they experimented and "did things" on court. Soon they controlled the tempo on the half-block of asphalt between Foster and Farragut, and the whites, who came as visitors the way the blacks once had, seemed ponderous and mechanical in comparison.

To Rodney it was simple justice. "Blacks own the city," he said. "They should own the game, too."

But as the talent escalated, so did the problems. Almost every boy now came from a broken home and was, or had been, in some kind of trouble. The athletic potential had multiplied but the risk had doubled.

I think about this as I attempt to guard my man, wondering if he's had it bad, if he has dreams. He blocks me and I push off, feeling his heart through his jersey, pounding hard.

There is almost total darkness now. Yellowish speckles from a street light fan through a tree at the other end but do not come this far. Teammates and opponents have merged and the only thing I can do is hold on to my man and not let him disappear. Rodney is still hollering. "Pass, dammit. Pass like Danny

Odums. Hit the boards! Looking for another Fly! Who's gonna fly out of the ghetto?"

Passes have become dangerous, starting off as dark orbs which do not move but simply grow larger and blacker until at the last second hands must be thrown up in protection. The first ball that smacks dead into a player's face is greeted with hoots.

Lloyd Hill unleashes his "standing jump shot" and the ball disappears into the night. It reenters, followed by a sharp pop as it whacks straight down on someone's finger.

"Oooh, god day-yam! Pull this shit out, Leon. Thing's all crunched up." The damaged joint is grabbed and yanked. There is a similar pop. "Eeeeee! Lorda . . . ahh . . . there, now she walking around a little . . ."

"Where's Franks?" shouts Lloyd Hill. "Where'd he went just when I'm shooting the rock in his eyeball."

Franks reappears from the side.

"It's gone."

"What's gone," Lloyd asks.

"The bike."

"What bike?"

"My bike."

"You ain't got a bike, fool."

"Friend gave it to me. Had it right over there."

The ball is punched out of Rodney's arm as little kids appear like phantoms out of the darkness to shoot and dribble during the break.

"Shit, Franks, that ain't funny."

"It's terrible."

"Can't laugh. Heh, he, he."

"Five seconds, gone. Man walks in and rides out."

"Hee ga-heeee."

"It's terrible and I ain't laughing."

"Hooo hoo ooooohhhh . . . they steal things in the ghetto."

"Niggers . . . hoo hoooo . . . they take your shit."

"Some little spook halfway to Fulton Street . . ."

"Hoo ha hoo haaa . . . peddlin' his ass off in the motherfuckin' ghetto . . ."

"In the for real Ghet-toe . . ." Franks is now laughing hysterically, doubled up and slapping palms.

The darkness is complete. The old people have gone home. Slow-moving orange dots point out groups of boys smoking reefers under the trees. Two other basketball games are going on, but the farthest can only be heard. I start to wonder what I'm doing here, in this game, under these conditions. Playing basketball in total darkness is an act of devotion similar to fishing on land. Soon, I know, someone will rifle a pass and shatter my nose.

"Come on now, let's be serious," says Eddie. "We down, twenty-four, twenty-one."

The ball is returned and the contest starts again. Laughter fades and the bicycle is forgotten. Everything is in earnest and yet I am blind; I cannot follow the game with my ears. Rodney shouts but does not exist. Quietly, on an inbounds play, I walk off the court.

"Hey, hold it," says Lloyd. "Where's that white dude we had?"

"Yeh, we only got four men." Someone counts. "Where'd he go, Rod?" The players look around.

"He went to get some water, I think. He's not used to this shit, he's quitting. Just get another man."

"Come on, little brother," says the tall player called "Muse" or "Music" to one of the hangers-on. "Put the weight to this dude and keep him outta the sky."

From thirty feet away on the bench, I can barely see the occasional sparkle of medallions as they catch the street lights along Foster Avenue. I'm exhausted and relish the chance to wipe my face with my shirt and rub my sore knees. I can hear the players' voices, and it sounds to me like they'll go all night.

2

It is a common saying in the ghettos of Brooklyn that if a boy is bad he joins a gang; if he is good he plays basketball. Indeed, outright crime or idleness aside, there is not much else a boy can do. To ask any sampling of young men from Brownsville, Williamsburg, Bedford-Stuyvesant, or East New York about their formative years, is to get variations on only two answers: "I ran with the wrong dudes," or "I played basketball."

Of course, the two roles are not necessarily exclusive. In Harlem, teen-aged members of the black mafia play games for a hundred dollars a basket, pistols bulging from pockets, their Rolls Royces parked like carnival wagons on the dirty streets. Ghetto memory is short but park-goers don't soon forget the flashy dudes, men like Pee Wee Kirkland, a lightning-quick guard who used to bring shopping bags of money to the Manhattan courts and have his bodyguards stand watch over the loot while he dazzled his opponents with a series of small man "shakes." Pee Wee was good enough to be offered tryouts with several pro teams but reportedly turned them down because the contracts made him laugh. When last heard from, Pee Wee was no longer on the playground scene, averaging, as he was, over 70 points a game for a federal penitentiary in Lewisburg, Pennsylvania.

In Brooklyn, most boys can remember a time when a gang took over the local playground, imposing a hierarchy that descended even to the lowest courts. Traditionally, some of the best undisciplined ballplayers have been members of groups like the Black Spades or the Jolly Stompers of Brownsville; and the basketball talent wasting away in New York prisons puts those programs on a par with many universities. As the coach of the Auburn State Penitentiary said, "What we have here in upstate New York is a transplanted ghetto playground."

Ultimately though, the two paths of behavior—call it the good and the bad—must split and a choice must be made. Basketball or not.

Jim McMillian, the recently-retired NBA star 6'5" forward, remembers when his family had just moved to East New York from North Carolina and he was forced to make a decision about his future.

"I was thirteen and I'd never played basketball before," he recalls. "I didn't know anyone, not a soul, and I was terrified of everything. I'd just go by myself to this park on Sutter and Ashford and shoot baskets alone. I had this vague notion that maybe I could be good someday, but I didn't really even like basketball at the time. I mean, I didn't watch it on TV or have any idols or anything. I took to it because I was so introverted. "I started playing all the time, weekends too, and when you do that it gets rough. Gangs, bullies, everybody gets on you. You take all kinds of abuse. You have to keep from getting pushed around. When you get down to it, it's hard to say what makes a kid stick it out."

Being a loner was a blessing for McMillian because it helped him avoid peer pressure. But the single most positive influence came from a fast-talking neighborhood man.

"This guy kept coming into the park that first summer, I guess he was about twenty-five, and I remember he had lots of money. At least it seemed that way because he had a big roll of bills and he was always peeling a few off to buy sandwiches and soda for everyone. He was always smiling and everybody seemed to know him except me.

"Then one day he came up to me after a game and just started asking questions, how old was I, how long had I been playing, did I want to go to other parks to play. He said he could get me into a good high school if I kept working hard.

"He seemed so knowledgeable, not just about the park or basketball, but about society, the whole world. I asked him what his name was and he said 'Rodney Parker' and that was the start of it all."

Rodney Parker, who lived just two blocks from McMillian, in the East New York district, would remain the young man's guide throughout his amateur career. Rodney would buy him shoes, teach him strategy, lose money to him purposely in shooting games so the boy wouldn't starve, then later try futilely to beat the flowering athlete as he went on to become All-City at Jefferson High and later an All-America. There were no strings attached. Rodney was always just *there*, giving the companionship and direction Mac might have received had he known the security of a real father.

When it came time to choose a college, Rodney was busy making sure McMillian went to the top. Deciding that the Ivy League would be a good spot for his gem, Rodney began riding the subway to Columbia University in Manhattan—visiting coaches, administrators, professors—literally talking his product into the elite school, then returning to hard-sell Mrs. McMillian and Jim.

Today McMillian, who earned a great deal of money in the NBA and has invested it wisely, shakes his head over his good fortune. "Rodney Parker was the *big* influence in my life. He just helped me grow up."

A mysterious benefactor is a highly suspicious thing in the ghetto where street rules maintain that above all, nobody does anything for nothing. Few players were as lucky as Jim McMillian but many, indeed, would not have been as gullible. Looking back, McMillian is amazed that money was never a factor in the relationship. "It's hard to explain, but Rodney is like a little kid. When he gets somebody into school, he feels like he's just put a puzzle together. He gets all excited. It's an identity thing. I have a hunch that what he'd really like instead of money is a title, you know, a telephone and a desk—his own little office."

Other playground players dealt with Rodney Parker simply because they had nothing to lose.

One of these was an exceptionally skinny, timid youth named Danny Odums, whom Rodney first noticed lurking around the Vanderveer courts in the fall of 1970. Danny was a senior at nearby Erasmus High, though he was obviously having problems at school. From his sixth-floor window Rodney watched him morning after morning, shooting alone in his street clothes.

Though a member of the Erasmus basketball team, Danny soon became ineligible and by spring had neither graduated from school nor received a single college offer. Late that summer Rodney told Danny he could salvage his future by getting him into a prep school for another year of precollege courses. Danny was too frightened to reply but he shook his head, yes, that would be nice.

Earlier that year, Rodney had heard from the head coach at Fordham University that Glen Springs Academy in upstate New York was looking for ghetto youths to polish up and send on to college. Rodney had contacted the prep school and all but guaranteed them the state's greatest basketball team if they let him do the scouting.

They agreed and by that summer he had garnered eleven players from eight different Brooklyn high schools. Two others he sent to schools in Pennsylvania and Minnesota. Not until late October was he able to find a place for Odums, at St. Thomas More in Colchester, Connecticut.

The biggest event of that summer, however, came about as an unexpected sidelight. While watching Danny warm up before a Hoboken, New Jersey, tournament, Rodney noticed a teammate of his—bowlegged, bony, shift-eyed, perhaps 6'5", with as much arrogance and razzle-dazzle as Danny had shyness. During lay-ups the youth floated to the basket, grinning at the crowd, and threw down stuff shot after stuff shot. Occasionally he whirled in midair and flipped in delicate jump shots or launched soft bombs from deep in the corners.

They called him "the Fly," a spectator said, or just "Fly." His last name was Williams and he was from Brownsville in Brooklyn. "He's got an attitude as bad as a killer," the man added. Rodney was blinded to all else except the sheer overpowering talent he saw in the boy's every move, every gesture.

"I want the Fly," he said to himself.

In the game, Fly, who got his name in the Brooklyn playgrounds because he let "fly" with the ball, started shooting almost before he came across midcourt. He waved his arms, he pointed at opponents, he showed a contortionist's range of expression. Sometimes he left defenders so entangled in their own legs he laughed at them as he drove past.

The game was a rout. Danny played with unexpected confidence, passing brilliantly and scoring 26 points. But it was the Fly who captured the crowd. He scored 50.

Like the young men already in Rodney's stable, Fly had his off-court troubles—no father, no diploma, no scholarship—and it was not difficult for the glib-tongued salesman to convince Fly he needed outside help, that Glen Springs was his best alternative.

Though their friendship grew, Rodney realized intuitively that here, indeed, was a difficult case—perhaps, though he didn't like to admit it, an impossible one. At times Fly seemed a near-parody of the ghetto man. Defensive, wild, unpredictable, his psyche seemed so entrapped by environment that it was nearly impossible to discern where personality left off and act began. At Glen Springs, Fly bragged about the gunshot wounds in his leg and fought whenever it suited him. During games he sometimes dribbled off the court to get a drink of water and once sat down on the floor because the other team was stalling. "Fly was not a normal ghetto product," said headmaster John Pulos. "Even the Brooklyn kids were scared of him."

Despite the turmoil, Glen Springs did achieve the number one ranking in the state, and Fly was awarded All-America honors. Rodney had mixed emotions about his biggest catch, but whenever he saw Fly perform, he lost control. "The Fly is unreal!" was his cry.

Even with his abilities, however, Fly was not besieged with college offers upon graduation. His reputation as a difficult case was well established. Though he would tell the press he'd had to sift through two hundred scholarship letters, the truth was that only two or three schools showed interest. From those Rodney had chosen unheard-of Austin Peay State University in Clarksville, Tennessee, partially because coach Lake Kelly seemed best prepared for trouble and partially because Rodney was able to send along Danny Odums and two other boys as baggage.

Once on the slow-paced campus, named after a Prohibition-era governor, Fly's behavior was predictable. "Excitement? Oh yeah," he said, "We go downtown on Saturday nights and watch the grocery trucks unload." To liven things up Fly told horror stories about the slums of Brooklyn and soon had the Southern press calling him "Flatbush Fly" and quoting his every word. In games he sported high-topped black shoes and turned his trunks around backwards. He waved to people in the stands, blew kisses, and several times during practice launched his frightening tantrums. None of the townspeople had seen anything like it. Nor had opponents, and halfway into the season Fly was averaging nearly 34 points a game, the highest in the nation.

By the end of the year Austin Peay (rhymes with "see") had clinched the Ohio Valley Conference for the first time in its history and proceeded to knock off nationally ranked Jacksonville before losing in the NCAA regional semifinals to Kentucky. Banners in Clarksville proclaimed: "Fly—Second only to Sex."

The next season, 1973–74, was more of the same—more points, more bumper stickers, buttons, and the inimitable Fly cheer ("The Fly is open. Let's go Peay!"), more tantrums (leading to a midseason suspension), and once again the league championship before a humiliating loss to Notre Dame in the NCAA regionals. Fly finished third in the nation in scoring, and some felt he was tagged for the All-America team.

In Clarksville, construction on a new 10,000-seat gymnasium was speeded up and rumors had it the building would be dedicated the next season before Austin Peay's first home game. Unofficially, it was to be called "The House That Fly Built."

Back in Brooklyn, Rodney knew that of all the players he had aided Fly was the one who truly could give him a name, make him a star in his own right. Besides the prestige, this time he stood to make big money as well; certainly whomever he delivered Fly to would reward him for the service. Indeed, pro teams had already come inquiring about Fly's availability. For Rodney, there hadn't been anybody like this since neighbor Jim McMillian six years before. The future, barring some unpredictable, impulsive move by Fly, looked as bright as a sunrise over Queens.

A rumor circulating that spring in college circles that Fly, Danny, and twenty-two other athletes in the Ohio Valley Conference might be ruled ineligible for further competition due to entrance-exam miscalculations had Rodney slightly worried. But even if Fly could not return to Austin Peay there were plenty of options—other colleges, the ABA, the NBA. A man with Fly's abilities had the sports world in his palm.

By the middle of May, when I arrived to play in that lightless game, Rodney was growing excited, waiting at the park for the return of his boys.

3

"What'd I'd like to do," says Rodney as he steps through his cluttered apartment, snapping a set of upper teeth into his mouth, "is start a farm system. Discover kids in the Brooklyn playgrounds at twelve and thirteen and work them from junior high into the pros. I'd take care of them, be their father image, the guy to pat them on the back and tell them what the hell life is all about."

It is a familiar theme. At best it is a confused vision, for Rodney, despite his street-level connections, has no idea how the real business world works—the miasma of negotiations, contracts, and legal interpretations.

His livelihood is ticket scalping; and he is good at it. Later in the season, I would go on scalping trips with him and marvel at the way he bought and sold, leaving me far behind his stumpy-legged scurryings as he went from gates to ticket booths to parking lots in a dizzying circuit.

Sorting through a pile of college T-shirts, he locates a sweatsock and an Ace bandage. "There's a goldmine of talent out there," he says. "Just in Brooklyn, just in Flatbush, just in this park. A college coach told me he'd recruit the entire block if he could."

Rodney gestures out to Foster Park which includes within its paved confines a baseball diamond; swings, a dry wading pool, a jungle gym, six handball courts, six basketball courts, and not one blade of grass. If only numbers are considered, the park demonstrates why basketball is the city game: the baseball diamond can accommodate 18 or 20 players, the handball courts 24, the basketball courts 60 or even 120 if the games are played on half courts. And though one could look endlessly for a wide, grassy field or a golf course or tennis courts in Brooklyn, one can scarcely go two blocks without passing a patch of concrete where a few poles, backboards, and rims have been erected.

The economics of basketball are also right. "For ten guys all you need are sneakers, a rim, and a ball," says Rodney. "And you can play without sneakers if you have to."

Rodney hangs his head out the window and stares at the crowded courts below. "What is it, ten o'clock in the morning? And the place is packed, see that? With good kids, kids who work themselves half to death because they know how lucky they are, I can do wonders. Jim McMillian was so poor he had to put cardboard in his shoes, but he had the best attitude I've ever seen. But that isn't what I always get. The playgrounds of Brooklyn are filled with sick people."

Two years ago, after articles had appeared in the New York papers about Rodney's aid for a few lucky boys, he suddenly had been besieged with pleas for help. Youngsters hounded him in the streets, begging him to get them into schools, to give them one more chance. Overnight Rodney became a magician, a miracle man. Mothers wrote pathetic misspelled letters imploring him to take their boys who were on drugs or in gangs and pull some secret lever that would turn them around, make them *good.*

But Rodney felt he had justification for turning the unfortunate down. "When I was scalping years ago I'd be at the Garden with maybe a hundred tickets for the circus. It's sold out. I'm selling them to people for twice what they're worth and they're going fast. But behind me are all these poor mothers from Brooklyn and Harlem who rode the subway with their kids and they can't afford ten dollars a ticket, and they're cursing me and begging me and their kids are crying. But what can I do? There's so many of them out there that I'd go broke if I gave in."

Still, he invariably made special concessions for special ballplayers, a weakness stemming from his tendency to hero worship. When he first watched Fly Williams preening and carrying on during games at Glen Springs he told the coach to send him home because he would ruin the program for everyone. But as time went by and Fly picked up honors and became the renowned *enfant terrible* of Austin Peay, Rodney wilted.

"Most of my kids get one chance in school," Rodney admits with a shrug. "But Fly, he could burn the whole damn place down and they'd let him back."

His full-throttle salesmanship of Fly included talking him into basketball camps free, pushing him on sportswriters and even getting Fly an interview at the halftime of a Knicks game. When the ABA Denver Rockets approached Rodney in early spring to discuss Fly's turning pro immediately, Rodney had gone to Manhattan sports agent Lew Schaffel for representation. "He came to me," Schaffel would say later, "because he said he'd heard I was the best. And he'd have only the best for Fly."

Meanwhile Fly had continued his normal routine in Clarksville, combining wildness on court with a cool casualness over schoolwork and the future. A few people began telling Rodney that Fly was using him. Indeed when Fly missed a meeting with Rodney and Schaffel in early May and offered no excuse other than that the plane took off without him, Rodney was filled with terror. "Maybe he's getting another agent! Maybe thirty agents. The kid doesn't know anything about advancing. All he knows is Brownsville and being a big shot on the corner."

Fly's name has been put in the NBA "hardship" draft coming up on May 29, a political move that will help Schaffel determine Fly's value in both the ABA and NBA as they bargain against each other. Fly will have until one hour before the draft to remove his name if he wishes to stay in school. When Rodney called Fly a week ago he was startled to hear Fly say he wanted to stay at Austin Peay for his junior year. "Don't tell me it's for your education," Rodney accused.

"I like it here," Fly said. "People are nice to me. I'm the man."

"The pros are killing themselves for you!" screamed Rodney. "Denver's talking a million, Fly. A million!"

He convinced Fly to at least keep his name in the draft until Schaffel could get some figures from the NBA. Fly seemed singularly unimpressed despite the fact pro ball and big money had been his lifelong dream.

"Just don't take your name out yet. And Fly, don't do anything stupid."

"It's cool, Rodney."

Finished taping his foot and tying his sneakers, a pair of which usually lasts him no more than a month, Rodney picks up a stack of bills for the scalping action at Shea Statium and heads for the subway.

Trotting past his park, he begins talking about the problems he sees in his players. Like a farmer who can tell the weather by an ache in his big toe, Rodney is at times a fairly astute psychologist.

"Ghetto kids can't handle authority," he says now. "And you know why? It's because 90 percent of them never had fathers. I know because I never had one. The only men they see are the guys on the corner being cool. They can't take being yelled at or embarrassed even for their own good because it's all part of this manhood thing, what they think a man is—never being told what to do."

Before dropping into the Newkirk station Rodney buys a paper, one of perhaps three or four he'll buy in a normal day. He reads slowly, but it is only the murder stories and sports pages that interest him. Jogging towards the stairs he stops dead.

He stares at a caption in the sports section of the *Daily News* that reads: "Williams Plans To Remain At Austin Peay." Slowly Rodney begins reading aloud the rest of the column. "James Fly Williams says he is snubbing all offers to play in the professional ranks. Williams, who averaged 27.9 points per game last season and 29.5 as a freshman, said he had just mailed a letter to NBA headquarters in New York asking that his name be withdrawn from the hardship list."

The draft is still six days off and the NBA offers are just starting to materialize. Nobody has told Fly to take his name out of the draft.

The approaching number 3 Flatbush train rumbles below ground like a gigantic mole. "That stupid idiot Fly," roars Rodney, leaping down the steps.

At the park the benches are lined early with the local ballplayers. The season is young and there is enthusiasm in the air for all that summer will bring—the warmth of the sun and the late-night dancing in the street, the ice cream trucks, the girls in halter tops, the beaches, the arguments and fights and beer drinking and marijuana, the competition out on the courts.

Danny Odums is just back from school and he sits, legs splayed, next to Mario Donawa, another of Rodney's boys just returned from his first year at St. Francis University in Loretto,

Pennsylvania. These are two of Rodney's favorites for their no-nonsense attitudes, continually held up as examples to the rest. Many of the park kids saw Danny on TV against Notre Dame and come by now to pay respects.

Next to Mario sprawls Calvin Franks, one of the players involved in the night game a week and a half back. He had been one of Rodney's boys originally, a phenomenally quick yet undisciplined swing man with a tendency toward buffoonery and unaccountable silences. Rodney had sent him to Glen Springs after his sophomore year at Boys High and upon graduation had gotten him a scholarship to a small college in Miami, Oklahoma.

Franks had lasted there exactly five days, not even to the opening of classes. Neither he nor his family had seen fit to pay the five hundred dollar bill for the several thousand dollars worth of education at Glen Springs, and the prep school consequently had withheld his transcripts, thus making him ineligible for college entrance.

"So you're the writer dude," he says, eyeing me. "Man, why don't you lend me fifty cents for a burger?"

I sit down and tell him I'll give him a quarter if he tells me what happened with his scholarship.

"Dig, man," he says. "Rodney said I was going to Miami, so I was expectin' palm trees and beaches. Damn, I get there and there's all these cowboys in boots and stuff." He looks down for a moment. "It wasn't bad, though. I got messed up every night. I had a nice week in college."

For one year now Franks has done nothing, living hand to mouth in the streets, playing ball when he can. His clothes are ragged, but at long last he has gotten his high school transcripts and is now begging Rodney to get him another scholarship. Yesterday Rodney laughed about it. "One chance per customer," he said.

Next to Franks is Lloyd Hill, a twenty-two-year-old high school dropout from Brownsville who spent three years in the merchant marines before moving to Flatbush with the rest of his family. He now cuts hair part time with his younger shaved-head brother, Cleanhead, in a shop out on Lott Avenue. The rest of the time he spends at the park. By his own admission he drinks too much beer and smokes too much "weed." In fact, as he demonstrates by his slurred speech and giggles, he is high now. Still, Lloyd has the reputation of being the best street ballplayer in the neighborhood, with a tomahawk stuff shot envied by every boy in the park.

Recently, he has started talking about the strange dream of going to college some day.

"Well, my friends are mostly in jail, you know," he states matter-of-factly. "And I don't really have no plans, but college must be something nice if you go there and do like Danny and Fly and them. I've held my own against Fly over in Brownsville but when these college kids come back they make me look silly 'cause I been playing dummies all year.

"I thought I'd hang around the park this summer and show Rodney what I can do. I won't talk. He'll know a player when he sees one. I can always take the high school equivalency exams, that ain't nothing, and if I get in I'll have a college rep and they'll say, 'Lloyd, how's school?' And I'll say, 'Yeh, it's sweet,' and I'll have books and all and then I won't be just Lloyd Hill, you know, the stupid guy."

The players relax and watch the little kids go through their routines, doing the trick shots and fancy ballhandling they equate with stardom, content to substitute flash for depth. Danny Odums once had a flashy game but no longer. Through coaching and hours of practice, he honed it down until it became tight and essential. As a result, he made first team All-Conference in the Ohio Valley last season and set an Austin Peay record for assists.

"Have you seen that fourteen-year-old kid that Rodney's biting on so hard?" asks Lloyd. "That Albert King dude who's 6'6"?" All the players nod.

Young Albert has been to the park several times for Rodney's games and has shown a grace and coordination utterly pheno-menal for a boy his age and size. Considering he won't enter high school until the fall, his talent seems mystifying, portentous; and the players defer to him like a god.

"Well, if I was fourteen," says Lloyd, "I'd be smarter than I am now."

The players are lost in the warmth of the day, like snakes on stones, and they make no comment. Soon they stretch and wander out to the courts, loose and ready for action.

Lionel Worrell, a dark-skinned, muscular eighteen-year-old from a few blocks away rides his bike up to the park fence and surveys the scene. He has a broad, sloping nose, high cheekbones, and a smiling expression that gives him the look of a cheerful Indian; when he spots the action on the main court he peddles toward it. Having just moved to the area from Bedford-Stuyvesant, he is new at the park but some of the players recognize him from street games and shakes hands. Lionel takes off his shirt. "Let's run it," he says.

As a freshman at the University of Michigan, Lionel had played sixth man on a team that reached the quarter-finals of the NCAA tournament. His colorful, all-out play showed signs of greatness and won him his own personal fan club—the University of Michigan Lionel "Main Train" Worrell Boosters, a unique honor not even All-America center Campy Russell could claim. And yet Lionel was not happy in Ann Arbor.

He has come to Foster Park today because he knows Rodney will be by eventually and he needs to discuss some things with him. Rodney had helped get him into Michigan by bringing scouts to the playground last year. Now, maybe, he can help get him out of Michigan.

EARLY JUNE

Winston Karim, a twenty-two-year-old Trinidadian immigrant settled in Flatbush and working on Wall Street as a clerk in a shipping firm, is known as Rodney's "man." He follows Rodney around, plays him one-on-one, chauffeurs him in his (Winston's) new Oldsmobile Cutlass Supreme. For his services he gets nothing. "I let Winston hang around with me," says Rodney, "because my life is so damn interesting." This is not entirely true. Winston is his own man, a friend who lets Rodney play the role; he stays around because he enjoys their association. Today, Saturday, Winston goes to the crumbling Fort Greene section of town to pick up young Albert King.

At Foster Park Albert steps out of the maroon car, seeming to unfold from the waist down. His long dark face emerges humming the melody of "Rock the Boat,' his eyes deep-set, eager yet cautious like a fawn's, his skinny arms attached to exceptionally broad though bony shoulders. He is wearing baggy gray pants, a tattered yellow T-shirt, and the inevitable Converse All-Stars, black and salt-crusted.

Rodney scurries up like a crab after fish.

"The King is here! I'll put you straight in the pros. The hell with high school!" Rodney laughs joyously over his prized possession, second only to Fly in importance. Albert smiles, embarrassed, as players stop shooting to watch.

The park is filled. There are games at every basket. Handball

and paddleball are being played on both sides of the cement wall
separated from the courts by rusting wire. Swings are screeching,
Haitians and Jamaicans are playing soccer in the asphalt
outfield, a few white kids are playing softball, screaming "foul
bool!" and "Trow it da home!" A crap game is under way
beneath the trees with dandies frozen in gangster poses. There
are babies in strollers, men in undershirts drinking warm beer,
women hollering at children, old men watching in silence.

Rodney clears a court and sets Albert King on one team
against Mike Moore, a 6'7" pro from the European League, on
the other. As the game begins, Albert opens his mouth in
concentration, moving with a dexterity that brings "ahhs" from
the small crowd. His boyish face looks misplaced on a body
stuffing two-handed behind-the-head, batting shots away, hitting bullet outlet passes, screening the heavier, older players
away to snare one rebound after another.

"Do it, Big Al!" screams Rodney.

People approach in disbelief. "Tell me the dude ain't fourteen,
Rod," says a small crapshooter outfitted like a tiny chunk of
rainbow. There are moans as Albert slides by his man and hooks
one in from the baseline, rolls of laughter as he smashes one of
Lloyd Hill's floaters back in his face. Albert stares straight ahead
and ducks his chin to sprint, not responding to the crowd noises,
embarrassed by his talent. After the game he hurries off with
Winston for orange juice.

"Yeh, he's good," admits Mike Moore to Rodney after being
soundly whipped. "But what about five years from now? The
streets have destroyed better talents than his."

Sitting under a tree, Albert clutches a borrowed radio and
presses it to his ear, soothed by the blasting vibrations.

He had met Rodney last summer in his neighborhood and was
convinced by the older man to visit Foster Park for some pickup
games. Rodney, who wanted Albert as badly as he once had
wanted Fly, began showing up whenever and wherever Albert
played in a game. He bought the youth hamburgers and gave
him subway fare, and at the beginning of this summer got him a
job working in the office of agents Jerry Davis and Lew Schaffel.

Their alliance has now become somewhat official, though

Albert is less than certain as to what it all means. "Rodney is always just hanging around," Albert states. "People tell me to stay away from him but I can't see why. He just seems to like helping kids."

It hadn't taken any particular genius on Rodney's part to know that the thirteen-year-old, then 6'3" and in the eighth grade at Sands Junior High, was a rare find. In one outdoor game against older players, Albert had snagged a rebound, dribbled full court, switching hands en route, and then stuffed the ball. His older brother Bernard was gaining All-City fame at Fort Hamilton High School (in 1977 he would be named All-American at the University of Tennessee) and another brother Thomas was a standout at West Virginia Wesleyan College. Already Albert was holding his own against his brothers; his potential appeared as unlimited as it was natural. After an early season park game I asked him how he developed his lefthanded hook, and Albert said, "I don't know. I tried it and it was there."

But perhaps his greatest asset was a natural intelligence and a humility that made him eminently coachable. Told to fake left, go right, and shoot from the key, he did just that. His teachers called him bright. He had no disciplinary problems. Ballplayers called his game "straight up" meaning it was aggressive, simple, effective—a rare thing in the ghetto where it is most difficult to get youngsters to perform the basics, to convince them that Walt Frazier is great not because he passes behind his back but because his jump shot is picture-perfect, his defense flawless. Albert seemed to grasp this intuitively. When as a thirteen-year-old he had dribbled full court and dunked, he had done it reluctantly, he explained, only because no one had been open for a pass.

Ever fearful of the city's destructive forces, Rodney had searched through his basketball grapevine until he found a sequestered high school in a small town in Pennsylvania where he felt the climate would be perfect for Albert's development. Away from the violence, the drugs, the peer pressure, the squalor of his decaying projects, Albert could put his energies squarely behind his game. He would never miss a class. His nourishment would be good. He would be a local hero. Indeed, wealthy benefactors had already offered to move the entire King household to Pennsylvania.

All this Rodney continually laid down in great detail. "He'd be like a goddamn white kid," Rodney claimed. "So what if they give him a car? Kids in California drive to school don't they? They don't worry about rats and junkies, they have money and good food."

But the young ballplayer had balked at Rodney's version of paradise, was balking now; and the indecision has added to his overall restlessness.

"I don't think I want to go to Pennsylvania," he says, drumming on the pavement. "I've never been away from New York and this is where all the competition is. The best players are out in the playgrounds, that's what I told Rodney. But then I guess you do get bad habits, too, like carrying the ball and fouling—I don't know. And then I was thinking about my knees and how the pavement messes them up. Especially since I grew too fast, a half-inch last month. And then I play so hard here lots of times I'm too tired to do any homework, and sometimes I worry about the guys over at Fort Greene, the guys on drugs who want to get me with them. Rodney says this is my best chance to get out of the ghetto. But I mean Brooklyn is my home, where I learned my game."

Behind Albert kids jump into the fence and hang there upside down like bats. A ball gets stuck on one of the rims and the young players yell for help. "That's how you learn to jump," hollers an older player, turning unconcerned, as the boys, none of them five feet tall, leap again and again pitifully short of the rim.

Albert fidgets, admitting he never realized there would be so much pressure involved.

"Everybody's trying to tell me what to do, coaches telling me to go to this school or that one, go to Long Island, go to Connecticut, go to the Catholic League, go to private schools. People call so much I have to leave the house. They try to compare me to Connie Hawkins, saying I'm the next Hawk and that I'll get myself messed up the way he did.

"But that makes me mad. I'm gonna fight it. I'm doing better emotionally than he did—I've got an 80 average now. And, wow, look at me, I'm just a kid, I'm not even in high school yet. They say, 'Albert, what you gonna do when you get rich and famous?' Like they don't even think about me as a human being, just some sort of . . . thing. Famous? A million dollars? I don't want nothing, except I wish I had my own radio."

By 3:00 the park is in high gear. At Foster, as in most of Brooklyn, the games are played to 15 by ones, with the losing team being banished and a new five taking its place. Today the wait for challenges on the number one court is nearly two hours.

Suddenly the afternoon rhythm is broken. A long silver Rolls Royce has pulled up to the curb, double-parking next to the fire hydrant. Bicyclists stop. People turn.

The passenger door opens and a tall young man wearing extra wide bell-bottom jeans and platform sandals emerges. There are metal bracelets on his right wrist and choker beads around his neck. He steps onto the curb with his white-hatted driver friend, and looking beyond the crowd spots Rodney, Danny Odums, Mario, Lloyd, Calvin Franks, and other familiar faces.

Smiling, bent at weird angles, grabbing his crotch with one hand and hollering "Show time!," he ambles up the sidewalk. Young boys scurry about, grabbing their friends, whispering, pointing. "Here comes the Fly!" they shout behind cupped hands.

Albert King, on another court, takes several steps backwards and stands still, quietly dribbling a ball. Rodney leaves him and rushes out to greet his most publicized product just back from school. They slap palms, but Fly's monologue goes uninterrupted.

"I ain't playing here. No sir. Where's these players you always talking about, Mr. Parker? Oh, that kid Alfred or whatever, forget it. Say, Danny-O, my man! Saw a dude catch a bullet in his teeth at the Garden the other night at a kung fu show. Now how's he gonna do that, how's he gonna chomp down?"

Fly looks all around, questioning the growing crowd, then laughs in a loud sibilant hiss which vibrates from his mouth like fizz escaping a soda bottle. He has no upper teeth except four or five on the left side, and he refuses to wear the dentures that were fitted for him at Austin Peay. "I got gums of steel, that's why," he once said. "I can crack bones on these here gums."

There is a battered yet not unattractive quality to his face, with its fine bones, its scars, wispy goatee and mustache, its missing teeth, and searching, wild eyes. It gives one the odd impression of confronting a cheerful mugging survivor.

But there is also something about his movements and rapid changes of expression that makes one apprehensive, as though next to a ticking bomb. In a picture-taking session last summer for *Sports Illustrated* at Foster Park, Fly had been jostled by Anthony Harris under the basket while positioning for a rebound in a staged game. "Get this big Baby Huey away from me!" Fly had screamed, backing off, waving his arms. "These are million-dollar legs he's fucking up!" Then he had fled the park in a rage, the photographer's film blank.

His entrance to the park last summer for the accompanying interview had been just as dramatic.

"They crazy! They crazy!" he had ranted when I asked him casually about the people in Brownsville. "They *seriously* insane in my neighborhood. I mean if you don't have a gun—maybe five or six guns—you in real trouble. The other night this dude's standing in a building yelling, 'Shoot me! Shoot me!' And this other dude was holding a gun in the mother's mouth the whole time. And he *shot* him. The shot dude comes staggering out on the sidewalk and lays there. And the people—man, the people on the sidewalk—they just stood around and laughed."

Fly was a good comedian, keeping his material part comic, part tragic; and the younger players, Rodney, Fly's friends, myself, were all transfixed.

"Now you stand here and ask me if I look forward to coming back to good old Brooklyn," he continued. "Well, I'll tell you, there are gangs in my neighborhood who will shoot an old lady in broad daylight just to see if she's gonna bleed. The Jolly Stompers and the Tomahawks, they ain't no Indian tribes. You tell all the readers that jitterbuggin' is coming back. Jitterbuggin' is the rage, man. And I don't mean dancing."

Here he had stepped back, laughing to tears, and done a

pantomime of someone pulling guns out of every part of his clothing and shooting everything in sight.

"The people around here," he croaked, laughing so hard I got the feeling he was covering a lot of pain, "man, the people all think they're Jesse James. Boom, boom, boom!" He raised his hands and swaggered like a drunken gunslinger pouring lead into the local saloon. "Boom, boom, boom!" He grew weak from the laughter and had to sit down.

Today he again talks about the Brownsville Homes over on Stone Avenue and the court there known as The Hole.

The area is an ugly, sad one, dotted as it is with the burned and boarded-up remnants of a once-flourishing Jewish community. The red brick housing projects have long since replaced the quaint brownstones, and the delis have fallen to cheap, grate-covered rib joints. The Hole, a single, sunken basketball court, stands in the midst of the Brownsville Homes like a pathetic, ill-advised joke for its thousands of potential occupants. Everywhere the feeling is of used-to-be, of poverty and lawlessness. From the narrow, low apartment he shares with his mother and assorted brothers, sisters, and in-laws Fly can witness shootings and muggings as through a nightmarish TV screen.

"They were fighting in my park the other day, like always. Phhht, phhtt! From down here." Fly demonstrates fierce body punches. "Me I just picked up my sweats and tiptoed out of there. They like to kill a man about every day. If they ain't fighting it ain't the ghetto, and if it ain't the ghetto it ain't my neighborhood. . . . Now you take the Tomahawks, whew-ee, they got guns and they ain't happy if they ain't shooting 'em. Think they're kids? Damn. The mother-fucking president's twenty-four years old. Shee-it.

"But we had crazy dudes at school, down in Tennessee, stealing bikes down there at the Peay. Remember, Danny?" Danny Odums nods, smiling. "They had so many bikes they were taking orders—'What will you have, sir? A red and white one? Yes sir, right away.' You know Danny says I didn't ever sleep down there. He was my roommate and after practice he'd be tired, everybody'd be tired. Tell 'em Danny. Except me, I'm still cooking, saying, 'Let's go Danny-O!'"

Fly continues his speech, hypnotizing the audience like a snake charming a bird. The people laugh and stare, seeming to reexamine their own vision of Brooklyn, finding it vastly different yet somehow the same.

Puckering his mouth, shooting his tongue out where his teeth should be, using his hands in great dramatic sweeps, Fly talks about players with "unbelievable shit," players who can stuff from half court. He plays three different characters at once. He grabs his crotch, doubles up, puts a leaf in his mouth, talks like a homosexual. The world he describes is bigger, uglier, more vivid than the one around us. He sits down, then sprints out twenty feet to demonstrate somebody pigeon-toed bringing the ball up court. He comes back and runs out again to show another shot, another murder. "Skinny? You think I'm skinny? I weigh 135 pounds soaking wet." He sucks in his stomach and shows his ribs. The routine is nonstop, pulsating, frantic—as though silence would be unbearable.

Fly turns to Rodney.

"Go get this kid, Rodney. You're so hot on him. Get this Alfred, Albert, whatever. I'll ruin his career today. He don't know what it's about. I'll kill him one-on-one. I'll break his heart just by talking to him. Go get your bankroll, too, Rod. You been talking too much jive. Fifty dollars and I'll bury this kid."

Albert King stands far away, out of earshot, shooting baskets and occasionally taking furtive glances in Fly's direction.

From the street an overweight, middle-aged white man in tennis shorts and red coaching shirt bounces toward the group. His skinny white legs and bloated stomach provide a strange contrast to the lean black bodies around him.

The man was once an assistant coach at Southwest Louisiana University until that school was put on probation in 1973 for over fifty recruiting violations including several involving Larry Fogle of Brooklyn. Fogle is well known locally, having occasionally played summer ball at Foster Park. Last season, after transferring to Canisius, Fogle led the nation in scoring while Fly (due mostly to his brief suspension) finished third. Ironically, the two had once been teammates on the same junior high team, living only blocks part. Some of the players claim that Fogle was charmed by the coach while playing summer ball in Brooklyn. "That fat honkey used to come sneaking around here all the time just looking for dudes," one of them told me.

The man walks up to Fly and greets him sarcastically. Almost immediately the two are arguing in loud voices.

"He says we got money at Peay!" screams Fly. "Tell him Danny, we got nothing. Going to the coach for cash was like asking Jesus Christ to summon the Devil out of hell!"

"Nobody plays fair and wins," says the man, turning as red as his shorts.

"Bullshit, we win. I wouldn't go near your campus."

"Fly, you're stupid. Admit it, they're using you and you're using them."

"I ain't *using* nobody," Fly shouts. On the benches a few of the players get up and move away.

"They're using you. They're using your ability," yells the visitor.

"So what! I'm using the coach's ability. Man, where's your head at!"

"Think they care about you? Fuck, no! And you say you're going back to school—you should just take the money and run."

Fly raises his hand and waves at the man in disgust.

The argument at an impasse, the ex-coach spouts to anyone who will listen.

"You *have* to cheat to win, to get to the Final Four. Give me a satchel of money and I'll get the best players in the country."

People drift away and the man is left without an audience. Corruption, the players all know, is one thing; in the ghetto it's just another way of getting by. But yelling about it is something else.

A new game begins on the main court and once again Albert performs brilliantly, easily the match of any of the college players on court. Rodney directs the game in his typical frenetic style and people laugh at him because he is so excited, so uncool.

Feigning noninterest, Fly dribbles a ball over to the court. He snatches pieces of the action between his monologue.

"That kid might be okay in a few years," he says reluctantly. "One year if he comes to The Hole. If he survives."

The afternoon wears on. Fly and his driver friend, Country James, a dark muscular man of indeterminate age, saunter away to James' Rolls and drive off, little boys following halfway down the block.

Later, at the McDonald's on Flatbush Avenue, Albert King stalks up behind a pensive Rodney and gets him in a stranglehold. Rodney's eyes bug. Albert lets go and starts dancing.

"What did you think of your first view of the Fly?" asks Winston.

The name stifles Albert, causes him to sit down and grow quiet.

"Does he always act like that?" Albert asks finally.

"Worse," says Rodney, punctuating his opinion with a loud greasy belch. "You got no idea."

By noon it is hot, in the 90s already. People's shoes leave imprints in the asphalt street like dots on a fresh cake. The benches are lined with park regulars but nobody stirs, nobody talks. Mac, the park supervisor, walks by, a handkerchief rolled around his glistening forehead. A little girl lies down on the sidewalk and screams, trying to stuff her foot in her mouth. The players turn and watch noncommittally, then gaze back out at the shimmering courts.

Outside the park the younger kids are still buzzing over Fly's first visit.

"Whose wheels was those, man?" asks a youth named Doodie who had followed Fly from the moment he entered the park.

"Country James, he one bad nigger," answers Pablo Billy. "Fly and him are tight."

"Dig it, a silver Rolls."

The boys ponder that for a while.

"What does Country James do to be living like that," one of them asks.

The others laugh and wink at each other.

"Shee-it," says Pablo Billy.

Doodie, a fourteen-year-old with crossed eyes and a head that seems too large on his long, coathanger body, speaks in undisguised awe.

"They say Fly makes dudes look silly at Axel Pay."

"Austin Peay, you moron."

"Yeah, well they say he could score a hundred if he wanted to, and he used to yell 'Sucker' every time he did it to somebody."

"Have you seen his Whirlybird?" asks a big, scarred-faced youth known as Sgt. Rock. "Where he comes down and spins around twice in the air like this."

The boys all snap their fingers and nod. Martin, a small, even-featured sixteen-year-old, remains seated and tosses a pebble off a hub cap.

"It's his attitude, though. Man, he's always in trouble."

"So what. He don't take no jive-assed shit is all," says Doodie. The players slap palms solemnly.

"Yeh, I wisht I had his ability," says Pablo Billy. "There'd be schools crawling for me even if I was choppin' people up with a axe."

"Sure, without ability he wouldn't have gotten all those breaks," continues Martin. "But it's a day-to-day thing. My mom tells me you don't get something for nothing. I mean, someday he's gonna have to pay it all back."

Farther down on a car hood by himself sits Calvin Franks. Staring blankly at the street, he looks sullen, mean, as though he has been placed on the hood for penance.

"I don't know what happened," he says slowly. "I had a scholarship and I was gonna get a summer job. Things were nice. What happened? Rodney says I got the quickest hands he's ever seen. I'm looking forward to school—man, I got my transcripts now—I'll just go away and won't bother nobody ever again."

Two drunken men stagger by, arms around each other, each clutching quart bottles in sacks. Suddenly Frank's expression changes to one of absurd good humor. He emits a loud, "Aaaaaaah," sound that I presume is to be taken as a laugh. He jumps to the ground and bounces an invisible basketball.

"Here's Calvin Franks, 6'3" and change and he does it all He'll turn your program around, just give him some hamburgers and orange juice. He'll shoot, he'll score. He's bad. On Saturday, man, you saw me take a bottle of orange juice from Albert King, because he had two of 'em. I bo-garted that motherfucker. Aaaaah! He was gonna hit me in the head with the other bottle, but I said 'Later rookie.' Gotta let my emotions come out, can't let 'em build up. That's how people commit suicide."

Franks's clothes are oddly ill-fitting, and with good reason. The pants belonged to Craig Smoak, a 6'6" center at Glen Springs, and the T-shirt was Danny Odums'. The shoes, with quarter-sized holes in the bottoms, are hand-me-downs from Rodney. Franks himself has no money, owns virtually nothing— a basketball bag, some socks, another pair of shoes Rodney gave him, his precious transcripts. His mother lives in New Orleans; his father threw him out of the house for harassing the baby-sitter.

For a while he ate meals at the Odums' until they could no longer afford him. Now he claims he doesn't have to eat. "I live off water if I want, or apples. Somebody gives me a quarter I'll buy some apples, but I can take nourishment from the air if I have to."

In reality he has been reduced to begging, to sleeping in the park or on friends' sofas, and to scrounging. At nineteen he has become a loser, and the people who aren't frightened of him simply ignore him.

A rhythm band of congas, shakers, and spoons has started up. Behind the park house one can see where three rims and two poles of the six courts are missing. The story is that when blacks moved into the neighborhood and started winning games, the local white kids tore the baskets down. "You'd see them at night," says Mario Donawa, "a bunch of 'em drunk, shaking the poles back and forth."

A game is getting started now, despite the heat, but Franks remains on the car hood. A couple of days ago the boy whose bike he had lost came around and asked Franks to get him a new one. "I'll kick your ass is what I'll do," Franks threatened. The boy had left and Franks had laughed hysterically.

Now Franks's clown mask crumbles away and gloom covers his

face once more. His voice is low, confused. "I had a brother who was bad. Your genes get mixed up and that's how it happens. He was in jail in Baton Rouge because he was always stealing cars. Way, way in the woods, deeper even than Glen Springs Academy, and they wouldn't even let me give him some gum when I visited. He always had to have a car, you know, he said it was the only time he felt good, like the real thing . . ."

Franks begins nodding his head slowly. He sits back down on the car hood, a flawed ornament. "Rodney'll get me in school. Yeh. Maybe UCLA. I can shoot. I can turn a program around . . ."

Today, perhaps for the first time, Rodney begins to seriously ponder his relationship with Fly. In general he is angry over Fly's behavior and hurt that Fly seems to be drifting away, but most of all he feels personally betrayed because Fly isn't living up to his potential.

Once, years ago, Rodney located a talent the equal of Fly's. It was in Bedford-Stuyvesant and Rodney was no more than fifteen years old, but he sensed that the small, anemic-looking boy named Leonard Wilkens, who played guard on his playground team called the "Aristocrats," was destined for greatness. True, the boy was frail and easy to run into the support poles or simply hold away with one hand, but he had a doelike agility and uncanny peripheral vision that enabled him to cope with the larger players. He would not even make the varsity at Boys High until his senior year, but by then his playground skills were nearly perfected.

"Lenny was my very first discovery," says Rodney of the youth who would go on to become an All-American at Providence College, an eight-time All-Pro in the NBA, and the head coach of several NBA teams. "I told him he was a great player before he knew it."

Now with Fly, however, even the vicarious thrills are dissipating.

"I had a talent, I could scalp tickets and sell things. That's the only reason I made it. But this city loves to toss away basketball players. Shit, the parks are full of old players who just let the city beat them down. Drugs, wine, crime . . . why talk about it. That's why I have to get Albert out of here."

Rodney is particularly upset with Fly's decision to return to school. He has heard from college coaches that the test score foul-up in the Ohio Valley Conference does not look good. Apparently, someone made the mistake two years ago of admitting Fly, Danny Odums, and twenty-two other athletes on the basis of SAT rather than ACT college entrance exams, an NCAA violation making their status in the Ohio Valley questionable. What's more, Fly will need to enroll in summer school to stay academically eligible even if the test scores are allowed. Indeed, he had quit going to class early in the spring, having decided this was the best time to turn pro with the two leagues still warring, his reputation (talent-wise, at least) established, and the money looking good. "The pros are where the action is," he told Rodney.

Now Fly is harder to pin down.

"I can't get a straight answer from him," moans Rodney. "Who told him to take his name out of the draft? He says he wants to play more college ball. Then he says he wants the pros. Then college. Why didn't he go to class like a normal person? All he's ever wanted to do is turn pro, to get his mother out of Brownsville, to play ball with the stars. Now he's turning it all down—a million dollars, I'm telling you—for another year of school."

Soon Rodney is spouting his own personal philosophy, a flexible high-pressure credo that stems more from his dealings with hungry ticket purchasers than from any intellectual bent. "Look," he says. "You gotta get things when you can."

The justification he generally points to is the older men he finds in every park he visits. Nodding on junk, wasted from alcohol, uneducated, self-pitying, stupid, they are proof in the flesh that time waits for no one. Just the day before Rodney and I had gone to another park in Brooklyn and Rodney had recognized two old friends. "You could have been a great one, Willy," he said, shaking a heavy-lidded man's hand. "And you too, Sam. You were big time. You had moves but you wouldn't listen. You thought the street corner was where it was at." The men had laughed and joked, offering up drinks from their sacks, but they understood.

"Fly had a friend named Booboo and he was just like Fly," says Rodney. "From Brownsville, wild, everything the same. Except he didn't have no talent. Last year he overdosed on heroin. So who cared? Nobody. Because he wasn't any use to anybody. That's what I mean!" Rodney throws his arms out and waves them as if drying off water.

"Here's how it is: People only want Fly for what he can give them—basketball. Nobody paying out the money cares what he's been through, what caused what. They don't care that Fly never had a father, that he lives in the ugliest place in the world, that he got beaten up every goddam day as a kid. It's just what he is *right now*."

Later, as Rodney and I take a bus to Bedford-Stuyvesant to watch Albert King try out for the New York City Youth Games team, Rodney seems back in healthier spirits.

He has just learned that a 5'8" youth under his guidance has gotten a basketball scholarship to Murray State University. The player's name is Derrick Melvin and he had been kicked off the Erasmus High team a year ago. Rodney had sent him to Maine Central Institute, a prep school willing to take a chance, where Derrick had "turned it on."

Fred Overton, the Murray State coach, has called to thank Rodney; and Rodney is now referring to himself once again as "the genius."

At the tryouts in St. Johns Recreation Center, Albert is so obviously the class of some eighty-five or ninety boys that spectators begin yelling to get him out of the game. "Ridiculous!" they scream as Albert blocks a player's shot so hard it knocks over one of his own teammates. Albert looks more embarrassed, more self-conscious than ever playing with boys merely his own age.

After his performance he tries to make a quick exit from the gym but finds that his shoes have been stolen. All around him he sees boys staring at him, people pointing and whispering. "I don't think they should cut these guys like that, in front of everybody," he mumbles, trying to hide. "It hurts their feelings."

And, indeed, there are several boys crying in the dusty hallway. One of them, a five-foot, 80-pounder who made it to the second cut, stares at Albert through his tears. "That big guy," he says several times. "That big guy . . . it ain't fucking fair. "

Back at his apartment Rodney calls assistant coach Nick Makarchuk at Providence and tries to sell Lionel Worrell as the man they need. "Worrell can play, Rod, but we're set," says the coach. "We're not even gonna recruit next year."

Late at night, when things are quiet, I take a walk through the streets encircling the Vanderveer Homes. It's a time I have come to enjoy here in this city. The wind is soft, from the distant ocean, and it stirs the litter into clattering spirals like leaves on a parched field. The traffic lights click on and off, but there are few cars to respond. In cities, I'm thinking, there are times when one can be alone, not places.

Down the sidewalk a man is approaching, arms churning at his sides, his head down. I can see from the short, bow-legged strides that it is Rodney, the man of boundless energy.

He walks up without slowing his pace. "Franks has been bugging me. He's crazy like Fly, I think he imitates Fly. I think all these playground kids imitate Fly."

We walk off. Rodney buys a paper at an all-night newsstand and reads the back page, then throws it away. He waves at a cab driver.

"Kids paint his name all over Brooklyn," says Rodney. "On backboards and telephone poles and right down their damn hallways. Did you know that?" I did, having seen several "Fly's" just tonight on the walls of the recreation center.

"Fly's the rage in the ghetto. Oh yeah. The big goddam hero."

The West Indians who have thronged to Brooklyn in the past ten years have left their mark on the ghetto environment. On any summer night the throb of reggae music pulses from the slum buildings, the spicy odor of tripe and Jamaican curried chicken wafts out of the screenless kitchen windows, and on the street corners black men speak in the singsong dialect of the islands. Each summer a lavish West Indian festival is held near

Prospect Park and several hundred thousand Jamaicans, Trinidadians, Virgin Islanders, and Haitians crowd Eastern Parkway to watch parades and dances and to drink to their native countries.

The American blacks, for their part, watch the islanders with a mixture of envy and distaste. They see the West Indians' traditions as foolish sentimentality but also as a privilege American blacks have never known. The English and French accents of the immigrants irritate the locals, particularly when they witness the preferential treatment given the West Indians by white employers because of their "culture." Even more, the naive, get-ahead attitudes of many West Indians gall native-born blacks who long ago quit seeing this country as the promised land. "Somebody's got to tell them dudes the white man runs it here," says Lloyd Hill.

In the playgrounds, where West Indians prefer soccer to basketball, the division continues. "Man, what kind of sense it make to be jivin' with your feet all day?" Pablo Billy had asked me as we watched a soccer ball fly over the fence trailed by half a dozen jabbering Jamaicans.

For their part, the immigrants are less than taken with Americans. "West Indians call us 'stupid' or 'trash' and we call them 'coconuts,'" young Martin explained to me. "But the whole thing's kind of funny because to the white man we're all just niggers."

In Foster Park the far court along the street is more or less reserved for the basketball-playing West Indians. The first ones to arrive in the morning set up camp, putting their radios, blaring the music of Jimmy Cliff and Desmond Dekker and The Aces, around them like fences. The court next to them is a buffer zone of the two factions. The other courts are predominately native black. The boundaries are not hard and fast—for instance, whites occasionally get a game up in one of the corners—but as a rule, they hold.

The friction that might seem overwhelming in such a condensed area is generally avoided because few West Indians are good enough to compete with the Americans in basketball. Fights have started, however, often on the buffer-zone court.

And nobody denies the fire power of the immigrants. More than a few of them have turned out to be armed; and many have weapons in their apartments only yards away.

One Jamaican cult, the Rastafarians, a group that worships Ethiopian Emperor Haile Selassie as the son of the Living God and smokes massive amounts of ganja in its rituals, can respond to provocation with extreme violence. "Don't fuck with the Rastas," was one of the first things the boys told me when I came to Foster Park. Indeed, when the Rastafarians come out to play, wearing high-heeled shoes and shouting in an indecipherable tongue, their Medusa-like dreadlocks flying, *everybody* gives them wide berth.

As fights go, though, perhaps one of the best-remembered occurred last summer and had nothing to do with nationalities.

A game had been arranged between Fly and a few friends and some other players, including Pete Davis of Michigan State and his brother Mike. In the course of the game Mike Davis and Fly's buddy Booboo got into a shoving match. Suddenly Fly erupted from silence into a mountainous rage and the crowd that had turned out for the game poured in to watch.

"Fly went wild," remembers Calvin Franks. "He smacked one of the brothers' glasses so far they almost disappeared. He was screaming and throwing shit left and right and those dudes was backing up *real* fast. The one guy is saying he doesn't want to fight but nobody could stop Fly. He's got real quick hands. Rodney couldn't do nothing and this cop who knew Fly was trying to settle him down, but he couldn't do nothing either 'cause Fly'd keep running back, screaming he was gonna get 'em all. Those guys got in their Cadillac, man, and they split. Whew, I enjoyed that fight."

To Rodney it was an example of the way Fly reacts whenever he feels threatened. "He can even start foaming at the mouth when he thinks he's being attacked. That's why the first thing his opponents in the Ohio Valley Conference did was push him or elbow him so he'd get mad and try to go one-on-one against the world."

Once when Fly was just a skinny teen-ager known by his first nickname, "Junior," he was knocked down and beaten by a much larger and older opponent during an outdoor game in Brownsville. Fly ran off and returned minutes later carrying a brown paper bag. Inside the bag was a butcher knife. Country James, Fly's longtime friend who had also been in the game, jumped in and grabbed the trembling boy. Only after several minutes of soothing talk was he able to prevent violence.

Danny Odums recalls that at Austin Peay the whole squad waited in anxious dread of Fly's next outburst. "You could see Fly wanted to get along, and he'd go five or six games and be straight. But then all of a sudden, boom, he'd crack. It scared everybody."

Today at the park, though, there is an unusually festive mood and nobody feels the least big combative. The atmosphere is noticeably similar to that of a country club, with parallels all around.

Instead of a golf course and tennis courts there are basketball courts and handball courts. Instead of a locker room there is a water fountain and a urinal. Instead of a clubhouse bar there are benches and bottles of beer and cheap wine. Instead of caddies and servants there are little boys to run errands. When I explain my thoughts to Lloyd Hill he replies, "Then I guess being a club member means you got 'nough money to walk here."

Having played little ball since my first night in town, I decide the vibrations seem appropriate to try again. I work my way into a half-court game on the first court and soon have the old juices flowing again.

In the middle of the game Big George, a fireman with a flare for the dramatic, suddenly holds the ball and stops to tell a story. "Now look here," he says, walking over and picking up a quart bottle of beer. "This lady, see, she started calling the firehouse last Tuesday asking for a truck to come and get her cat out of a tree. The fire chief gets on the phone and tells her the thing'll come down by itself. Then a little while later she calls back. Don't worry, the chief says, the damn cat will come down when he wants to. So she hangs up, but ten minutes later she calls again. 'Please, my poor pussycat's stuck in a tree.' Well the chief, he's all pissed off now, he's got veins popping in his head, and he yells at her over the phone, 'Goddammit, you stupid bitch! When was the last time you saw a fucking cat skeleton in a tree!'"

Big George looks around at his audience, takes a drink of beer and the game continues.

In the high-level game at the other end Lloyd Hill plays very well against several college players including Bernard Hardin, who has just been drafted by the NBA. "He's got some raw talent," Sam Stern, a visiting coach from New York Institute of Technology, says of Lloyd. "I think somebody could use him."

In his apartment Rodney reads a letter from the coach at Guilford College asking if Danny Odums would like to finish his two years there if he is declared ineligible in the Ohio Valley Conference. "As I recall, Danny was an extremely nice guy who had good grades and who would fit in well . . ."

Though Fly obviously would also be available in the event of a negative ruling of the OVC, there was no mention of his name.

MID-JUNE

"I had a friend," Doodie tells me in his most serious tone, "and he was growing just like King. Thing is he been drinking wine since he's thirteen. Dollar-nine wine, too. His guts is all erosion and he can't sky no more on account."

As a fixture in Foster Park I'm beginning to blend in. I'm no longer a stranger; boys expect me to be around. They think I play basketball funny but that, as I tell them, is only because I happen to play "white," the way I've learned.

Pablo Billy is giving me pointers on dribbling between my legs while looking a man in the eye and other tricks to liven my game a bit. I'm picking up a few things on my own. Yesterday I saw a player make six shots in a row from half court. I asked him how he did it. "I pretend I'm only ten feet from the basket looking through glasses that make things little. Then I squint and pretend there's a fifty-mile-an-hour wind blowing at me."

Over next to the fence Albert King sits by himself looking glum. He has on long pants and a white Fruit-of-the-Loom undershirt over which is draped an imitation-silk shirt patterned with tiny men in various karate poses.

Behind the park benches are the local teen-age "slicks." Decked out in ruffled shirts, sunglasses, jewelry, and white panama hats, they serve as counterpoints to the functionally attired ballplayers. For them the park is a place of swagger, a hideout, a place to shoot craps and smoke dope and discuss petty crimes. They strut and point and act out roles they've seen in the movies; periodically they remove their sunglasses to look at themselves in the reflection.

The slicks, of course, seldom set foot on a court. One of them, Joey, though now "all superfly" in his talk, dress, and actions, was once a promising backcourt man. Two summers ago in a midnight chase with the police he ran into one of the low iron fences that protect certain patches of Vanderveer grass and shattered his leg. The leg never healed properly, leaving Joey with a pronounced limp, unable to run. His basketball days at an end, he joined the other crowd and artfully turned his limp into a first-rate gangster shuffle. When he walks now he sways back and forth almost in a slow dance, "all cooled out."

"There ain't no *good* wine," interjects Music Smith, whose name I am now sure of, having finally asked him about it. "Music Claudell Smith," he said. "My mom gave it to me 'cause she dug tunes. My aunt said if you gave mom a radio and a place to stand she'd dance all night."

Music used to live in Brownsville near Lloyd Hill and Fly, and the junkies were so bad there, he claims, walking the sidewalks one had to step over them like bottles. "But that wine," he continues, "it all rots your insides. There was guys in Brownsville used to dribble up court and pass out. Wine can do you as bad as the junk."

After a few minutes Sgt. Rock comes out of his apartment on the fifth floor of the Vanderveer, one below Rodney's, and joins Doodie, Martin, and several other boys for a game. They ask Calvin Franks to play but he declines, saying he's too hungry to shoot the ball. He has on the same clothes he's been wearing for the last four days except that now the left shoelace of his sneakers has been replaced by wire.

The group asks Albert to play but he also declines, staring at the ground. "No thanks, I'm tired," he says.

He has my radio and he holds it in both hands like a sun reflector. Everytime I bring the radio to the court he politely asks if he can borrow it: "Let me keep your box, Rick," and then he retires alone to a secluded spot. If there is a cassette in the tape compartment he amuses himself by taping his favorite songs directly from the radio and playing them back at full volume. One night after he returned the unit I played the tape out of curiosity and heard "Jungle Boogie" five times.

The players accept his excuse without argument, realizing as Albert does, that they are only a year or two older than he and it would be a waste of his time.

When his buddy Winston arrives at the park, still in his coat and tie from work, Albert hops into the car. I climb in, too, and we drive off. Albert slumps in the seat and turns the radio up until it sounds like a mudslide.

"Hey," says Winston, "I can't hear anything." Albert taps a beat on the radio.

"Albert," yells Winston above the noise, "when you're a senior in high school, you'll be worth a million and a half."

Albert stares in front of him, drumming on the radio.

"Maybe two million!" screams Winston.

Albert still shows no response.

"How about two and a half million and naked women." Winston turns to look.

"You're sick," says Albert.

We tour Brooklyn aimlessly, its heights and its depths, past isolated mansions on Ocean Avenue, down Flatbush where decay lurks like fungus on cellar walls, up Fulton Street where the wreckage is nearly complete. On a similar tour it had struck me that the nice parts of town and the bad parts vary only in their upkeep—structurally and architecturally they are the same. I realized that blacks in Brooklyn are passive invaders, hermit crabs, living in shells built for other animals. Except for sporadic housing projects nothing has been built for them. It's a land of hand-me-downs.

Finally Winston drops Albert off at the Fort Greene projects on Myrtle Avenue about a half-mile from the Brooklyn Bridge. Albert lives in the red brick building with his parents, four brothers and a sister in a tiny apartment on the twelfth floor. Albert often has to take the stairs to his apartment since the elevator, like many of the other conveniences, seldom works.

Albert, who is all too aware of his station, once gave a reporter directions to his home by saying, "You go to this project then take a right to the next project, go past two more projects, and it's the first project on your left."

Today Albert has no humorous comments. The irony between his current situation and the one predicted for him because of his basketball skills is becoming ponderous. Just yesterday he received a letter from coach Lefty Driesell's office at the University of Maryland urging him to have an enjoyable summer and to fill out a basketball questionnaire. There is also the fact that his girlfriend just moved to Arizona. He feels so down he declines Winston's offer of a free snack at Colonel Sanders'. "I don't feel like eating," he says. "Or anything."

It is nighttime at Foster Park and the younger players are lazily shooting baskets in the weak glow of a street light, softly, gently, the way resting campers will toss chinks of bark into a campfire.

"You hear people talking much about sixty-nine?" offers Pablo Billy.

"Naw," says Pontiac Carr, a fourteen-year-old with a Kool behind each ear. "White folks be doing that mostly, not niggers."

Pontiac lives a few blocks away in the Jackie Robinson Apartments on the site of old Ebbets Field, where the Dodgers played until they moved West. Back in the fifties, Ebbets Field was a landmark to Brooklynites, a source of pride equal to the bell in Philadelphia. When the stadium was razed, people lined up for seats and chunks of wood. The entire playing area is now part of the housing complex. "Pontiac, he lives on second base," Doodie told me.

"My friend says it tastes like pie," says Doodie now.

"What kind?"

"Didn't say. Just pie."

They dribble and shoot, bouncing the balls off the rectangular blue blackboards, winding down. Pontiac seems to be drunk tonight. Whenever he is, I've noticed, he does pirouettes. He spins now each time after a shot.

"Had a dude told me it's a lot like grape jam," says Sgt. Rock.

"Friend of mine from Brevoort said it's awful, like fish."

"What do you know about it, Rick?"

My jump shot misses by about five feet. I tell them that in a truly dedicated ballplayer's life there isn't room for such notions. This gets a few laughs, some hand slaps.

"I hear you get a good one, you be eating watermelon," says Pablo Billy. "Gimme five."

"If you want to know the truth," says Martin, always the expert on abstractions, "they put different flavor things in there—fizzers—so you get anything you want."

The boys roar with that statement, but it's accepted.

They continue shooting, happy in the warm night air, basking in friendship, their futures before them like bright city streets.

Last night Rodney had returned home hot and tired from a hard day of scalping at the Mets-Pirates game. (There was a time when Rodney tried to go straight, working as a salesman for a large company, with a company car and a trunkful of samples. The experiment had failed to bear fruit, however. Rodney quickly piled up reams of traffic citations from his habit of throwing the car into park and dashing off whenever he spotted a basketball game, leaving the vehicle in the middle of the streets, in front of hydrants, wherever. It was a blessing of sorts, and a firm statement on his future, when he finally demolished the car in a multi-vehicle accident.)

Sitting on the couch last night he wanted to read the sports page and then casually mull over the problems with Mario Donawa (unhappy at St. Francis), Lloyd Hill (untrained, uneducated), and Calvin Franks (unstable).

To his chagrin the first thing he read was that "Brooklyn's Fly Williams" had played in the Baker Professional League in Philadelphia. "Ga-awd damn!" shrieked Rodney and he ran out of the house.

The preceding afternoon a game had been set at the park and Fly was supposed to have shown up. No one had gotten overly excited when he didn't arrive; no one depends on Fly. Lloyd Hill had been strolling about singing a tune he had just composed entitled "I Must Get More Sweeter on My Jams," and stopped to point out that some buddies of his in Brownsville had heard Fly was in Philadelphia. Still no problem.

But the fact that Fly was there playing with professionals in a professional tournament was news to all. In so doing he was breaking a cardinal NCAA regulation. Amateurs are allowed to mix with the pros only on an informal, pick-up basis.

Rodney was beside himself with rage, calling first Lew Schaffel, then Fly's house (not in), then Winston, then a string of random people upon whom he vented his fury. Fly had taken his name out of the NBA draft, thus eliminating himself from that league for at least a year. Then the ABA Denver Rockets had undergone a coaching change and had rescinded their original offer which Rodney claimed was $1 million—this having taken place within the week. And now Fly had played in a pro tournament meaning he was no longer eligible to play NCAA basketball. He couldn't even go back to *college*.

Rodney calls Fly's number, muttering to himself about dumping the "schizophrenic" off the Brooklyn Bridge.

"Where's the madman!" he shouts.

"I don't know," says his sister. "I don't take care of him."

Rodney tries all afternoon and finally settles for a harangue with Mrs. Williams, Fly's mother. She is in her mid-fifties and still carries traces of the South Carolina accent she brought with her on a "sleep-in" job back in 1955.

"Oh, Rodney, I don't ask Fly what he does, 'cause whenever I do he hits the ceiling. I say, what's with Rodney? and he gets up and leaves so I don't mention you no more. He don't fuss with me but he's still got that nasty attitude. He's born like that, just like his daddy. I never hurt my hand on him, I always beat him with a strap, but now he's twenty-one, Rodney. Can't be no more excuses. See, he's like his daddy, he was worse than Fly. Fly don't care 'bout nothing—about money, anything. Just basketball, that's his life. He got suspended from school in kindergarten—you know a boy don't like school if that happens. He wouldn't even go into the room. I had to sit with him for days, and when the teacher ask him a question he wouldn't answer. So you say he knowed he wasn't supposed to play in the game? Why'd he play, then? I just don't know that much about basketball, Rodney. He came in at noon today and said he'd get some sleep. So that's how it stands."

Rodney knows better than to force her to wake the sleeping Fly. When denied certain things Fly can become extremely volatile. Once at Glen Springs someone stole some food from the cafeteria and the teachers would allow no one to eat until the culprit turned himself in. Fly began getting hungry, then angry. "He wrote it on the blackboards that he'd destroy the place if they didn't let him eat," remembers Calvin Franks. "They let us eat."

"He probably figured Philly was far enough away so nobody would find out," mutters Rodney. "Ninety miles. Lew was going to use the school as a lever against the ABA for negotiation rather than the NBA against the ABA. Now he can't do one or the other."

Later, at Coney Island, where Rodney has taken his family and Winston for a brief Father's Day celebration, Rodney runs into Curley Matthews, an old friend from the Connie Hawkins-Lenny Wilkens days. Curley made All-City in 1959 at John Jay High School and then played four years at Virginia Union College. After school he became a practicing Muslim, changing his name to El Haj Abdul-Malik and making several pilgrimages to Mecca. "I still play some ball," he says, "but I pray more."

"Man, you had a jump shot," says Rodney.

"Yeah, it wasn't raggedy, it was nice. It was a gift from God and I was thankful to Him for allowing me to get it off. You know, I figure I spent 75 percent of my time as a kid playing ball, Rodney. Otherwise I would have been the average Negro from Brooklyn—robbing candy stores, trying to be Super Fly. Yeah, I had a shot all right. All praises are due to the Lord."

On the ride back Rodney admits that at age thirteen he, too, had changed his name and was practicing to become a Muslim. "I wasn't emotionally prepared, though. Here I was shining shoes for the Mafia on Pitkin Avenue and getting ready to visit Mecca. Yeah, Mecca Avenue in the Bronx, is more like it."

Though it is midnight Rodney calls Lake Kelly, the basketball coach at Austin Peay, to get his reaction to Fly's misadventures.

"Way-ell, I don't know," drawls the coach in a resigned tone. "I wish he hadn't done it, narrowed down his choices like that. I think he would have been ruled eligible back here, too. Now he's got no negotiatin' power. What was he gonna do, was he gonna come back to Austin Peay? You think he was. Way-ell, we can do without Fly but I don't want to lose Danny. Absolutely not. I'd like Danny to have the chance to play without him. The other felluhs have expressed more enthusiasm about playing without Fly, too. The public will miss Fly, I mean he was the big name, but we just can't take another chance on him. He wouldn't do anything anybody said—he's so wild and free, like a deer rambling through a meadow. I'd like to see him graduate anyway, but if he doesn't come to summer school he's through forever. Other than that, Rod, we look super. This may just give these other kids a chance to blossom, know what I mean?"

Rodney hangs up. He is depressed. The business with Fly is affecting him deeply, more deeply than he'd like people to know. Beyond the money angle and the pride and the anger is real heartbreak, the same as in the disintegration of an affair. For three years Fly has been his project. Rodney has fed him, handed him money, cheered him at games, pumped him with philosophy. They both would be famous. Fly would become All-Pro; Rodney would be the Super-Agent. They both would conquer the ghetto, together, making money hand over fist; successes to the hilt.

"That was the coach of a player who led his team to back-to-back Conference championships, the third-leading scorer in the nation," says Rodney. "And he's not even upset. He's almost glad Fly isn't coming back. It's just sickening."

On Thursday, the high school in Pennsylvania calls about Albert. They want him so badly they're ready to make him mayor. All the wealthy people in town are behind the project and there's big money to back things up—free clothes, free food, an apartment, undisclosed luxuries.

"Rodney," the man says, "we can take *care* of the boy."

Rodney calls several junior colleges looking for player openings. He's got four more kids from the playground right now who need schools. One of them, Eddie Campbell, never played organized school ball. As a boy he was hit by a car and had his leg broken. When the leg came out of the cast it was nearly three inches shorter than the other one, necessitating an operation on the good one to even the length. Recently, however, with both legs in working order, his game has been methodically developing.

Another boy known as "Possum" dislocated both his shoulders in a fall and was unable to play at Erasmus because he could not extend his arms for rebounds. A third player, Craig Martin, only played football in high school, but has shown a natural basketball ability in his summer games. None of the players can be called hot merchandise, and the best Rodney can get are a few reluctant "maybes."

Just before dinner time Myra Parker grabs the phone. "Stop calling!" she pleads, pointing to a four hundred dollar phone bill.

Rodney grabs her arms and hollers to Winston who has just come in the door. Winston takes the phone and dials the number and the process continues.

At 9:30 P.M the park is dark and nearly deserted. Standing by the fence is an old man wearing a green cap, a German who comes to the park frequently to watch the games, carrying a radio from which wafts the classical music of Wagner and Beethoven. He seldom speaks, indeed there is no one for him to talk to. He is always alone, content to watch.

Under the first basket there is a bit of commotion as Cameron, a fifteen-year-old park regular with legs as thick as stove pipes, is being taught the rudiments of stuffing. Eight or nine other youths are all trying to explain their personal techniques for palming the ball, approaching the basket, hooking over the rim, returning to the pavement.

Cameron listens to each intently, nodding his head as the points become clear. When the last man is finished Cameron backs up, wipes his hands, and runs at the basket.

At 5'8" he is an exceptional leaper, but on his first attempt the ball slams into the back of the rim and bounces ten feet in the air. Cameron remains above, hanging on the rim.

Lloyd Hill, who has been walking down the sidewalk, steps through the hole in the fence onto the dark court. He looks up at the body dangling above. "Get off there, boy," he orders. Cameron drops.

Lloyd points back to the free-throw circle, "Now try the dunk again."

Being the master leaper and stuffer of Foster Park, Lloyd's word is a solemn and valuable thing. Cameron backs up and snorts like a bull before charging down the lane. Though he seems to rise beyond all normal boundaries for a man his size, Cameron's second attempt is a repeat of the first, with him again hanging like wash on the rim.

"Don't be scared," says Lloyd. "Man, that first time you gots to overcome. The dunk is something, specially for a little man." He pats Cameron paternally on the head.

"Now I know you is kinda scared of falling over ass-backwards and smacking your head on the floor. But it ain't gonna happen if you just let the ball go once it's over the hole. See, you doing the two-handed power stuff, which is cool because you kinda squatty and all, and so you make the run a little different than if you was hook-dunking or behind-the-head-dunking."

Lloyd simulates a takeoff without leaving the ground. The other players begin dunking the ball to show how it's done, and soon they form two lines as in pregame drills. Cameron joins the group and gets closer than ever to dunking but is not quite smooth enough to flip the ball down.

The boys become earnest, silent except for loud "aahs!" as they jump into the night air. "Yeh, I hear you!" they shout to each other, sweating and tossing off their shirts. "In his face!"

There is an atmosphere of ritual surrounding the event, as though Cameron is in the company of braves, with Lloyd a chief watching from the perimeter. What I have seen of dunks in playground games has made me realize their importance: a man can leave his opponent behind with fancy dribbling or he can embarrass him by blocking his shot or stealing the ball, but nothing makes a statement of dominance better than a resounding stuff shot.

After one shot the ball bounces into the street and one of the players chases it, nearly getting run down by a bus. "That's the spirit Leon," they yell. When the player returns, Lloyd asks for the ball. He takes it and saunters to the front of the line. "You just not cool enough, Cameron," he says.

Carefully removing his shirt and folding it into a square which he places on the sidelines, Lloyd palms the ball and looks at the basket ten yards away. He puts the ball down and reaches into his pockets, pulling out an Afro pick, some change, and a dollar bill. He places these things on top of his neatly folded shirt and then picks up the ball. He rolls his shoulders two or three times and starts loping toward the basket. When he is close enough, his skinny legs uncoil and he sails into the air, cradling the ball in the crook of his elbow before casually smashing it through the hoop.

He slowly returns to the front of the line. A player hands him the ball again. This time Lloyd runs in a little faster. While in midair he waves the ball around his head like a bolo before dunking. Again, he returns.

On his third approach he cocks his arm like a pitcher in his windup and throws a strike straight through the rim at the pavement.

For his final attempt Lloyd walks back an extra ten paces and blows on his hands. He grasps the ball in front of him and takes an all-out sprint at the basket. He cuts sharply through the row of silent boys like a halfback turning upfield and then, nearly ten feet from the hoop, flings himself into the air. As he floats slowly to the rim he rubs the ball on the back of his neck like a man with an itch under his collar and then slams it through the rim so hard it caroms wildly off to another court.

Lloyd walks silently back to the sideline. He picks up his comb and change and puts them in his pocket. He picks up his shirt and puts it on, buttoning it as carefully as he removed it.

The lines start moving again, with added energy and a sense of respect. But Cameron has peaked and will not dunk tonight.

From the shadows the old man is laughing and shaking his head. "Ooooh, that was great," he says, clapping his hands quietly. "How high they go and hang there."

I walk over and sit next to him because I'm a little excited myself. The middle chords of Schubert's *Unfinished Symphony* weave from his radio.

"They're just like flies, eh, buzzing. Different bodies—see, the short one and the long one with his shirt on—like the green flies and the blue ones and the big horseflies. They come right out of the pavement, that's what I say. Flatbush was never like this, but now there is such a pretty game and so good to watch. Flies all summer."

LATE JUNE

Calvin Franks has been bothering Rodney so much that Rodney reluctantly watches him in a game to see if Franks' renewed efforts merit attention. Franks' belt is pulled in another notch and he now wears a green beret that gives him the look of a deranged artist. "The lid," he says. "I got the lid in Vietnam." He struts back and forth for a few moments. "All right," he says stopping. "I got it in a trash barrel at the bus station. So what?"

After the game Rodney is less than pleased.

"He's the worst player in the world. There were four men on him and he wouldn't pass, just dribble and do everything himself. Danny tries to give him some advice, just friendly stuff, and Franks says, 'You play your game, I'll play mine.' He doesn't deserve another chance but I know he won't leave me alone."

In the early evening a white man with a gleaming new Cadillac parks in front of the Vanderveer on Foster Avenue. He walks up to Rodney's apartment where Albert and Winston are waiting with small overnight bags.

The man is a representative of the school in Pennsylvania, and his eyes nearly burst from their sockets when he sees the 6'6" teen-ager for the first time. As though fearful the boy may fade like a mirage, the man hurries both him and Winston out to his car, casting nervous glances the length of the uneven sidewalk. Once in the car they roar off into the night.

They are going to Pennsylvania for two days so Albert can

look over the school and get "the feel" of the town. Winston is coming along as Albert's guardian.

In a coincidence of sorts, tonight's paper reveals that the massive recruiting battle for nineteen-year-old high school superstar Moses Malone has been won by the University of Maryland. Albert met Moses a few weeks ago at the Kutscher's All-Star Game in upstate New York, a showcase event for the nation's best seniors. Though only a spectator himself Albert was forced into a one-on-one confrontation with Moses by Rodney, who called the occasion "a meeting of basketball's future." Wearing his street clothes Albert showed a quickness at least the match of Malone's. The scouts in attendance drooled, as Rodney knew they would.

Looking at the headlines Rodney decides to give Moses a call.

The phone rings and is answered by Mrs. Malone, who lives alone with her son in a sixty-five-dollar-a-month apartment in Petersburg, Virginia. Moses isn't in, she says.

After the trauma he has been through it seems likely that Moses may never "be in" or speak to strangers again. Weird stories have circulated about the no-holds-barred recruiting blitz of the last few months, of secret signs and knocks, of scouts crawling through the Malones' back yard, climbing their house, of mysterious payments, of coaches taking up permanent residence in nearby motels, of Moses cowering silently beneath his bed.

"I wasn't gonna let my baby get too far away," says Mrs. Malone in a weary voice. "That's why we picked Maryland. If I get sick or if he does we can see each other. And all that money the pros offered—he can get it later. His education is only four more years. We can make it. We've slept on couches a long time. I told 'em my child wasn't gonna play no pro ball."

After hanging up Rodney sneers. "I wonder how much Maryland's paying him."

Tonight as a diversion Rodney and I go to the movie theater on Flatbush and Church across from Erasmus High School. The movie showing is *The Lords of Flatbush*. It's a fifties nostalgia piece about a street-corner greaser named Stanley, played by Sylvester Stallone, and his gang of leathercoated hoodlums who do nothing but suck egg-cream sodas at the malt shop and beat up "wise guys" in pool halls.

It is movies like this, I find myself thinking, that stick in the mind. No wonder people in California and Illinois see Brooklyn as the land of a thousand yucks.

But from my own recent experiences I find the movie oddly archaic, foreign beyond its time period, a fantasy world that couldn't have existed even in a time warp like 1958. In the entire show not one black person appears.

"Believe me," says Rodney. "That's how it was."

The day starts out dreary and overcast, but not until bolts of lightning start flashing and the rain gushes down is it certain there will be no ball today at Foster Park. The players who are out early this Sunday scurry in all directions, pulling shirts over their heads like canopies.

Underneath the awning of Ray's Luncheonette on Nostrand, Lloyd Hill stands staring at the swollen gutters and the streets oily as licorice. He shuffles in place and sings to himself, ". . . diamond in the back, sun roof top, digging the scene with the gangster lean, oo-weee . . ." The decrepit three-story house where he lives with his mother, nine brothers and sisters and assorted in-laws is only three blocks away, but he would get drenched trying to run there now.

"You know, Rick," he says as a bus squishes past with a sound like giant rolls of paper unravelling, "I wouldn't mind having me a nice Cadillac or Bonneville to drive home in. With a TV antenna in the back and gangster white walls." He nods to himself. "Long as I didn't have to work to death to get it."

The other thing Lloyd fantasizes about is a college education, actually playing on a university basketball team with uniforms and cheerleaders and locker rooms and fans. The collegiate experience is immensely confused in his mind, being a composite jumble gleaned from what he has seen on TV, what players have told him, and what he envisions words like "campus," "fraternities," "liberal arts," and "philosophy" to mean. But he knows it is a valuable thing, that its meaning may be hidden too deep for his understanding, but that without it he is just another "dumb chump."

He works sporadically toward the goal, sometimes running miles through the park and working out feverishly at his homemade bench press. "I do it five hundred times in a row sometimes to build up these little muscles, whatever they are," he says. But then in typical ghetto fashion the impossibility of it all weighs on him—he becomes apathetic, resigned, and hides for days behind clouds of marijuana and liquor. The picture of Lloyd's fifteen-year-old brother on the living room table next to the artificial flowers and the cracked mirror reminds him too well of realities.

Once, after drinking a lot, he had talked about it.

"There he was, my little brother, and he was just starting to get up, to start to *leap*. You can't see it in the picture but he was gonna be nice, you know. He wasn't strong or even as big as me, but he had a strong stomach. I held the school record for sit-ups—I did around three hundred, but my brother could do them for as long as you held his legs.

"Some things you shouldn't think about, just let pass by because they'll only make you crazy. But one day he went back to Brownsville where we used to live and this gang came up to him. They said they had 'drafted' him, you know, like the army drafts somebody? I knew some of them. They were punks. He said he wasn't gonna join so they beat him up and threw him off the roof of an abandoned building. They killed him."

After the incident, Lloyd and his brother Cleanhead had gotten guns, but Mrs. Hill had begged them to do nothing. For the brothers it was a terrible blow—in the ghetto it is up to the family to even the score, to show exactly what is sacred. Music Smith remembers that Lloyd became sullen and withdrawn, but eventually bent to his mother's pleadings and "let things slide."

When I mentioned the incident to some of the regulars in the park I was surprised to find that nobody looked on it as anything extraordinary; most players were not aware that Lloyd even *had* a fifteen-year-old brother. When I told young Martin that Lloyd's younger brother had been killed, he asked if it took place recently. About six months ago, I said. "That's not recent," he replied, and continued dribbling the ball.

Yesterday Rodney and I had taken the subway over to Manhattan and then up to City College in Harlem to watch the Harlem Professional Basketball League, commonly known as the Rucker Tournament. In the games, which were originally started by the late Holcombe Rucker to showcase New York's play-ground talent, street legends and legitimate professional stars such as Julius Erving, Nate Archibald, and Larry Kenon find themselves side by side. The tournament, in many ways, is a display of what is and what might have been. The thrill, as the fan sitting next to me put it, is to see "millionaires and bums on the same court."

For Rodney, however, it merely points out the ease with which the undisciplined and the unguided fail. "It would kill me if in a year or two Fly is out there playing for free for Vitalis or Mr. B's."

Before the subway ride over, I talked to Lew Schaffel about Fly. Lew had finally gotten hold of the youth and asked him what in the world he was doing. If he wanted to make an ABA team, Lew said, there still might be a chance for decent money because the ABA might not know he played in the Baker League. Lew asked Fly to stay out of pro tournaments for two weeks so he could try to solidify a deal. Fly mumbled that he couldn't "sit around home doing nothing," but then, reluctantly, he agreed. "My God, it's the guy's only chance!" Lew said.

At the Rucker two of the most renowned playground stars ever, Earl Manigault and Herman "the Helicopter" Knowings, have come by to watch the action. To Rodney they are simply losers, men with fantastic abilities who didn't capitalize; but to others they represent the all too human weakness of the common ghetto dweller—men beaten down by fate, frailty, and circumstance.

That they have become symbols at all is more the work of an analytic white press rather than anything the players or their fans have done. Neither Earl nor Herman played college ball; Herman did not even play in high school. But their stature on the courts of Harlem was never questioned. In his book, *The*

City Game, Pete Axthelm called Manigault "the classic play-ground athlete," a symbol of "all that was sublime and terrible about this city game." Herman he describes as a "playground phenomenon," a "demigod."

The Helicopter, aged thirty now, sits in the bleachers and watches the games silently. He is rock-solid at 6′4″, with a beard, huge arms, and coal black skin. Like a stone, his body seems deeply at rest, as though movement would take the work of levers and sledges. His face is expressionless, as blank as an aquarium drained of water.

Ever since a childhood attack of meningitis he has had hearing only in his right ear, but until the pavement ruined his knees, that seemed to be his only infirmity. His game was built around his muscle and an almost superhuman leaping ability.

In games at old Rucker Park on 155th and 8th near Yankee Stadium, Herman used to outjump all the pros, being able to dunk the ball easily in one step from the free-throw line. Many people claim to have seen the Helicopter block shots a yard above the rim, a move that would put his feet nearly five feet off the ground.

Milton Wadler, an assistant coach at Hughes High School, swears he once saw Herman jump higher than any man ever has. "It was up at Rucker against Nate Bowman, Tom Hoover, and Willis Reed, three big men. They had him boxed out and Herman just went over all three like a huge bird. I'd say he could have put his chin on the rim."

Why he never made the pros can be seen partially in Herman's self-effacing character. "Basketball was a hobby," he says, waving his hand as if to clear the air of annoying smoke. "I didn't have anything to do so I used to play in the alley behind my home on 100th Street. I took a basket out of a park and put it on a telephone pole behind my place. I just climbed up one night with some pliers and took it home. It was so heavy it fell off the pole every week but I'd keep putting it higher and higher until it was above the first floor. I could still dunk easy." He drifts off into the game, motionless again, except for his eyes. Then he returns.

"I don't know why I didn't play high school ball, I just liked blocking shots and didn't think about much else. I never really thought about making a living at it either. And people said I was a hero, I don't know why. Why should I be a hero? I never did nothing. I could jump, yeh, that's true. I used to pick quarters off the top of backboards, a wallet a few times and dollar bills, and I was careful not to hit my head on the rim."

I ask him if it is true about the three-second stories. "Yeh, a couple of times guys would fake me in the lane and before I'd come down the ref would call three seconds on them. But I don't know, it's all talk, talk. It's nothing."

Earl Manigault at a slender 6'2" had a game more spectacular than Herman's, if not as physically overpowering. At eighteen he had such control on a basketball court that observers said only one other New York youth showed as much promise, a giant by the name of Lew Alcindor.

Earl, as vocal as Herman was reticent, became a favorite of young boys who followed him in parks wherever he played. Because they couldn't pronounce "Manigault," they changed his last name to "Nanny-goat" and then just "Goat," which he still goes by today. Though he could dazzle any crowd with his speed and moves, nothing tore people up as much as when he leaped, dunked the ball, caught it in the other hand, and dunked it again, all in the same floating vault. The Goat was becoming a legend in Harlem, but at the same time he was drifting into the world of drugs. One reason was that he did not appreciate the real worth of his skills.

"It all came so natural," he says. "I mean, can you dig that one night I had a dream about stuffing the ball and then the next day I went out to the park at 129th and Seventh and jammed behind my head, *two-handed*. I was only fourteen and 5'9" at the time. On the courts it weren't nobody but the Goat; I didn't have anybody to push me here or there. I didn't care."

The ninety-dollar-a-day heroin habit Earl got into led him to crime, the courts, and eventually a year and a half in jail. When he came out, his game, once so freewheeling and fluid, had deserted him as mysteriously as it had appeared.

"I was at my best at eighteen or nineteen," he says.

"Afterwards I knew what I'd lost. Maybe I got some raw deals along the way, but I'm not bitter. No, I just couldn't deal with the whole situation. And the worst thing is that when I went on drugs I took a lot of people down with me. I have a debt."

As penance, Earl now works free-lance with kids he spots in the teeming playgrounds, particularly his own at 99th and Amsterdam, an ugly, cracked place known as "the Junkyard."

Manigault is still finding his way, which may be one reason his players are so important to him.

"I got a kid at the Junkyard now, Alonzo Jackson. He's 5'7" and he can tap dunk on a man 6'9"," says Earl, his eyes bright, recalling a feat they once said was his alone. "He's the baddest dude in the world. I call him God. I want to help him before he falls asleep and wakes up to nothing. But I want to do more, to show all these kids by my attitude not to be slick dudes, not to be Super Flies. But man, it's hard, very hard. You got no idea."

On Saturday in Foster Park, some boys sitting next to Lloyd Hill had offered him a cup of thick orange juice-like liquid. It was a gesture of friendship, free of challenge. Lloyd declined. "It was methadone," he said later. "Same high and all as heroin."

Today Lloyd and his brother Cleanhead play in a game against some players who have come by from Bedford-Stuyvesant. Like most playground games this one has an added dimension of drama that comes from the roles each player assumes.

There are two strong, hard-working players who hustle for position and play hard defense. There is a small, left-handed guard with yellow socks and matching wristbands. There is a "sissy" who catches abuse for calling fouls whenever he is jostled. There is a bully, a clown who insists on continual razzle-dazzle, a "chucker" who shoots whenever he gets the ball and one tall, awkward boy, a "fool," who is always a step behind the action. Lloyd himself is the star, playing "above the rim" and tossing in shots from all directions. Cleanhead, with a stony expression and frenzied, overaggressive movements, is the wildman. Twice he causes collisions that nearly erupt into brawls.

"Brother, don't do that no more," warns an angry opponent after the second crash. Cleanhead stares at the man, his eyes opening wider, his fists slowly folding into knots.

Lloyd runs in and takes his brother away. He speaks soothingly, walking his brother in a circle for a while, arm in arm, before returning to the game. Back in the action, Cleanhead glowers at everyone, teammates and opponents alike, running silently, his reckless flailings belying some inner turmoil.

"He skinny, but you don't fuck with Cleanhead," says Ernie, one of the park boys who hangs on the periphery of Sgt. Rock's and Martin's crowd. "He don't want to take shit no more."

After the game Lloyd talks with his brother again and pats his smooth-shaven head. "He's the only one can cool out Cleanhead," says Ernie.

Cleanhead stands in front of Lloyd, without saying a word. He apologizes for nothing, makes no excuses, looks his brother in the eye. People who "won't take shit anymore" in the ghetto have retreated as far as they can. Murders over petty insults or debts appear ludicrous in morning newspapers, but not to men deep in corners wearing their dignity like skin. Lloyd continues in a low hum.

"Okay, Lloyd," says Cleanhead finally, lowering his eyes. "Okay." And he walks slowly out of the park.

In the evening Albert plays in his first interborough Youth Game competition in Queens. Of the five boroughs—Queens, Brooklyn, Manhattan, the Bronx, and Staten Island—Brooklyn is far and away the class team with the Bronx running a distant second. The reason for Brooklyn's dominance is its fourteen-year-old, 6'6" center who blocks shots harder than most boys can throw them up, and is so quick that his first fake is frequently missed completely by defenders.

The five boroughs will play for several weeks until director Abe Raskin can pick the twelve best boys to represent New York City in the United States Youth Games to be held in mid-August in Baltimore. As he watches Albert King demolish his opponents, the director appears mesmerized. "For the record I will say we have one player right now. We're looking for eleven more."

The same sort of amazement had been waiting for Albert when he and Winston arrived in Pennsylvania. Local businessmen had come out to pay their respects as to some new deity. At the sparkling gymnasium Albert had combed his Afro in the center-court reflection, and then tried a new dunk where he stood with his back to the hoop, jumped up and smashed the ball against the backboard before tossing it through the rim. It was a trick he had learned from watching Julius Erving on TV.

"When he did that the coach got real nervous like Al was from another planet or something," says Winston. "He said if Al came there he'd let him do the dunk and just take the technical foul."

A sixteen-year-old boy, one of the starters on last year's team, then had been brought in and Albert played him briefly one-on-one, disposing of him as easily as one of the children from Foster Park.

By now the coach was sweating with anxiety. Shortly after that he made a call to Rodney.

"The man is nearly crazy," Rodney cried to me afterward. "They'll pay for everything—apartment, food, clothes, they'll even move Winston out there and give him a job. They have a spotlight to use on Albert."

In a tour of the town the school representative had shown Albert a few of the many stores he owned. "The man kept saying 'Which one do you want?'" recalls Winston. "'I've got twenty-seven. Go ahead, pick any one.'"

"It's a perfect place for a kid to grow up," claimed Rodney. "It's small, there's no ghetto, the coach is excellent. It'll make Albert humble. And it's none too early, either. Before they left I asked him if he wantd Winston to come along and he said, 'Yeah, I need somebody to carry my bags.'"

But if anything, Albert had been the picture of humility and courtesy on the trip. He opened doors for people, excused himself when necessary, and maintained a profile so low that he even asked Winston to turn down "Rock the Boat," his favorite song, when he felt it might be too loud for the others. "They couldn't believe this was a ghetto product," says Winston.

After an immense dinner cooked by the coach's daughter (Albert had offered to eat at McDonald's), Albert and Winston went to a theater to see *The Exorcist*. Albert feigned disinterest, laughing at the frightening parts, as he was sure his friends in Brooklyn would have. That night at the motel, however, with the lights out, Winston got down on the floor and began shaking the legs of Albert's bed, mooing like a cow.

"Yaaaah!" screamed Albert, picking up a lamp.

"I had to grab him and say, 'Al, it's me, Winston.' He woke up people next door he was hollering so loud."

Though it was 2:00 A.M., Albert was up by seven the next morning to watch the Saturday cartoons. Before checking out he carefully made his bed.

After a farewell talk, the coach asked Albert if he wanted to come to school in the fall. "I'll have to talk to Rodney," he answered.

But personally, he had not been sold, primarily because the place seemed too foreign, too eager, too bewildering for a youngster whose housing project was larger than the biggest building in town. "What would I be like if I'd grown up out here," he wondered in deep seriousness.

He also was not pleased with the way Winston had cynically depicted life in Brooklyn. "You should have heard him, he kept saying how bad New York was, like it was the worst place in the world, like you got your car stripped in five seconds . . ."

Rodney, nevertheless, is still confident that Pennsylvania is the place for Albert and that with prodding Albert will see it as a once-in-a-lifetime opportunity.

"Yeah, I know, everybody says leave him alone. Bullshit, he needs guidance before it's too late. They say he's doing fine now, but so was Manigault, so was Hawkins, so was, hell . . . so was Fly and a million other guys until the city swallowed them up. If he goes to Pennsylvania he'll be like a white middle-class kid going to a normal high school."

The fantasy of the white middle-class upbringing is a strong one for Rodney, appearing again and again in his conversations. That trying to simulate it might be a traumatic experience for a black youth like Albert never enters his mind.

"In a small town Albert will see the same people day after day and he'll get to know them as people, not just faces in a huge crowd. Here it's all appearance—nobody knows anybody. Friends will hurt you as fast as enemies. And there's no controls—it's too hectic and it blows kids' minds.

"Ghetto kids don't go to school, they don't learn anything, they don't even eat right. Hell, Albert gained five pounds just on the trip. I mean this could be the start of the American Dream."

Albert, still brooding about his girlfriend moving away and beginning to be hassled by Rodney's constant directing, went straight home after the trip. The fuss that is being made about him now is bigger than ever before and he is not enjoying it. The week before he had told Winston that he was sad and just wanted "to be like everyone else." Among children his own age he is stared at and pestered by moronic questions. "Basketball, basketball, basketball—that's all I hear," he moaned.

After the Youth Games' tryout, Albert is mobbed by the other players and forced into a position of authority which he handles awkwardly. He becomes loud and abrasive, but he lacks conviction. I can sense that he sees through his own act. He talks about girls and money like an expert and tells one of the boys to carry his bags. He accepts their praise although it seems to make him uncomfortable.

At a candy store across the street the Brooklyn players eat dinners of strawberry ice cream, cake, and orange sodas.

"I think I'll tell Rodney I want fifty dollars," says Al loud enough for them to hear. "Yeh, I'll do that."

He continues to act cool like the others, several of whom are secretively pocketing candy bars and potato chips.

"I've got to tell Winston and Rodney to quit calling me," he adds. "Winston wants me to go to Pennsylvania so he can get a house and a job. I'm staying right here. I'm from New York."

* * *

Early Saturday morning Calvin Franks is wandering around Foster Park looking for all the world like a petty criminal, a purse snatcher catching his breath, a second-story man plotting a move. His mouth is set in a scowl, his eyes dark and foreboding.

He is carrying the cheap plastic briefcase he now keeps with him at all times. Inside is a two-day-old New York *Post* and his precious grade transcripts from Glen Springs Academy, a ragged piece of paper he occasionally withdraws and scrutinizes with furrowed brow.

He sits on the bench by the empty court for a few minutes and then walks down the sidewalk and up the stairs to Rodney's apartment building. The entrance buzzer and lock is broken so he walks in and opens the door to the battered elevator which, as usual, smells heavily of urine. The basement of the building smells even worse. "It's the closest place to the park," explains Music Smith.

On the sixth floor Franks gets out and rings Rodney's bell. Myra Parker slides open the viewer.

"You can't come in," she says and closes the viewer.

Ever since Franks talked Myra's baby-sitter into letting him in to wait for Rodney and then proceeded to eat every piece of fruit in the refrigerator, Myra will neither speak to him nor let him in the house. She calls him "rude, ingrateful, and mean."

Franks sits down in the hallway and reads his transcript again, then walks back out to the park. Albert King is there but he walks away from Franks and sits by himself.

The park is just starting to come alive, with a few girls playing handball and boys walking their dogs. Rodney is still sound asleep, having spent the last three days traveling to the Providence College Camp in Rhode Island where Mario Donawa is working as a counselor and to Howard Garfinkel's Five-Star camp in the Pocono Mountains where Danny Odums is on the staff—both placed by Rodney.

I went with Rodney to get a look at the summer basketball camps which are a sort of luxury alternative to city playgrounds. While at the Providence Camp, I heard Rodney receive a rare accolade. In front of nearly three hundred campers Providence's head coach Dave Gavitt introduced him as "one of the outstanding college talent scouts in America, Mr. Brooklyn himself—Rodney Parker!" Rodney's smile had been so immense he had been forced to stop and readjust his teeth.

Nick Makarchuk was also there, the man who received one of Rodney's biggest sales jobs ever. Now a coach at Providence, Nick had been the head coach at St. Thomas More Prep School three years before when Rodney was searching desperately for a school to take Danny Odums.

Despite the fact that the young coach had never heard of Rodney, had no scholarships left, and wasn't even looking for a player, Rodney broke him down. "I knew there was something wrong," admits Makarchuk. "Schools had been going a month, why wasn't this 'super guard' in some place? Who was Rodney Parker? I didn't know. I was naive. My God, this unknown man sold me an unknown player unseen, over the phone."

Rodney even convinced the coach to give Danny $1,100 off on the $3,100 tuition fee.

For the additional $2,000 Rodney called a Manhattan organization known as the Metropolitan Applied Research Center. Informed that helping impoverished schoolboys wasn't their line of work, Rodney nevertheless got Danny and dragged him off to the MARC offices on 86th Street and burst in on worker Dixie Moon. She remembers the scene well.

"In came Rodney, whom I didn't know, with this slinking, frightened, skinny, nonverbal boy. Rodney was the spokesman and he said over and over this was the boy's 'only chance.' I had no confidence in this kid, although Rodney was bursting with it. I took the boy upstairs to Dr. Lewis who's in charge and though Danny didn't volunteer any information, we decided to try to salvage him. At least, we figured, he had remained drug free."

Seldom did a hard-sell ever work out so favorably for all parties involved. By the first marking period Danny, who had failed virtually everything at Erasmus High, had made the honor roll. On the court he quickly became St. Thomas More's number one guard, leading the team to the New England Prep School Championship.

When Danny stopped in to see Dixie Moon the next summer, she was astounded by the change. "He was standing tall, he was self-assured and friendly, he liked himself. They'd made a fuss about him and that was all he needed."

At Providence, while Rodney was engaged elsewhere, I had a chance to talk to Ernie DiGregorio, a graduate of St. Thomas More himself, the 1974 NBA Rookie of the Year, and one of professional basketball's most unlikely players. Six feet tall, chunky, slow, with short arms, chubby fingers, and no jumping ability, "Ernie D" made me think almost immediately of his opposite—Fly—and all the dissimilarities in their makeup.

"You know," Ernie said, taking a seat by the tennis court, "nobody gets up at six in the morning to play ball. But I did. At twelve years old my mind was made up that I was going to play pro ball. TV did it to me, I think—watching fans go crazy. I started practicing nine, ten hours a day. By myself. With gloves. And I loved it. They could've cut my right hand off and I'd have played one-handed."

I asked him what gave him the insane notion that with his lack of physical tools he could ever be a basketball star.

"Well," he said, thinking a moment, "I remember the last day of class my sophomore year in high school, it was ninety-five degrees out and everybody was going to the beach. They said come on Ernie, you'll turn into a basketball. But I went to the court on Smith Street by myself, as usual, sweating like hell. I started smiling because I knew, I knew right then, I'd put in so many hours, there just couldn't be anybody better than me."

In the big game this afternoon Derrick Melvin makes his summer debut at Foster Park, having just come back to Brooklyn from California where he was staying with his brother. He is quick and passes superbly, but at 5'8" Rodney has definitely pulled a major coup by getting Derrick a full ride to Murray State.

Lloyd Hill is the tallest man on his team and is forced to guard George Berry, a 6'6" forward who plays for St. Johns. Lloyd stuffs over the top of Berry once or twice, but gets badly beaten on rebounds and tip-ins.

"Well," says Lloyd philosophically, drinking beer and puffing on a reefer after the game, "if Berry catches me on a day when I'm good and my knee ain't hurting, I'll tear him a new asshole."

As I sit in what has become my favorite spot under the maple tree, watching the patterns around me, I suddenly hear my name being called. Doodie and Martin are standing almost in front of me, but my eyes have been focused beyond and, like the leaves on the tree, their bodies haven't registered.

"Rick, we see you out here every day, writing and listening," Martin continues, "and we—Doodie, myself, and some of the others—well, we wondered if you'd like to be our coach."

I look at the boys and allow their features to sharpen. Doodie's mouth is half-open and his arms hang limp at his sides. Martin's arms are folded on his chest. Proud and intelligent, he once refused a soul handshake I had awkwardly extended, saying some things must be reserved for brothers.

"What?" I say.

"A coach," answers Martin.

"A coach?" I ask.

Martin looks to Doodie as though perhaps none of this is coming through.

"A coach," he says again.

"Of what?"

Martin shakes his head. "Whew, and I thought colored people were dumb. Rick, take a guess."

"You want me to be the coach of a basketball team?"

They both shake their heads. Doodie's mouth clicks shut on the downward swing.

"What basketball team?" I ask.

Doodie takes a small step forward and points at his bony chest. "Ours," he says.

Martin explains the concept of the team which is to be composed of young park regulars, players of approximately the same age and skills who are looking for action beyond the low-level games they are resigned to at Foster Park. He points off vaguely to where Pablo Billy, Sgt. Rock, and a tall sixteen-year-old named Vance are half-interestedly watching some slicks shoot craps.

"We thought we could travel around and visit other places," says Martin. "We'd play anybody with enough guts to try us. Maybe get some uniforms, have practices, enter in some tournaments. Something to keep us occupied."

I tell them it sounds like a fine idea, something to be proud of.

"Then you'll do it?"

I didn't mean that, and I try to tell them that the team idea sounds good but that I'd really rather not be a coach.

"What's wrong with coaching?" Martin asks.

"I don't know anything about coaching." This was true.

"You don't have to do much. Just run us through some drills, put dudes in and out and, you know, keep some order."

I ask Martin why they've chosen me.

"Well, you've obviously got a lot of time on your hands or you wouldn't be sitting around on the bench all day."

I mull this, involuntarily. I'd promised myself not to get involved this summer. Even marginal objectivity is a fragile thing. And positions of authority, well, there you're just asking for it.

"It'd be like social work," says Martin. "You'll like it."

Doodie is agitated. He's been wanting to say something for a while now, forming silent tentative words on his lips. He takes the same small step.

"You could just coagulate us a little," he says.

I need time to think. I excuse myself and walk over towards the bustle of Nostrand Avenue, trying to piece this out. If I become a coach objectivity will be shot. But then, who's objective anyway? Of course my working relationship with the park youth might disappear once I become a coach. And Martin has been talking about trips to Bedford-Stuyvesant and other dangerous areas. I might get killed. But then anything short of death might make good copy. Involvement? I'm already involved just being here.

Returning to the park bench, I pronounce to Martin and Doodie that I'll do it.

Doodie slaps palms with me, and Martin extends the traditional businessman's grip. We walk over to where Sgt. Rock and the others are waiting. They have already asked another boy to join the team, and he stands there now, a skinny fifteen-year-old, perhaps 6′2″, with pronounced holes in his Pro-Keds. His name is Mark and his bedroom in the east Vanderveer overlooks Foster Avenue and the park.

That makes six players and the boys feel eight is the best number for a touring team. They decide to add a swingman named Arthur, a shy, graceful sixteen-year-old with braces on his teeth. Arthur is deeply interested in electronics. This summer he is building a color TV from scratch.

Pontiac Carr, a happy-go-lucky fourteen-year-old who could easily pass for someone three or four years younger, is deemed too unskilled to play, though his cigarette smoking and familiarity with hard liquor seems invaluable. I mention that I could probably use an assistant, so Pontiac is made the team manager and trainer.

"How you doing, coach," he says, extending his palm.

That leaves one position open and the players consider asking Albert King to join the team but then drop the idea.

"He won't want to play," says Pablo Billy. "And besides if we ask him we might as well ask Danny and Mario and Lionel and them."

Seeing our discussion, eleven-year-old DeMont suddenly bursts into the center. Already known as a "bad nigger" overly prone to fighting and bottle breaking, he now begins shouting that he should be on the team.

"Get outa here, 'fore I bust your skull," snarls Sgt. Rock.

"I'll be good! I'll be good!" DeMont screams, looking from face to face.

A while ago I had been walking down Bedford Avenue with DeMont and he had abruptly broken off a car aerial and thrown it at a bus, laughing fiendishly. He was bad, but then there was something about his spirit I liked. I thought he could be salvaged.

"DeMont can be the ballboy," I state. The players groan. DeMont yelps with joy, then runs over and puts his arms around me, sticking his tongue out at the other players.

The boys hold a short debate on two other possible players, a Haitian known only as Champagne and little Ernie, the five-

foot, sixteen-year-old with a gold star in his ear. Martin asks for
my opinion. I tell him that since this is supposed to be a
pleasurable experience why not invite your friends.

Champagne, the boys decide, might come in handy. He is still
learning the game and doesn't know about such things as three-
second violations or palming the ball, but he hustles and plays
defense. Little Ernie, they decide, should not be allowed because
he sometimes hangs around with older men and because they
already have enough guards.

"The dude is just a little *too* small, you know," says Sgt. Rock.
"But he thinks he's a big man."

Over on the bench Lloyd Hill has reached a mellow stage. His
arms are crossed, his legs are stretched in front, and his head is
cocked back.

"I think I may put my bed out here under that basket, sleep
right there, and get up and take a few jams in the morning," he
says to no one in particular. "Hmmmm. But maybe I'll move it
over here by the fountain so I can splash some water on my face
when I get up. Uh-huh. I just might do that."

EARLY JULY

alvin Franks is becoming a joke at the park. Nicknamed "Mooch," he no longer holds respect except on court, and even that is fading. Whenever he walks by someone whispers, "Here come Mooch, hide your food." Today his buckle-less belt is tied in a knot. He begs a dollar from me saying he won't bother me ever again, and then heads off to the ABC Burger House across the street.

After much argument our new basketball team has decided not to call itself the "Foster Park All-City Borough-to-Borough Traveling All-Americans" because of the length, or the "Afro-American Hit Men" because of my vehement rejection. I remind them that we might have to play in white neighborhoods some day.

Instead we have settled on the title "Subway Stars." This confuses Doodie.

"Does that mean we're stars that shine in the ground?"

"Damn, you homely" answers Vance. "It means we're great players who ride the subway."

Two o'clock this afternoon has been set as our first practice session; and as I clean off one of the far courts and line the players up for some basic drills, with Pontiac Carr holding a ball confiscated from smaller boys, half the population of the park comes over to watch. Everyone wants to join the team—not just teen-agers, but little children and men as well.

Little Ernie asks if he can play, but Martin and Sgt. Rock inform him that the roster is set and nobody new can be added. "Is that how it is, Rick?" Ernie says turning to me.

"I guess so. We sort of decided on eight players," I mumble. Martin offers to let him practice against the team but Ernie walks away, his head down.

Starting the players off on one of the few drills I remember from high school, a pattern called the three-man weave, I quickly realize there are going to be problems. Arguing with each other even before they start, the players refuse to perform even the rudiments of teamwork once the ball is handed over, lacking the discipline for anything but one-on-one confrontations. When I demonstrate the basic pick-and-roll, a routine straight out of fifth grade, they act baffled.

Doodie sets his picks sideways, a ludicrous response since his paper-frail body blocks little enough even head-on. Champagne rolls backwards to the basket, once stumbling straight into the pole.

Feeling that a short scrimmage might straighten things out, I divide the team into fours and announce, "fifteen baskets wins." Instead of calming things down, it makes matters worse. The players taunt one another, elbow, push, refuse to pass, mope when they don't get the ball. Periodically, Sgt. Rock snatches the ball and defies anyone on either side to take it from him. Pablo Billy insists on dribbling between his legs every few feet and yelling, "So sweet!" each time he shoots. Mark stands in the corner calling various players "motherfucker" and refusing to participate.

Never in my life have I wanted to be a coach. And here I am now wanting only to let things happen of their own weight, a near riot on my hands.

When Pontiac hollers, "Seven!" I call the game and the practice, telling everyone we'll try again in a day or two. "We don't mean to get like this," says Martin apologetically. "We'll straighten out."

Eddie Campbell, one of the older park players, walks over to me, shaking his head. "You've got nothing but attitudes on that team," he says. "I'd cut 'em loose if I was you."

* * *

In today's late paper a small story is tucked in with the rest of the sports news. "Fly Soars In, Paces Win," it reads. "Fly Williams soared into town yesterday. The Austin Peay superstar made a 32-point Harlem Professionals League debut to pace Brooklyn (his hometown) to a 137–116 win over the Courtsmen."

"Oh, well," says Rodney with feigned non-concern. "What difference does it make? We ask him not to play for two weeks and he can't wait one. Not only that, he's playing in Washington, D.C., and Newark, too. Plus Philadelphia. *Four* professional leagues! Lew is ready to go out of his mind.

"And now Albert is starting to act strange. People come up and tell me I'm ruining Albert, that he doesn't need me. They say I'm just a money grubber. Maybe that's what I ought to be. I could have sold Fly *myself* to Denver way back there, and he'd never even have known the difference."

Rodney is having problems with another one of his charges, too. Coming home for lunch after hustling tickets, he gets a phone call from Mario Donawa who says Derrick Melvin hasn't shown up at the airport yet and their plane to Murray State is getting ready to leave. Rodney, who had finally convinced the coach to accept Derrick and to give both the players a recruiting trip to the campus, can't believe it. He tells Mario to catch the plane and to hell with Derrick forever and ever.

"I spent *hours* on the phone going to bat for that kid. And he can't even put in the effort to catch a goddamn plane. What's Overton gonna think—that I'm a jerk, that the kid's a jerk, that everybody in Brooklyn's a jerk."

Derrick Melvin arrived at the airport moments after his plane had left. Suddenly frightened about his future, he remained at the airport all day long, without eating a meal, and caught a plane eight hours later to Murray, Kentucky.

Today Lloyd Hill is drunk before 10 A.M. He sits on the park bench finishing a beer and singing up at the blazing sun, his eyes as yellow as bananas. "Fancy lady, you walk a little shady. Got

them skintight peaches doo-dah . . . and some real sweet
breeches. . . ."

Globules of gum melt on the sidewalks and string out behind
people's shoes like elastic thread. In the apartment buildings
crowded along Flatbush Avenue people hang their heads out of
windows and gasp for air. Only the very little boys, who take no
notice of the heat, have ventured onto the Foster Park
basketball courts.

Lionel Worrell rides up on his bike, parks it, and greets the
players on the bench.

"Wha's happenin'," he smiles.

"You got it, Nel."

A spot is made for him on the bench and he gets comfortable.

"What's going down with Fly?" he asks.

"Don't know," says Danny Odums. "Last summer he was out
here all the time. Now he plays in those tournaments. I haven't
heard from him in weeks."

They sit quietly, waiting for a friend with a car to take them to
Riis Park out on Rockaway Beach where the breeze blows
steadily. Playing ball today on the Foster courts, a person would
lose so much water weight that cramps and nausea would quickly
set in. Heat waves shimmer just beyond the first court, making
the little boys shake like dancers.

"Now I ask you this," says Lloyd, his voice slurring. "Here I
am 6'3" and 165 pounds. Why should any man be that skinny?"

He looks at each player but gets no answer.

"I weigh 168 on a full stomach and two days' rest. But the
more I eats the more I shits. If I go to college I can't be fooling
with no big guys. Those coaches be saying, 'Lloyd, you some
kind of bone, here, eat some of this steak, have some pie. Get
big.' I'll come home huge like Batman."

At Riis Park the players walk slowly down the sidewalk to the
basketball courts that are set back from the beach and surrounded by a low fence.

Lloyd dances in place to the music blasting from the hundreds
of radios. "I'm getting all down and boo-tiful," he says,
demanding to guard the big 6'9" man with the straggly hair.

"Nobody with that kind of Afro can check my shit. I'll block his shots with my forehead."

Calvin Franks declines to play, looking malevolent as he sits by himself on a bench, wearing a pair of cheap, badly scratched sunglasses. Suddenly he bursts into laughter. "I'll turn hardship after two years. Aaaaaaah! Rod said they wouldn't take me at that Florida school. So I'll hit St. Johns for a couple years, then the big time."

He savors the last bit of candy bar, his breakfast and lunch for today. Last evening Danny Odums showed up at Rodney's and asked if he could please eat dinner. "Franks turned up at our house and ate almost everything on the table," he explained.

Danny, like most of the other players, is very slender, skinny except for the exceptional wiriness of his build, with veins that protrude from calves and forearms, washboard stomach muscles under taut skin. As a boy growing up in the Sumner Houses in Bedford-Stuyvesant he was painfully gaunt; in fifth grade he stood 5'2" and weighed 65 pounds and had to wear suspenders to hold up his pants. With his ragged, unfitted clothes and sad eyes he presented a pathetic image. "I'd be feeling fine but people were always coming up to me and asking what was wrong," he remembers.

Despite his appearance Danny didn't want to gain weight. He was an outstanding runner in the Police Athletic League and other organizations where the classes were determined by weight and height. At eleven he had already run a 58-second quarter mile, the fastest in the city for his class.

There was also the fact that nearly everyone else his age was equally as bony. One day, when Danny and two friends decided to play hooky from school, they tried to sneak out the basement doors of P.S. 59, knocking over stacks of garbage cans in the process. The crashes alerted the principal who was listening to a violin class in the next room. He came running out and Danny gave himself up, but his friends disappeared. "Those two guys hid in lockers," says Danny. "That's how skinny they were."

Danny's family moved to Flatbush shortly after his suspension from school for that incident, and he began to spend more time

playing basketball than running track. Rodney noticed him and
gave him sporadic encouragement, but Danny paid no attention. He was terrified of the neighborhood, of the world in
general. "If somebody said something to me, I'd just keep on
going."

At thirteen, Danny met Calvin Franks, then eleven, and the
two became friends. Franks was the better ballplayer and showed
Danny a few of the moves he was working on. One day he took
Danny with him to an outdoor clinic at St. Jerome's School
around the corner from Foster Park. The coach there pointed
out flaws in Danny's shots, helping him develop the picture-
book form he has today. Danny feels indebted to Franks and it
bothers him to see his friend becoming so strange and his future
gone astray. But he knows that in some things there is little one
person can do for another.

Danny realized it at Austin Peay when he played next to his
friend Fly and saw things happen there that seemed beyond
anyone's control. There were days when everyone on the team,
the coach included, had to back off and let Fly's excesses go by.
"To win two conference championships we had to be tolerant,"
says Danny. "That was the main thing. Fly did something, got in
one of his attitudes, well, we all overlooked it."

That was the way the program was set up at Austin Peay.
Indeed, that seemed to be the only way anyone could be certain
of Fly's services. Some blamed Lake Kelly for being too lenient
with the superstar, but others realized his predicament. When
Kelly suspended Fly for arguing and lack of hustle four days
before Austin Peay's first game at Madison Square Garden, he
was pressured into reinstating him for the New York trip. "If he
didn't put me back on the team the townspeople would have
fired him," says Fly. "Hell, yes. The bankers and that told me
so."

But Fly claimed the special attention was not his doing.
"There was more than just me on the team. But you could tell
the coach was the kinda guy that just wanted one dude. He
found out I could jump and had the best shot he'd ever seen, so
he made me that one."

In Fly's mind even the brief suspension, the last of several, was not his fault. In that game, which he had entered as the number two scorer in the nation, Fly went 0-for-6 from the field before Kelly benched him and they had words. "Western Kentucky was playing a box-and-three on me and the coach wanted me to go in there and do it all," says Fly. "There was one guy in front of me and one on a side and one guy chasing me. I couldn't do nothing. So I told the coach. I said, 'Man, I just can't do nothing.' He said, 'Don't call me "man".' And I got dressed."

For the coach it was more involved than that. "It was a matter of me having gone as far as I possibly could in two years," Kelly told a reporter. "I felt I had to take these steps for my personal self-preservation."

Indeed, whenever Kelly dealt with Fly he confronted a paradox, for Fly was the team *and* its problems. And Fly, it seemed, was equally perplexed. When he did his thing, hogged the ball, shot whenever he pleased, performed his antics, the stands were packed and the people shouted for more. Not only that, the team usually won.

"We knew we were taking on a hard case when we recruited him," Kelly says. "But I made up my mind to work as hard as possible with him—harder than a lot of other places would have. I'd worked with his type in high school, and I just felt that to turn him loose wouldn't be fair because I knew the environment he'd have to go back to."

But for Danny and the others, the bystanders in the turmoil, very little seemed fair. "To keep the coach off our backs and to keep Fly cool everybody had to do what they could," says Danny. "And what I had to do was give up the pill. And everybody else did too."

Even though he shot 50 percent from the field, Danny was forced to become an assist man, taking shots only when it would have been ridiculous not to. Some of the other players seemed to suffer more from the emotional effects of Fly's presence than from the crimp in their own styles. "Before Fly came to school Howard Jackson was averaging 18 points," Danny recalls. "You could tell Fly's appearance on court was affecting him—he was missing lay-ups, he wasn't taking his jump shot, he was uptight and nervous all the time. All he was doing was rebounding.

That was something he could do without thinking. And this other guy, Percy Howard, whenever Fly sat down he played really well. Fly fouled out of one game and Percy scored forty-three. In the second half against Western Kentucky, with Fly out, Percy came on and got twenty."

Despite the team's general unhappiness, Lake Kelly felt the players were more fortunate than they knew, that they actually depended heavily on Fly whether they admitted it or not. "There at the end, why, they were standing back and letting Fly do it all," he says.

But a more accurate assessment, one that became obvious to a national TV audience, was that they didn't know what else to do. In the last game of the 1974 season against Notre Dame in the NCAA playoffs, the Austin Peay players went to Fly again and again even though he was bottled up by the aggressive defense of Adrian Dantley and John Shumate. Covered as he was, Fly soon quit moving and proceeded to launch ridiculous off-balance, long-range shots. The game rapidly turned into a rout, but the players continued to pass to Fly, to look to him out of habit and fear. It was an embarrassing display by a horribly unbalanced team, and the Governors lost, 108–66.

Back at Foster Park, late in the evening, the players are cooling off, resting on the hoods and trunks of several cars. Mario has gone home, having gotten sick from playing all day in the heat.

When Rodney comes out for an evening stroll Calvin Franks approaches him, grabbing his T-shirt, touching him, imploring him with pathetic seriousness to get him into school. "One more time, Rod. One more chance to get on my feet."

When Winston drives up with Myra and a car full of groceries, all the boys trudge wearily over and grab the sacks to carry upstairs. All of them have eaten at Rodney's table at one time or another and they do this now as a gesture of thanks.

Franks alone remains in the street watching the group march off. When they are gone he climbs into Winston's car, pretending to be driving.

"Zoom! Vroom! Errrrrrt . . ." he says as he whips the car

through mock turns and waves at imaginary people. "Reeeeeeee. . . . Zoom! Zoom!"

When Winston comes back out a few minutes later and starts his car, the wipers, radio, heater, tape deck, and flashers all go on at once.

Two days ago the Subway Stars had been sitting in the park talking excitedly about their coming game against the Flatbush Flyers on Sunday. Pontiac Carr had located the challengers, a team of white boys approximately the same ages as the Stars.

I liked Pontiac and felt good having him as an assistant. His street knowledge filled a glaring void in my own makeup as head coach. He knew the subway lines and the bus lines and the shortcuts and the cheapest stores for soda and which movie houses showed kung-fu on Saturdays and where the bargains for damaged sneakers could be had. He knew the inner workings of the park world as well. He knew who had the strongest reefer and where the best place to shoplift was and how to bluff a policeman so he thought you were the victim and not a criminal. He knew the easy marks at cards and where holes in fences were and guard dogs and who was kicking whose ass and who not to mess with and who just might be carrying a gun.

One afternoon I asked him for a cigarette.

"I'm out," he said. "But I'll get you some."

I told him I didn't want a whole pack, just one.

"I'll get you one. What kind?"

I had nothing particular in mind so I tried to think of something difficult. I asked for Old Golds.

"Straight?"

"Filter."

He started to run away but then came back. "It's a nickel for one," he said. "But you get three for a dime."

I gave him a dime and watched him disappear through the gate. A minute later he was back with the three cigarettes. I gave him one to put behind his ear and one to smoke and we sat on the bench and lit up. I didn't ask him how he did it. I liked the mystery of it all.

In general, the situation with the team was somewhat better than at first. We did have another practice filled with fights but then we had one that seemed nearly under control. I blew that one, however.

"All right," I had said, "let's get a few of you boys over here for lay-ups."

"Rick, you see any boys around here," said Pablo Billy in a loud voice, "you smack 'em in the mouth."

They began laughing and shouting and talking in pseudo-white voices. "Boys? Boys? Are there boys on the premises?" "Gracious, send the boys home." Martin came over, tears in his eyes, shaking his head. "Rick, wake up. This is modern times."

One solid breakthrough, though, was the ordering of our team shirts from a sports shop on Fulton Avenue in Bedford-Stuyvesant.

We spent an entire morning debating over and designing the logo, figuring out placement of stars and numbers and agreeing on colors. Then all eleven of us went to Freedman's Sporting Goods just down from the park, streaming into the store with the noise and curses that seemed to follow us like background music. The clerk took one look at the group and another at the open boxes of gym shoes, shirts, and socks on display and immediately ordered everyone out. One representative would be allowed in, he said, as we scattered onto the sidewalk. I deemed myself that person and went in to negotiate. Periodically, Martin was allowed in to run suggestions out for a quick vote of the group.

When the haggling was over we all decided that sixty dollars for eleven shirts was too much and we'd have to find another store. Vance rode off on a brakeless bike, using the toe of his shoe against the tire for stopping. He returned after ten minutes, his sneakers smoking and half the toe rubber gone, without having found a store.

Pontiac mentioned the shop on Fulton, and we went there by bus not knowing what to expect.

The neighborhood was dark and ugly with sinister-looking men lining the sidewalks like gargoyles. Many of the store windows were hand-painted and a few were smashed. The insides of several buildings looked charred, like casks waiting for fluid to be pumped in and aged. But the sports shop was what we wanted, and for thirty-eight dollars Lester Roberts, the black owner, promised us shirts in two weeks.

The thought of those shirts and the first game had made the players excitable and a little cocky; they watched the park night life with a pronounced sense of aloofness. Even I felt somewhat singular, sitting next to my team in what must be considered, at least in the limited scope of certain recent events, as my park.

"Now listen," said Pablo Billy in a somber tone. "We gotta be careful. We can't have other dudes getting our jerseys and walking around the city, you know, like they're us."

The players all nodded, except for DeMont.

"No, no. Let's make a hundred of 'em and sell 'em for ten bucks apiece," he cried.

"Boy, shuttup," said Sgt. Rock.

"I figure we can get shorts, too," continued Pablo Billy, "to match our jerseys. And buy plastic numbers to stick on, and spell our names across the back just like . . ."

Doodie interrupted, waving his arms.

"Man, if we get too much shit on there it'll look like shit."

For once I had to agree with him. I was footing half the bill already and the players, I knew, couldn't afford anything more for frills.

"We can sell 'em!" cried DeMont. "We'll get rich! Tell 'em, Rick. Tell 'em."

Vance turned to me. "Why don't you just take his ass over there and kick it till it matches coal."

I looked at DeMont, but he was already backing away. "You never do what I want," he yelled. "Everybody else says stuff. But I just gotta shut up. Fuck all you!" And he sprinted out to the street.

The players laughed and waved good-bye. The discussion of the uniforms started again and continued in desultory fashion until being briefly interrupted by a fight near the main gate, which ended with two Puerto Rican girls waving nail files and chasing a slick down the block.

Shortly after that Rodney Parker came walking into the park

in what was obviously a foul humor. Scalping was down due to poor showings by both the Yankees and Mets, and just tonight Coach Overton of Murray State had called saying he had heard some bad reports from Derrick Melvin's prep school. He was no longer certain he wanted to take the youth, but he might come to Brooklyn for a first-hand appraisal. Rodney had exploded, furious that the coach could doubt his judgment. He made up a lengthy story about Derrick being the greatest point guard in America, that he couldn't protect him forever, that several major colleges were ready to take the youth immediately.

Rumbling into the park, his jaw thrust forward, Rodney resembled Scrooge in search of Bob Cratchit. Spotting Sgt. Rock smiling on the bench, he walked directly up to him.

"You'll never be a ballplayer!" he shouted. "I saw you in practice. You can't listen to advice. You can't be coached. You're scum! You're just another ghetto nothing! You'll be shoveling ditches the rest of your life!"

The players were caught off-guard. I didn't know what to say. I felt awkward, sensing that no one would benefit from this anger.

Sgt. Rock sat up straight, then stood up, trying to defend himself. But before he could get off more than a few curses, Rodney had wandered away toward the subway station.

"Where's he get off saying that stuff?" asked Vance. "What's he ever done for us?"

I told the players not to worry about it and tossed in some lines about us being a unit that had to function as a whole and couldn't be upset by outsiders. It sounded awful as soon as I said it.

"You think I'd let that motherfucker help me?" shouted Sgt. Rock. "Huh? Carr, go get one of those mats."

Pontiac Carr ran over and picked up one of the rubber mats from under the swing set.

"Hold it there," ordered Sgt. Rock. Pontiac held the mat in front of him like a shield.

"Mmf! That's his head," Sgt. Rock grunted as he slugged the mat as hard as he could, sending the Subway Stars' trainer flying. Pontiac came back.

"Mmf! That's his big mouth!" This time Vance and Mark

caught Carr before he crashed into the drinking fountain. He walked back again.

"Mmf! That's his fat stomach."

"Save it, man," said Vance putting his hand on Rock's shoulder. "Use it against those dudes on Sunday."

Today is the Fourth of July and Albert comes by because Rodney has invited him to a picnic at Manhattan Beach. Since the beginning of the summer Albert has changed—becoming at once more timid yet more prone to anger and sudden bursts of sarcasm. He is wary, edgy, and continually on the watch for false motives. Rodney's threats of imminent disaster if Albert stays in New York have become almost a form of challenge to him. He is talking less and avoiding discussions of his future almost completely. He speaks to me still, but not without measuring his answers first. "Winston told me how you get on the phone and listen in," he said.

When Fly drives up to the park in a rented car, Albert backs away, moving to the other side of the fence. Fly terrifies the youth. Once, in a pensive mood, he had told Winston that he was afraid of turning out like Fly, of having his career twisted in the same way.

"Don't get in my car or I'll have to go to my trunk and get my gun," Fly shouts to some bystanders.

As usual a crowd quickly gathers around him, and Fly begins telling his stories. Even Rodney, who is trying to act disgusted, soon drifts over and listens.

"I know I look tired, it's because I slept in the park last night. It was hot and the neighborhood was jumpin', man there was about nine fights going on. They beat up this dude—bam, bam—and when the cops came they told them this guy was crazy, he was on acid. They blamed it all on him. Sssssssssss."

Albert finishes playing a game and starts to come out to buy a soda. Seeing the street vendor is next to Fly, he calls me over.

"Here's a quarter, Rick. Will you get me some grape soda?"

"Why don't you get it?"

"Oh, I just kinda want to stay here. I'll be right over by the court."

Rodney sits down on a car. "Fly throws away a million dollars and he's happy driving a rented car," he mumbles.

"Hey, Rod, my man. Gimme five dollars, will you," shouts Fly. "I'll be needing some gas soon."

Rodney tells him he doesn't deserve any money and Fly starts to chase him through the crowd. Rodney dodges between the parked cars, keeping one between him and Fly. Grinning like a cat, Fly suddenly runs up the hood of the car, over the windshield and roof and down the trunk, grabbing Rodney in a bear hug and snatching a wrinkled dollar bill from his shorts.

At Manhattan Beach, crowded and hot under a scorching sun, Rodney drags Albert along with him, first to the basketball courts and then through the masses of humanity to talk to some coaches he has spotted. Albert is reluctant, wanting simply to wade in the murky brown water and play with Rodney's children. Rodney is unconscious of the boy's feelings, leading him back and forth like a float in a parade.

Rodney gossips basketball in a ceaseless wave, stopping on the way back to chat with George Murden, a black coach in the Bedford-Stuyvesant Restoration's youth division. George has had teams play against Albert and is convinced Al is unique. "He's much better than either Jabbar or Hawkins was at that age," he says. "In fact, I believe he's better than any high-school player in the city right now."

George is also familiar with Fly, having once coached him in a summer league. "He gave me no problem because I *demanded* respect." Indeed, George, with his stab wounds and rugged physique, is well known for openly battling the toughest kids, with fists if necessary. "If you can shut them up, you've got a chance," he says.

Out of curiosity and a growing sense of kinship towards other coaches, I ask him what he thinks the biggest problem with ghetto kids is.

"No doubt about it," he replies. "The absence of male leadership. In the typical absent father home, the mother doesn't have time to give the kids self-confidence. The boys see men acting like kids, so they never grow up. Like with Fly, all this arrogance is a facade. In that Notre Dame game on TV I don't think he was being cocky. He was scared."

Not an earth-shattering revelation, I think to myself, but probably a realistic one. Indeed, from talking with Pontiac Carr I've found that half the Subway Stars are not living with fathers and several of the others have fathers only in the token sense.

For many ghetto boys, George Murden implies, the first contact with a father-figure is through their basketball coach.

Back at Foster Park in the late evening, Lloyd is at his post on the bench working swiftly through a six-pack of beer. He is telling little Ernie and a few others about a kung-fu movie he just saw in which the hero was walking around on one finger and leaping over buildings. "It was nice," says Lloyd. "The man could definitely jam."

DeMont occasionally flashes onto the scene, throwing fire-crackers at cars and dropping cement blocks on rolls of caps. As the evening wears on, the noise output increases noticeably, with sirens and horns joining the crackle of small explosions. Over the buildings sporadic pinwheels of fireworks from Brighton Beach and Coney Island drift towards the sea; and down the block Chinese boys launch whizzing bottle rockets.

The streets have become front yards. On Flatbush Avenue Puerto Rican families carry living-room furniture down to the sidewalk and play dominoes on coffee tables. Over by Doyle's Tavern, a young man beats his girlfriend with a belt, and from a fifth-floor window a bucket of water is dumped on a staggering, singing drunk who sits down in the gutter and stares at his shoes before curling around a parking meter to sleep. Throughout Flatbush residents celebrate America's 198th birthday.

I'm having a small problem of my own. A few days ago I loaned my radio-tape recorder to Albert King and said it would be all right if he took it home with him. Today, though, I need it for an interview.

I call Winston at work and ask him if Albert would have the radio with him now. "He takes it everywhere," Winston says, and offers to call Albert at work to make sure. He does and then calls me back to say that if I need the radio I'll have to ride into

Manhattan and see Albert where he works as an office boy for sports agents Lew Schaffel and Jerry Davis. "I told him you'll be coming," Winston says.

I wish I didn't have to take the radio back. Albert, I know, is at his wits' end, having nowhere to hide from the pressures of the basketball world—whether at school, the playgrounds, or work—and the radio is a soothing balm for him. Yesterday's aggravation at the beach had unnerved him, and working in the offices of two major pro agents obviously eyeing him for the future has put him right on the edge.

When I walk into the office, Jerry Davis calls Albert out from another room. He enters looking oddly sinister.

"Hi, Al," I say.

He says nothing. His face is tight and creased in a way I've never seen it.

"Listen, I have to borrow my radio. I hope you don't mind."

Albert's eyes flash.

"What do you think, I stole it?" he yells.

I look to see if he's kidding. "No, who said that? I just need it for a while is all."

"So who told you to come over here? I don't need your stupid radio!" He glares at me.

"What's going on?" I ask, confused and a bit scared. "What's happening, Albert?"

Suddenly he begins to yell and curse. He goes into the other room and brings out the radio, thrusting it at me. "Go back to Brooklyn!" he screams. "Leave me alone. Take it! Get out of here!"

"Al," I stutter. "I don't understand. I'm not accusing you of anything . . ."

"Leave me alone!" he roars. "I don't want to talk to anybody. Not you, not Rodney, not anybody!"

He grabs his jacket and rushes out of the office, slamming the door.

I look over at Jerry Davis and ask him what is happening.

"I don't know," he says like a man who has just seen his prize cow sink over its head in quicksand. "I don't know."

A short while later Albert calls Winston.

"All people are sick, Winston," he says. "I hate them. I'm not talking to anyone anymore. I don't even think I should play basketball anymore."

Winston tries to settle Albert down.

"Hey, Big Al, you're the man," he says.

"No, I'm *not* the man. I'm just like everybody else. And tell Rodney I'm not playing in his park anymore."

In the afternoon Rodney had come back to the park to send Lloyd Hill off to the Providence College Camp, giving him instructions on how to act, how to dress, and how to deal with the hordes of young white kids he would be helping to supervise for one week. To Lloyd the trip was a magic occurrence. Never had he been on a college campus and never had he been given so much authority.

He sat solemnly listening to Rodney's speech and promised not to smoke pot or get drunk. Rodney gave him some money for the train and Lloyd picked up his bag and walked to the subway. He was wearing a long shirt, buttoned at the sleeves and collar, plaid shorts, platform shoes, and two different colored socks.

"Some people say I look funny," he said on the way out. "But I feel nice."

With the heat of midsummer now resting on Brooklyn's carcass like a collapsed tent, the tempers of the Vanderveer residents and the players in the park have begun to rise accordingly. Close games that once would have ended peacefully with handshakes and good-natured ribbing now finish with shoving matches and threats. Several fights have started over incidents as trivial as an out-of-bounds call or a player's refusal to share a can of soda. "This is the time of year when a person shoots somebody he wouldn't notice in December," says Music Smith.

Last night little Ernie had been lounging in front of the park, feeling the heat like everyone else. In the course of a discussion he had gotten into an argument with one of the slicks and the boy had feinted as if preparing to throw a punch. Ernie hit the boy several times in the face, pushing him into the street. Suddenly the boy dropped back and pulled a knife from his boot.

Making a dash forward he grazed Ernie across the stomach and stabbed him once in the upper leg before grabbing his girlfriend and running off.

Ernie tried to flag a taxi but each time a driver stopped and saw his bloody and torn clothes he drove off. Finally, Ernie limped to the corner of New York Avenue and Foster and waited for a bus. When one came he begged the driver to let him on even though he had no money. At the hospital the doctor sewed up the leg wound which Ernie reported as having cut while climbing a fence.

Today, sitting in the park with his leg bandaged in gauze and a cane at his side, Ernie is a minor attraction.

"Rest up, Ernie. You don't want no limp like Joey's."

"Bernard did it? He's crazy."

Ernie squirms, flexing his short muscular arms, the homemade tattoo on his left bicep stretching. "He'll be something when I put a bullet up his head."

"That's right, Ernie. Pay back."

Last summer two policemen had grabbed Ernie's thirteen-year-old brother off a court, handcuffed him, and taken him away for purse snatching.

The incident hurt Ernie who saw in it a desolate vision of his own future. "That ain't me," he told his friends. "It ain't gonna be me."

He had redoubled his efforts on the basketball courts, ignoring the fact that at barely five feet tall he lacked enough size even to be an effective playmaker. He took the abuse and the physical beating the larger players dished out, and he pleaded with Rodney to find him a prep school somewhere, anywhere. "Please, Rod," he said. "The ghetto's gonna do it to me."

Later, hobbling off to watch a softball game he looks even shorter than he is, a crushed old man with a limp. He has calmed down.

"The real reason I was fighting was, yeh, because I wanted to get on the team. I was runnin' with my head down, Rick. The Subway Stars was gonna be cool."

I tell him I'm sorry, I really am, that the team was already set.

"Hey, man, it's cool. Don't pay no nevermind. I can dig where folks are coming from."

He watched the pitcher's warm-up tosses with exaggerated interest, his face fighting to remain blank.

"You aren't going to try to get back, are you, Ernie?"

He bites his lip. Indecision is written in his posture, in the very clothes he is wearing. His shorts are threadbare and his sneakers salt-crusted but his wide-collared shirt is iridescent and a new earring glitters brightly from his left ear.

"Naw, man, what's the use of pay back." He looks at his leg.

"This ain't nothing, a few stitches. They come out in ten days and then I gotta get back in shape. Gotta play a lot of ball this summer."

Mario and Derrick have returned from Murray State in triumph. Coach Overton was so impressed with their games that he called Rodney to shout his thanks. "Mario's really super, Rod. And Derrick, why he reminds me of Nate Archibald."

Derrick, who runs seven miles daily through the Bedford-Stuyvesant ghetto surrounding his housing project just "to remember," says now: "It's serious. No more late planes. This is the new Derrick going to school."

Mario tells the other players about what a "healthy" situation the town and the people present. "The bitches, man, they got asses this wide. You *know* they're healthy."

Rodney, smarting from Albert's absence since my Manhattan visit and Fly's continued erratic behavior, is only too pleased to pat himself on the back. "My genius," he spouts to anyone who will listen.

"Now I'm really going to lay into those guys. There've been problems before, but no more. Now comes the Parker Pep Talk."

Ever since I met Rodney I have been trying to determine exactly what it is he gets from all his wheeling and dealing, why he works so hard discovering downtrodden boys and sending them to schools, compiling massive phone and food bills in the process with no apparent recompense. Does he simply get money under the table for delivery? Is he looking for the one big apple to make him rich, or is it something more prestigious, that mythical "super-agent" job? Or is it simply goodwill?—Rodney the hyperthyroid samaritan in gym shoes.

I've begun to believe it's all of them, perhaps in fluctuating, unknowable degrees: Rodney the Mystern Man. "He could keep an analyst busy for years," says Manhattan friend Bob Kalich, a part-time author. "He's an angel with unhealthy parts."

Whatever, I have to wonder at times about the returns. Absentmindedly running through the tape Albert King had left in my recorder, I came to a section that needed several replayings. There, between recordings of his favorite songs, after several scratches and clicks, was Albert's voice. "I'll kill him," it said in a low monotone choked with rage. "I'll kill him."

Kill who? Me? Rodney? Lew Schaffel? Winston? Someone else? I felt sad to think there could be so much misunderstanding between a group of people, all of whom quite possibly were motivated by good intentions, all of whom wanted only the best for each other.

Out on the court little Ernie is already hobbling around, shooting stiff-legged in a crowd of older players. He is unable to chase any of the balls down so he asks one of the players if he could toss him one.

"Beat it, punk," says the man.

"Now why you saying that?"

" 'Cause you just a little punk."

"Man, don't call me a punk," says Ernie, his face clouding over with anger.

"Why? If you weren't a punk nobody be calling you no punk."

Suddenly Mario is beside Ernie, putting his arm around him and leading him off court.

"Man, he don't even know me," cries Ernie, trembling with hurt and impotence. "Why's he call me a punk? I'll cut his fucking head off."

Mario holds Ernie and pats him on the back, saying nothing. Ernie slowly calms down and, fighting back tears, limps out of the park.

Late at night, Teddy Wallendorf, a white youth from Sheepshead Bay whom Rodney had sent to summer camp several times, drives Mario, Calvin Franks, Craig Martin, Rodney, and me out to a park near his house. The court there is dimly lit by a street light that happens to be pointed slightly askew. The boys pair up and proceed to play game after game of two-on-two, with Rodney watching from the sidelines.

I walk off and from a distance the pat, pat, pat of the ball sounds very soft, almost delicate as it floats through the sleeping residential area. The game looks small and somewhat strange, as though four people are simply gyrating in front of a fence. But it also looks intense, filled with hidden meaning. "Sometimes in a game you get so close to what's going on you forget who you are," Music Smith had told me.

As I watch Rodney watching what must be his umpteen-thousandth hour of the game, I can tell he is troubled by uncomfortable thoughts. Fly and Albert, who knows where they may be. And Calvin Franks, even normally noncommittal Mario has noticed the changes in him. "He just stares at you," says Mario, "and then breaks into that 'Aaaaaah' laugh. He almost looks like he could kill someone."

Rodney wanders away from the action. "Everybody is insane," he states, leaning against a pole. "Or maybe it's just that nobody in the ghetto knows what 'sane' is. How can I send Franks anywhere? The coach would know in a minute the kid isn't right." He looks in at the court.

"And now this little Ernie has started pestering me. He's sick too. How in the hell can I send a kid five feet tall somewhere and still have any coaches or scouts trust my judgment? I'm not a magician. Who's gonna be the first kid to come gunning for me when I turn him down?"

MID-JULY

The Subway Stars are having their problems. Organized with great expectations, they have so far reaped nothing but frustration.

On Sunday they waited eagerly for the arrival of the Flatbush Flyers. I kept them busy shooting lay-ups and chattering for nearly an hour and a half. But the team didn't arrive. Drawing Pontiac Carr to one side I asked him what he thought the problem was.

"I don't know, coach. Want me to find out?"

I told him I did. He hopped on a bike and pedaled furiously out of the park. Thirty minutes later he returned, sweating and bedraggled.

"I saw one of the guys. He said two of their players had to go to New Jersey and another of 'em's sick. They ain't coming."

The Subway Stars began moping, then acting surly and ridiculing one another. I tried to tell them to relax, that it wasn't that important. But as usual my halfhearted advice went unheeded. The boys became sullen and wandered off in various directions.

I felt angry for the position I'd put myself in. Half coach, half reporter, I was becoming not much of either. I didn't feel it was my duty to be a disciplinarian, but then how else could anyone run anything. I stood there looking stupid.

DeMont was agitated. "I don't know what to do," he said. "I'm bored."

He began smashing soda bottles against the bench and lining them up in jagged rows. Mark came over and slapped him on the head. "They'll put your nigger ass in jail so deep they'll have to pump in daylight!" he shouted. DeMont, angered and crying, tried to stab Mark with a bottle.

I felt more frustrated than ever. Several days ago DeMont had come up to me all excited. "Sit down, Rick," he said. "Listen to this. I'm playing third base on the new softball team. Third base!"

I told him I was proud.

The very next day he got into a fight in the first game, swinging a bat and taking on boys twice his size. "They threw me out of the league," he said that night. "I didn't want to play anyway." When I tried to tell him he'd made a mistake by fighting, DeMont waved his hand at me. "You don't understand anything," he said in disgust, walking away.

At the gate, Sgt. Rock approached me.

"I don't see how the Subway Stars can make it," he said.

"But you haven't even played a game yet."

"I know. But we're mean and we argue too much. We're not together. It's like we can't help it."

In the evening, Rodney calls a nineteen-year-old named Mark Harris, a player he helped send to a small college in Michigan a year ago on a full scholarship. Rodney has heard from other players that Mark is not going to return to school despite his great basketball potential.

"I don't know, Rod," says the youth. "I don't want to play anymore. I don't want the college degree. Nothing. I don't want to work that hard."

"Man, I got a lot of *major* colleges interested in you," says Rodney.

"I just can't do it another year. I give the coach a hard time, I talk back and fight. And I don't really mean it. I just stand there and think to myself, 'What am I doing here?'"

"You're only nineteen once. You'll never get another chance."

There is a long silence.

"You'll look stupid getting on the subway every morning at 6'6"."

More silence.

"Mark, I can get you a good job after school, maybe even pro ball. Why mess up now?"

"I don't know, Rodney." The young man's voice is pained, filled with stifled emotion. "I mean like last winter the heat went off in the dorm and I had to sleep in my pants and socks. I just don't know, I can't explain it."

Though Rodney makes the youth promise to think it over, he knows when he hangs up that it's futile. He bounces a sock off the wall as though shooting a basket.

When Rodney was nineteen he had sent letters to a number of colleges offering his services as a high-scoring guard. The letters were written on cheap tablet paper and showed the grammatical skills of a second grader. At the time, as now, Rodney was over three years away from a high-school diploma.

The old German with the green cap is sitting in the park today watching the games. He has seen a great deal of transition in the neighborhood but unlike most of the white residents he has stayed on and on.

"Twenty years ago, before they built these apartments, this was the Water Works, a big hole," he states. "The water, *ach*, it tasted like salt, very lousy. Then they built the Vanderveer and give us city water. It was a nice neighborhood. No black people, but there was a small section way out on Lott Avenue. But you can't blame things on them. Or the white people moving away. No, not on anybody. Even me I think this fall I have to move to Miami because of winter. Who's fault is winter?"

Another visitor for the day, Joe Iaquingo, sits on an adjacent bench and looks at the park where he grew up. Eight years ago Rodney had gotten Joe and a couple of his buddies tryouts with the Mets.

"When I was a kid this place was *all* white," Joe begins. "I'm speaking of the fifties to mid-sixties. Real pretty area, too, with flower gardens around and crap like that. Everybody I knew was either Jewish, Italian, or Irish. No Protestants. You either went to temple or mass. And usually you hung out with your own gang. There were the Skulls, the Good Guys, the Fugitives, the East 31st Street Boys . . . we'd name our softball teams after our gangs. As we got older we had fights and all, but not with chains and zip guns and that garbage. We were more a group that stuck together.

"Sometimes my friends and I would go to other parks in the Bronx or Lower Manhattan looking for competition. Over there you actually had to fight to stay alive. If somebody says something to you, you can't look around, you just gotta swing at the nearest head so they know you're not afraid.

"Back in those days Mac used to lock the front and back gates to the park every night. Some nights we'd tell him to go ahead and close up and then we'd climb out. That fence is over ten feet high, too. As a matter of fact, I broke my ankle one night and had to climb out of here.

"But don't get the idea it was all roses before the blacks came. There used to be a lot of junkies hanging around—drugs really hit hard in the sixties, believe me. Finding guys dead on the rooftops and all that. To give you an idea, I played grammer school baseball for St. Jerome's on Nostrand and of the twelve guys who could start on that 1962 team nine of them right now are dead or in drug programs. And then the regular kids starting sniffing a lot of glue. That's why Mac began leaving the park open at night, so these french-fried kids could sleep it off in here.

"But even before that was going on Rodney used to come around. He was the only black as far back as 1960, and he used to bring a fivesome in here for the games. I mean he brought some *players* with him—Oscar Robertson, Jim McMillian, this great leaper named Summers, and, of course, Lenny Wilkens. Man, three of those guys were All-Pros. But players didn't get all excited and lose their jocks over it, we just played ball. And the games we had? Two-hour battles that were tied all the way—my five against Rod's—rough as anything you'll ever want to see, but honest and clean. The crowd didn't just cheer for the white guys either. This black guy named Joe Bush used to put a show on, dribble between his legs, run down court, cock the ball behind his ear, and then lay it up off his bald head. The crowd went apeshit over that.

"And this one white guy, Roger McGann, who's about 5'7", blew the black guys' minds. One day Jim McMillian, 6'5", is here and McGann throws the ball over McMillian's head off the backboard, runs around him, grabs the ball in the dead corner, and set shots it through, swish. Then the next time McGann brings the ball inbounds he takes two dribbles and looks McMillian in the eye. Real casual-like he hits a two-handed bomb from full court. Jim just picked up his bag and left.

"It was great for everybody, but it had to end, I guess. My family finally moved from our place on Flatbush and 26th because there was this arsonist going around one winter throwing burning Christmas trees through store windows. He tossed one in our hallway and that was that."

Lionell Worrell rides his bike into the park around dinner time and locates Rodney shooting for quarters on a center court.

Even though the Providence deal he had hoped for fell through, Lionel tells Rodney he has torn up his scholarship re-offer at Michigan. Playing behind Jerry Grote, a white guard who directs the attack without the flair Lionel feels he can offer, has soured him completely.

"I want to showcase my thing this summer and go to a place where I'll be the man," he says.

Rodney suggests Fairfield College in Connecticut, a school that has shown great interest in Danny Odums if he is ruled ineligible at Austin Peay.

Lionel says that sounds okay but he'd like to find out something concrete soon. "Like it's getting late and I'm kinda scared. This is serious business."

At 10:30 P.M. Rodney gets the call he had been anticipating from coach Lake Kelly at Austin Peay.

"Bad news, Rod," says the coach glumly. "They turned it down. All the boys on probation because of the test scores have been ruled ineligible. Danny, Fly, and all the others. We're pretty upset down here. The NCAA really stuck us."

Rodney hangs up. Instead of being upset, he is ecstatic. He can wheel and deal again.

"The visiting is on!" he hollers, leaping across the room. "Got to tell Danny!"

Rodney dashes out of the building and runs the few blocks to Danny's apartment on Bedford and Avenue D. He has to make the announcement in person because the Odums family does not have a telephone.

"Danny! Danny!" Rodney screams up at the window even though it is eleven-thirty and the lights are out. "We're in good shape! Come on out!"

Danny walks out on the front steps rubbing his eyes, wearing only a pair of long trousers. Devoted to his sport, he gets up at six o'clock every morning before work to shoot baskets.

"You can go anywhere," blares Rodney. "You can sign at ten schools and go anywhere!"

Danny smiles and nods.

"After this it's the pros and money rolling in," yells Rodney, who is making so much noise that a number of neighborhood dogs have begun howling. "Then you move from Bedford and D to Bedford on the sea!"

The Subway Stars have managed to scrape up a few teams to play, and so far have won one game and lost three. The victory was a narrow win over a handful of rag-tag park regulars. And the losses, two of which I missed, being out of town on other business, were to equally unimpressive units. Music watched both of those losses and felt that the Stars were better players than either of the teams.

"See, when they start losing they don't try harder, they just get mad and try to start fights. Then the other team just ignores them."

"I know that. But why do they fight each other?"

"Well, I believe it's because they know each other."

"That doesn't make any sense."

"No. It sure don't."

I had induced Eddie Campbell to coach one of the games I had to miss. He resigned immediately afterward. "I screamed and screamed but it didn't do any good," he says. "You can't dribble through a press hollering 'Sucker,' every five feet, but that's what they try to do."

Today Fly comes into the park with Country James. He is eating from a bag of cherries, mashing them on one side of his mouth and shooting the pits out the toothless side.

Tomorrow Fly is taking a plane to Washington D.C., for a summer league game. The team he plays on is sponsored by the Moorish American League of Brooklyn, and all the uniforms, tickets, and expenses are paid for by wealthy black business entrepreneur Joseph Jeffries-El, who is also the Grand Sheik of an Islamic Temple in Brownsville. Fly has come by just to look around, and as usual, the park seems to energize with his presence. Fly has read in the paper about the Ohio Valley Conference suspensions and feels certain the players will be upset knowing he can't come back.

"I know all of them wanted me to stay at Austin Peay," he says. "Rodney's lying when he says they're happy I'm not coming back. Anybody who talks too much always lies."

Country James, Fly's companion with the silver Rolls Royce, stands off to the side watching his friend. I ask what has happened to ruin the one-time rapport between Fly and Rodney.

"Rodney always tries to joke with Fly and then slip in things that are serious right afterwards," he says. "From what I've seen the only way to get anywhere with Fly is to talk like a man."

"Hey Ed-dee," chuckles Fly. "You are West Indian, I see. We go back to Bom-bay soon?"

"Panama. It's in South America, Spanish," says Eddie Campbell.

"How do you like America, Ed-dee?"

Fly continues to prance about, seemingly without a care, heedless that agent Lew Schaffel is running into wall after wall in his attempt to find him a professional team. Just the other day, Carl Scheer, the new general manager of the Denver Rockets, said that despite Fly's talents "his terrific maturity problem in crucial situations" made him expendable. "We've had our fill of street players," said the GM.

LATE JULY

s the plane takes off from La Guardia Airport, Fly closes
his eyes tight and grabs the armrests. I'm sitting in the
seat next to him, having come along to do a story about
him for *Sports Illustrated.*

"Good-bye Brooklyn," he moans. "Good-bye world." He
remains motionless until the plane reaches cruising altitude. His
fear of flying normally would be covered by a layer of
braggadocio, but today Fly appears to be in a rare pensive
attitude. More developments have occurred in the last half year
than at any time in his life—doors to the future have been
routinely opened and closed—and though most of it seems to
have sailed over Fly's head, apparently some of the vibrations
have touched.

"It's all a big joke to Fly," Rodney had said. There were the
trips he had made to Lew Schaffel's office, bringing with him his
rowdy street friends, "those Brownsville bandits," Lew called
them. And there were the continued common-sense directions
he ignored, even went out of his way to disregard.

At times Fly seemed to be parodying the ghetto product,
doing his best to be the shiftless, broken, hell-raising type he saw
on the street corners of his neighborhood. To be just like them
he needed to eliminate choices, and he was zeroing in on that
goal. As I watch him staring down at the clouds I wonder if he
realizes that the process has gone far enough.

"I know everybody thinks I'm a real, real superbad-attitude

case," he admits. There was the time he sat down at half court during a Madison High game and the time he went berserk during a Glen Springs game and grabbed a chair to fight off the entire crowd and the times he waved to the crowd and the tantrums at Austin Peay. . . . But there also has been the way he has handled himself in the few months since the '74 season ended. He seems to realize that the "attitude" label has to do with that, too.

Trying to explain the recent series of events, he shows a near helpless confusion.

"Okay, see, I took my name out of the NBA hardship draft in May because I listened to the coaches, and as far as I knew I was going back to school. The Denver thing with the ABA? Well, nobody contacted me about no million dollars. Then the suspension hit and I couldn't go back to Peay. I didn't want to go anywhere else, so I didn't go to summer school to make up classes so I could transfer.

"I figured I'd go to the ABA and just take what I could get. I know I lost a lot of money but, man, Rodney ain't helping by saying they're gonna blackball me in the pros. He was supposed to be helping me. . . ."

I suggest that maybe Rodney is acting strangely because he is mad, because he thought Fly was going back to school.

"Man, I *told* him I wasn't going back to school. I hadn't gone to class for two months. He called me at the time at Peay and I told him. See, I knew about the ineligibility thing right after the season. It was getting around and they were talking about forfeiting all our games."

But in a phone conversation back in May, Fly had told Rodney specifically that he would be returning to Austin Peay in the fall. I mention this to him.

He ignores it.

"Well, then why did you take your name out of the draft if you knew you weren't going back to school?" I ask.

"Why'd I take my name out of the draft if I knew I wasn't going back to school? Well, see. . . ." He struggles as though it's all really so obvious, if people could just understand. "See, I *didn't* know . . . I mean, it was . . ." He stops and shakes his head.

Along with Fly on the flight is his longtime friend and fellow Moorish American League teammate, Greg "Jocko" Jackson. A recent graduate of Guilford College, Jocko, a 6'1″ guard, was the fifth-round draft choice of the New York Knicks this year. Around Brownsville he is known as "the Rocket Man" because of his amazing spring. In a game I had watched last summer at The Hole I saw him jump completely over a man's back and pin a lay-up at the top of the board.

With his polite, educated demeanor he seems worlds apart from Fly, and yet he was raised in the same Brownsville project and nurtured in the same squalor. Though no one can say what makes people different, Jocko feels that for Fly the small, immediate victories within basketball are directly linked to his self-esteem, that they have become substitutes for the other larger types of success.

"Scoring is the thing with Fly," he says. "Making points. He gets upset, *real* upset when he doesn't score."

Knowing this, Jocko frequently bends his own game to soothe his friend. "I do things to keep him happy. I'll tell him over and over that he could take his man if he wanted to, even if he isn't. He likes that."

As the MAL team begins to warm up for their game against a Maryland team which includes young high-school graduate Moses Malone and Indiana Pacer rookie Len Elmore, a change comes over Fly. Through his arrogance has seeped a cold earnestness. He is serious, preparing for something more than a game. Unsmilingly he sinks one jump shot after another, displaying over the unmistakable playground gyrations a classic form, hands high, eyes riveted on the rim.

Coaches who used to feel that Fly was indifferent to the game itself misunderstood his actions. "I *love* basketball," Fly has said again and again. "It's my life." It is an irony proved, as much as anything, by his unpredictable court behavior.

When the game starts, Fly takes the opening tip and goes directly at the 6'11″ Malone and 6'9″ Elmore, the obvious challenges. The two men, sensing the attack, prepare themselves for battle. Fly takes almost every one of his team's shots, dribbling the ball up the floor, switching from hand to hand, driving from side to side, maneuvering in towards the larger players like a colt charging into a forest. His mouth is open and the sweat pours off him as he works frantically, maniacally. With every gesture he tries to prove something. With every shot he attempts to assert himself.

Moses steps out and leaps high above the rim to bat away one of Fly's twisting lay-ups. Fly returns and drops in a fallaway over Malone's outstretched hand. The crowd roars its appreciation, sensing the spirit of the night, that here is something closer to private warfare than sport. Amazingly, of Fly's first eight shots two are blocked, three go in, and three are goaltended.

By the quarter Fly has fifteen points, but he is unhappy and storms off the floor. "Already I got two fouls," he fumes. "It happens every week. The refs don't want me to play, that's why I only get 30 instead of 60." He throws a towel and walks out of the gym to sit alone on the cement steps.

Back in the game later he continues his private assault on the basket, gaining his biggest victory just at the halftime buzzer. In a mad dash against the clock he takes a giant step at the free-throw line, going up and beyond Len Elmore, and smashes through a stuff shot that nearly blows the doors off the Pentagon five miles away. At Foster Park they would call it a perfect "in his face."

Two men dance past me out of the stands and onto the floor with the shot as the whole gym rocks. "He say . . . *shut up!*" says one as they slap palms madly.

In the second half Fly's intensity does not slacken for an instant. He yells at the refs, throwing his hands up to symbolize his persecution; and at one point goes one-on-one so blatantly that three other players come over to help guard him. As the game ends Fly puts up the last shot, a swisher from thirty feet away. He finishes with an even 50 points.

Though Fly monopolized play, scoring nearly half his team's total, the other players are not upset. "We all understand what he's doing." says Jocko. "We all went to college, we should have some smarts."

The story I wrote that night was not an easy one. I tried to be fair, but I really didn't know what Fly was doing. And I didn't know if he knew what he was doing. I started out with the graffiti.

Fly Williams knows he is becoming a folk hero in New York City because he has seen the writing on the wall. On the handball courts and playground walls and backboards of his native Brooklyn. On the red-brick projects of the Brownsville district. On the sidewalks and telephone poles. "Man, I saw FLY WILLIAMS, STONE AVENUE, painted on a *brand* new subway car the other day," he says, "I couldn't believe it. These kids write my name everywhere."

Then I told about the problem—the test scores and the attitudes and the fact that he wasn't really wanted back at Austin Peay and probably not in the pros.

Then I gave him the benefit of my doubt.

Fly is now finally aware of his situation and for the first time is giving very serious thought to his future as a pro. "All I've got now is basketball. I want to show people I can play with anybody, mold to fit any team. I'll take whatever they offer to let me play. I have to."

But did he really have the situation that broken down? It seemed unlikely. What about his childish antics at Foster Park, and the fact that his game tonight was as one-sided as any I had ever witnessed? There was a lifetime of problems hounding Fly each time he stepped on court, not just a few missed opportunities.

I told the story of the two men slapping palms and then ended by saying that Fly's loss to the game would be everybody's, that he had too much to say on court.

The story ran the next week in *Sports Illustrated* under the heading, WHERE CAN THE FLY LAND? The photo the editors chose to run with the piece showed a silent, worried Fly gazing into the distance, his hand over his mouth, his eyes wide and thoughtful. It was very convincing.

Albert King did not return to work after walking out in a fit of rage two weeks ago. "He could have at least called," says Jerry Davis, the nervous, elderly partner of Schaffel and Davis. "I guess he was too embarrassed, though."

Nor does Rodney understand how he personally could have been in any way responsible for Albert's flare-up. "I think that's just the kind of kid he was inside all the time."

About the fact that Albert was working all along in a veritable pressure cooker Rodney only says, "Hell, it was a good job and he worked hard."

Through his grapevine sources Rodney has learned that Albert has a new job working in a park not far from his home. He is being employed by Gil Reynolds, a small, tough ghetto coach who is good friends with Joseph Jeffries-El. Somehow, Rodney says, the two have combined to pay Albert fifty dollars a week for doing nothing. "Some days he's supposed to work on his shooting. Other days he works on his dribbling."

With Fly playing on Jeffries-El's MAL team and Albert now apparently in the wealthy minister's camp as well, Rodney feels a conspiracy has been laid against him. Yesterday afternoon he called Albert and told him he was being bought, that the time would come when Jeffries-El, who recently has begun represent-ing pro players, would own him. "He wants you for himself," said Rodney. After that Rodney yelled at Albert for being rude and for walking out of his job. Albert replied that he didn't care. Not about that, not about anything.

Bad happenings seem to be in the air, all of a sudden. Two days ago DeMont, Pontiac Carr, and I had taken the bus to the sports shop in Bedford-Stuyvesant where our Subway Stars shirts were being made. One of the heavy plate glass windows on the side of the store was boarded up and there were bloodstains on the pavement.

"What happened?" DeMont asked the clerk.

"Some boys tried to break in last night."

"Didja catch 'em?"

"Yeh, the police caught 'em. The alarm went off. One of them nearly lost a finger."

"Wow!" said DeMont.

"What were they after?" asked Pontiac.

"Got me. We don't keep any money here."

The boys looked around at the store's contents. Basketballs, posters of Julius Erving and Abdul-Jabbar, sneakers, tube socks, sweatbands, shorts and bags, uniforms. A paradise.

The man followed their eyes.

"Maybe some Pro-Keds," he said. "Seems funny to do five years for that, though."

Despite the incident our shirts were ready. I paid the man the balance due, approximately fourteen dollars. The players had all paid me their share, a dollar apiece. Yanking a shirt out of the box DeMont held it up and began yipping with joy.

"Oh, man, look at my jersey! Number thirty-two! Dr. J! That's me, Number thirty-two!"

Back at the park the shirts were instant sensations. Red with black stars and the logo: "Subway Stars, Foster Park, All-City, Brooklyn, N.Y.," they drew boys out of every nook and cranny like a pied piper's flute. Pontiac had to fight to hold onto the box, but within minutes each team member had arrived and gotten his own shirt. Personally I was quite pleased with the shirts, enjoying the sight of the red splotches spreading through the park as the players made the rounds.

It was in that same spirit of enthusiasm the next day, Sunday, that I suggested the team take a trip to Manhattan for a ball game. The players were all for it and immediately began shooting craps for subway fare.

"Where we going, Rick?" Pablo Billy asked.

I didn't really know. Someone had told me there was a park with a few decent courts on East 18th Street. On Sunday, I figured, there was bound to be some action, and if we wanted to get a game it should be easy.

We got on the subway at Newkirk, with Pablo Billy, Mark, and Sgt. Rock, hopping the turnstile and diving through the train doors as they closed. The man in the booth shook his fist in anger. At West 14th Street in lower Manhattan we got off.

"Where did you say those courts were on 18th Street?" Pontiac Carr asked.

"Eighteenth and Lexington, I think the guy said."

"Well, goddamn, Rick, we're on Eighth Avenue."

It was a bright day and there were artists and sculptors and dogs scattered along the sidewalk. The paintings hanging on the fences resembled skylines done in a hurry and the sculptings looked to have been welded from hangers and spoons and carburetors. The dogs were mangy and half-rabid-looking, but there was a cheerfulness lingering over the area as tourists came and went and the bells in a nearby church chimed the hour.

We started walking crosstown, a loud defiant group openly evaded by pedestrians. DeMont jogged in the front, kicking cans and rattling car doors. I wasn't sure how far we had to go but I wanted it to be short; I felt this could be a strong, unifying day if conflict was meticulously avoided.

Pontiac Carr walked on my left, and Doodie, his large ball-peen head trembling with excitement, clung to my right arm.

"Rick, we gonna donut 'em," he yelled in my ear, "put the skunk on they ass! They ain't gonna believe it when we walk in, they be so petrolized, all these nasty niggers jackin' and jivin' . . ."

He got on my nerves sometimes, all eagerness, malapropisms and stupidity. And his gawky body only added to the effect. All of the boys were growing, but Doodie seemed to be haphazardly elongating, like a rubber figure grabbed at each end and stretched. I worried that some day his threadlike neck would no longer support his head and the entire affair would simply wilt on his shoulders like a bloated sunflower.

Doodie did not have an easy time of it at Foster Park, and his jabberings and false cockiness were mostly reactions to his lowly status there. Under the basket he was pushed around by much shorter players; on the bench he was the brunt of the jokes.

"Hey, you cross-eyed motherfucker," they teased him. "What's it look like outa that eyeball." In the photos I had begun taking of the park boys Doodie always tried to hide half of his head behind another player or under a towel or jersey in an attempt to keep from looking ridiculous.

His one hero was Fly Williams, whom he called "my man" and imitated both on and off the court. He worked endlessly at "finger-rolling" the ball and dribbling through his legs and other useless tactics which he equated with Fly's court prowess. In all debates Doodie defended Fly's honor with his own. Whenever Fly came to Foster Park Doodie followed like a shadow, grinning with reverence. Whenever Fly drove off Doodie watched the departing car until it vanished. Fly, for his part, never noticed the boy.

We reached 17th Street and Second Avenue but there was no basketball court in sight. This made me nervous. En route the players had demanded we stop in a candy store and had then proceeded to shoplift the place blind. Now, after the long walk they were in a rather volatile humor. Without stopping I turned left. At 18th Street, where the park was supposed to be, there was nothing. "You on your own now, coach," Pontiac Carr whispered to me.

At 19th Street I could see an asphalt, treeless park a block away on First Avenue, and I led the boys there without a hint of the relief I felt. The players in a basketball game on the far court turned to watch us file in through the fence.

"Who you guys?" a small Puerto Rican boy asked as the Subway Stars changed into their shorts and red T-shirts.

DeMont told him we were a basketball team from Brooklyn looking for a game, so why didn't he go find some suckers for us to play.

The boy ran off and within moments we had our challenge. The entire park and its mixed Puerto Rican, black, and Italian population mobilized into a unit, putting together a ragged squad of ten players varying in age, I estimated, from thirteen to thirty-five. The remaining locals stood at one end of the court and shouted out insults. One of the Manhattan players, a barrel-chested black man about thirty years old with a razor scar from his nose to his ear, came up to Sgt. Rock. "We don't lose in here," he said.

I gathered the Stars together and told them to go out and play team ball, to hustle on defense, to pass the ball and wait for the good shot on offense. "Just like we worked on in practice," I said. "If you get a chance to run, go ahead and run." I was amazed at how easily the cliches rolled out of my mouth. I was a little scared. I sent the first five out: Martin and Pablo Billy at guard, Vance and Arthur at forward, and Sgt. Rock at center.

The game started and soon passersby began drifting up to the fence to watch the action. Cabbies pulled over to look, and men in suits and ties stepped up, shading their eyes with newspapers.

The Stars, unable to figure out the swirling air currents or the bounce of the unfamiliar rims, quickly fell behind. They made only five baskets before crumbling completely and being swept away. From the park crowd came a din of humiliating catcalls. "Subway assholes!" they chanted. "Go play on the D train!"

Attempting to regroup, the Subway Stars stood in a cluster yelling at each other. Lloyd Hill, who had come along as assistant coach, tried to calm them down while I went over to the other team and asked hesitantly if they'd like to play another game.

"Hell, yes," said a tall red-haired kid. "We'll send you back to Brooklyn in baggies if you want."

As the game began the Subway Stars seemed to realize they had little to lose by playing as hard as they could. I'd told them as much, asking them to perform as though they were back in the confines of Foster Park. DeMont had looked worried. "I'm gonna break some bottles," he said, tugging on my belt.

For a while the Stars played wildly, taunting the other team and elbowing them under the boards. Pablo Billy opened his eyes wide and shook his head back and forth as he stutter-dribbled through a fast break. Sgt. Rock and Vance combined to block a shot so hard that the entire rim, backboard and pole spun around in its foundation. Mark, talking all the way, threw in a blind reverse lay-up. But soon the disorder returned.

Doodie attempted a Fly-style whirlybird which disintegrated in midair like a watch exploding. Then Mark got so disgusted with Pablo Billy's dribbling that he stood statuelike in the corner, facing the street. I called time out and told Mark to start playing or he'd sit on the bench.

"Man, how'd *you* like to play with that yo-yoing punk nigger?"

Lloyd held Pablo Billy, but I knew the day was lost. Shortly after that, Champagne, still uncertain of the rules, called time-out while the other team had the ball and then watched from the sidelines as his man went in to score.

By the end, with the game again turning into a rout, I could hear crashes of glass against pavement as DeMont started breaking bottles. "They gonna fight, I know it," he said, slipping the necks over his fingers like claws.

But there were no fights. While I placated the Manhattan team in my most diplomatic voice, Arthur, the quietest of all the Stars, grabbed Sgt. Rock who was muttering about "caving someone's chest in," and Martin grabbed Doodie, who was squaring off with a bowlegged Puerto Rican. Lloyd Hill directed the squad out the gate and I quickly joined them as we beat an angry and embarrassed retreat toward the subway.

Back at Foster Park Rodney Parker watched as the Subway Stars entered their territory. He was feeling sorry for himself of late, I knew, but his words were even more contemptuous than usual. "Look at them, every one of them an attitude case and not one of them a ballplayer. Worthless trash."

He closed his eyes and feigned deep thought. "Don't tell me. I bet they just got their asses kicked by a team half as good as them, but if you ask them they'll say the game was stolen, the refs were crooked, everybody cheated." I said nothing, but he was very close.

Earlier in the day Rodney was supposed to have taken Calvin Franks with him to Manhattan to talk to the coach of a small northern Arizona college. Before it was time to go, Calvin played in a quick half-court game, and Rodney, who had ordered him not to shoot "even a lay-up" for a week, was utterly disgusted by Calvin's display of dribbling and shooting. "The kid thinks a pass is like a Christmas present," snapped Rodney. Then Calvin got dressed for the event, wearing checkered slacks three inches too short, huge, outdated, round-toed shoes, an Austin Peay T-shirt, sunglasses, and his green beret. In his arm he clutched his ragged briefcase.

"The guy looked like a goddam clown," said Rodney, who told Franks the coach had called and wasn't coming to town after all.

Watching the Subway Stars invent stories about their journey to a foreign park, Rodney sneered and fluffed out his beard. In some places white curlicues mingled with the black. Three boys bumped into him as they walked by checking attendance figures in the paper to see if their mothers had won anything from the numbers runners.

It hadn't been a good journey. Everything was the same as before. The Foster Park courts were jammed, as usual. I wondered if Dr. Naismith would recognize the sport he invented in 1891 so athletes could have something to play "indoors in the evening and during the winter season . . ." Maybe. Having nothing better to do I wandered out onto the number two court and joined a game of taps with three teen-agers in multicolored platform shoes and vinyl hats.

At noon Rodney gathers Mario, Craig Martin, Teddy Wallendorf, Lloyd Hill, Possum, and two other players together and leads them off to a game he has arranged in Englewood, New Jersey, with the highly ranked Dwight Morrow High School team. The game is a clandestine affair, played behind locked gymnasium doors. The high school coach and several college scouts are present.

Rodney hopes a few of his players will be noticed, but the reason the scouts have come is to see Englewood's seventeen-year-old William "Poodle" Willoughby, an unstoppable 6'7" forward. Within a year Poodle will become one of the few basketball players in history to be drafted straight out of high school into the pros.

Before the game Lloyd Hill looks worried. He sees the white men with their clipboards and whistles sitting and chatting in the bleachers and he knows that this is important, that some of them will be watching. Though loud and brash at Foster Park, anywhere outside Lloyd becomes humble and wide-eyed.

When Rodney announces his staring line-up, Lloyd is placed at forward because Mario, Craig, and Possum are more natural guards. Lloyd goes out and takes a couple of dunks to show the men he can jump. But his natural confidence seems to have disappeared with the mysterious feel of hardwood under his feet. He tiptoes over the polished floor as though afraid of scuffing it with his ragged sneakers.

In the game the scouts ooh and ah over Poodle's shooting and ballhandling abilities. When he chases a loose ball, sliding out of bounds with the force, the men dive to their reports to write about his excellent aggressiveness and hustle. When he passes up an easy ten-foot jumper to hit a man open for a lay-up, they scribble about his selflessness and team play. They take little notice of Rodney's boys other than to admire Mario's fine long-range shooting and to comment on a strange, somewhat bewildered-looking player wearing a T-shirt with a large red tongue on it.

"You know that guy?" one scout asks me.

"Yeh, he's from the park. His name's Lloyd."

"What is he, on drugs or something?"

Down on the floor Lloyd is meandering about like a lost dog. His "standing jump shot" looks foolish next to the disciplined shooting around him. Several times when he goes up for one-handed rebounds opponents snatch the ball away before he can pull it in. On defense his pushing and hacking earns him foul after foul. He looks toward the bench for help, something to give him balance in these surroundings.

His moves that are so devastating on the rough asphalt of Foster Park seem to lack purpose in this gleaming gym; his fakes against Poodle seem as ludicrous as poker bluffs on a croupier.

"He can play," I tell the men, wanting them to understand.

"He doesn't seem to have a real good 'feel' for the game, does he?" says a scout.

"And he looks awful old," adds another.

They watch the game, forgetting Lloyd for the present.

"Makes you wonder if he could play organized ball," says one of the scouts finally.

"But a lot of school programs aren't too organized either," comments an assistant coach from North Carolina State. "I always say there's a college for everybody if you look hard enough."

After the game Lloyd mumbles to Rodney that he couldn't get his shot off too well today. His two or three stuffs at the end of the game, he realizes, didn't impress anyone.

On the way back to Foster Park Lloyd stares out the window as though deeply interested in the scenery.

Connie Hawkins used to call his little friend Eddie Simmons "the Çzar" because Eddie was one of the slickest operators he knew. A young man with all the lines, angles, and toughness necessary to dominate the ghetto heap, Eddie was also one of Connie's earliest playground mentors in Bedford-Stuyvesant. "Ed took me under his wing for six years," Connie stated in his biography, *Foul!*. "I thought he knew everything. I depended on him for advice. He was like an older brother that knew everything."

A premier street player himself, it was only after Connie left town to play pro ball that Eddie Simmons started the slow, ugly descent into drugs, becoming yet another ex-playground hero with tracks on his arms.

Two years ago he died under mysterious circumstances, and as a tribute to him and his tragic yet familiar story the annual "Eddie Simmons Memorial Game" was organized at Long Island University in downtown Brooklyn by Connie and other friends.

Yesterday the event was held again and there were two games, one for professionals and the other for just-graduated high school stars. Rodney had heard that Bernard King, Albert's older brother, was playing in the high school game, so we took the subway to the gym.

In the game which pitted Brooklyn against Manhattan, Bernard, a 6'5" forward, played with a combination of grace and muscle so similar to Albert's style that at moments Rodney began shouting his old battle cry, "Do it, Big Al!" So transfixed was he by the game that when halftime came he continued to stare at the vacant court for several minutes.

Shortly after the game ended a very tall man in street clothes walked across the court. The crowd immediately recognized Connie Hawkins and started cheering and whistling. "Put a shirt on the man!" they cried. But Connie had flown in only to pay his tributes to Eddie Simmons; his knee was strained and he was unable to play. He waved and the people in the stands, many of whom had watched him develop on playgrounds only a few blocks from the gym, stood and stomped and applauded.

Sitting behind the officials' table, Connie, at thirty-two, with furrowed brow and graying muttonchops, looked like a man who had seen a great deal in his time, perhaps more than he wanted to. But as people in the stands continued to wave and shout he smiled broadly, slapping palms with old friends, talking about the old days.

"They stuck by me through the years," he said. "Even before *Foul!* came out the Brooklyn people were into me. If they hadn't seen me play themselves then they'd heard about me. Older brothers would tell kids and stories got passed down the line all through the neighborhood."

As a boy Connie lived in as much poverty as anyone in New York City. Though his road to success was often troubled, including banishment from college and, for years, the NBA for allegedly taking money from a man who was later identified as a gambler, Connie always had a basic sense of "direction."

"I don't know why but I never thought about drugs and that. It was basketball no matter what. I was skinny, too—for a while there I was 6'6", 140 pounds, that's just bones, man—but I didn't think about that either. I just thought about stamina and playing ball.

"But I guess a few people are mainly responsible—my mother, Gene Smith at the YMCA, Micky Fisher, the Boys High coach. And my friend Eddie Simmons."

Suddenly Connie is deluged by young boys begging for autographs. Aware of his status in his home community from previous trips, he had brought hundreds of postcard-sized pre-autographed pictures of himself in his Lakers uniform. He distributed handfuls of them and then returned to deep thought.

"Eddie was amazing. He always seemed to know what he was doing, and he loved helping me. He took me around with him and when I was only thirteen he had me playing against grown men. Eddie was a friend; I guess he talked to me more than anyone else."

The circumstances surrounding Simmons' death are as uncertain to Connie as to everyone else. Perhaps because the older youth was Connie's leader during those formative years he still prefers to think of him as the feisty backcourtsman rather than the scratching, nodding junkie he had become at the end.

"It happened in South Carolina and one story going around is that he was beaten to death by some locals. The other is that he O.D'd on junk," said Connie watching the pros and semi-pros get started in their game. "I really hope the first one is true."

Today I walk into Foster Park holding a male stag beetle by its rear legs. I found the insect in a gutter, apparently drowned by one of the recent thunderstorms.

It is perhaps an inch long, russet-colored, shiny, with long, jagged mandibles; and when I hold it out as though still alive two entire benches clear.

Slowly a few of the players drift back for closer looks.

"Day-yam," says Doodie. "Where'd you get that thing, New Jersey?"

The boys crowd in to observe, every so often one of them darting off from fear. The bug is something beyond their normal range of experience, as is virtually all of nature. One night I had decided to show them some constellations, but looking up all I could see was an orangish pall. Every night that week I looked for Orion's Belt, but the smog and glow of the lighted city made the heavens as opaque as dirty water. "Rick," said Martin to me one evening while I craned my neck, "don't worry about it. I've seen stars in books."

Some of Glen Springs Academy headmaster John Pulos' fondest memories are of the days the ghetto ballplayers recruited by Rodney were sent into the fields around the prep school to hunt for insect specimens.

"The biology teacher knew the only bugs these kids were familiar with were roaches so he had them label twenty insects," recalls Pulos. "Well, after the fly and the ant they were in trouble. I'll never forget seeing 6'6" Gary Jackson and 6'5" Fly Williams tiptoeing around in the woods. They'd heard there were insects under rocks so they got these ten-foot sticks to tip them over with. They'd turn one rock, drop the pole, and run through the woods faster than I'd ever seen them move."

The concept of the outside world for most of the Brooklyn youths is extremely distorted. A few days before the kids on the bench had been talking about the Chicago Bulls and had tried to pinpoint Chicago in relationship to the rest of America.

"It's kind of connected to San Francisco, ain't it?" commented Doodie, always the first to offer solutions in any kind of jam.

"No, Michigan State's in Chicago, stupid," replied Pontiac Carr.

"So what."

"Well, San Francisco's near Hawaii."

"On TV it seems people always be in Chicago and the next second they in San Francisco," Doodie rebutted.

Even Martin, who was wearing a ventilated golf hat in honor of Lee Elder being the first black accepted to the Master's tour, could only place Chicago "near Detroit somewhere." Calvin Franks, hearing the discussion, walked over to point out a few things.

"Some school in Ohio, a junior college near Chicago, wants me real bad," he said. "They play big-time ball there. The coach says they're NCAA champs but I'll tear the place up, give them my boom! hit from twenty, put the place on the fucking map. It's right out there in Iowa."

One night Rodney, who is no great shakes at geography either, had explained the park boys' outlook. "If you asked one of these kids to draw a freehand map of the United States, they'd cover half the page with Brooklyn, a quarter of it with the rest of New York City and on the far edge they'd jam everything from Jersey City to California."

The boys are not stupid, merely limited. The Subway Stars appear to be as intellectually diverse as any random sampling of teen-agers anywhere except that their world is smaller and its boundaries more defined.

Sgt. Rock visited relatives in Florida recently and came back astounded. "Man, Rick, black people were working in *all* the stores. Wow! And the white people are so strange. They don't get dressed up to go on the plane or anything, and there were

X-ray machines around and guys with shaved heads giving out books."

Most of the Stars talk about going to college some day. Doodie, though, says he'll be satisfied being a chef, and Pablo Billy looks forward to a job on the city payroll. "Those guys who clean the streets make a lotta jack," he says.

Arthur, who is still working on his color TV, would like to be an electrician, or—he is almost too shy to say it—an electronic engineer. Martin, who uses words like "tenacious" and "temperamental" in his conversation and who once became furious waiting for the Stars to arrive for practice, saying he could have been home polishing his furniture instead, is dead set on college.

"It's the only way to advance," he says flatly. "I might like to be a politician, everybody says I should be."

Like everyone in the park, the Subway Stars see basketball as the springboard for their dreams. I watch them as they show total confidence in their skills, bragging and carrying on much like Calvin Franks, but underneath I notice they have begun to realize some cold facts. Martin feels that even if he makes the varsity at Tilden High this winter, at 5′8″ he is too short to expect college scouts to fight over him.

"I'd rather go to a good school on my own than a mediocre one on a ride. There's too many kids in the ghetto trying to make it, too many who are going to be disappointed."

Mark, gangly at 6′2″, and Vance, who has grown an inch this summer to 6′3″, are both concerned about getting taller. "If I can be 6′6″ and nasty I'll be in there," says Vance.

All the Stars have their eyes secretly trained on Rodney, knowing the near-miracles he sometimes performs. But his open contempt for them and their skills has made them defensive.

"He thinks we have to kiss his ass to go anywhere," says Sgt. Rock. "Screw him. I'll get into a college on my own. Then some day I'll punch him out."

While the players relax on the bench, Champagne walks into the park, grinning from ear to ear. He is wearing his Subway Stars shirt, on the back and shoulders of which he has carefully glued labels from a dozen champagne bottles.

"Thees mah new shirt," he says proudly. The players gather

around to admire the handiwork but are suddenly interrupted by loud cursing at a crap game behind the backstop.

"No man! I ain't got no money!" comes DeMont's high voice from the center of a group of older slicks. "Lemme go, lemme go!"

I walk over to see what is happening. Music Smith is there already and he explains that DeMont tried to turn a seven into an eight when he thought no one was watching. "Catch that shit," says Music. "In two years some dude'll blow him away for trying that."

I peer into the center and see that DeMont is being held by a slyly smiling crapshooter at least twice his size. Slowly bending over, the man grabs first one, then the other of DeMont's wildly thrashing feet.

"What you doing!" he cries. "I ain't done nothing! I'm broke, I got no money! Help, help!"

DeMont begins kicking his legs as hard as he can but it has no effect as the crapshooter hoists him into the air upside down and shakes him like a sack. DeMont continues to screech, but the man merely smiles as nickels and pennies clatter out onto the hot pavement.

Today is Sunday. I have gotten the Subway Stars free tickets to a pro summer league game at City College featuring the Washington, D.C. All-Stars against the New York All-Stars. Fly is playing for the D.C. pros and the Stars are excited about seeing him in an indoor game for the first time.

Getting off the subway at 135th Street in Harlem, I realize again that we are not where we want to be. The gym is at least a half-mile to the west. Though several of the players have relatives in Harlem and most of them have visited the area before, I am surprised to see how openly frightened they are of the place.

Brooklyn, even in its worst pockets of decay, is familiar ground; but Harlem with its profound poverty and infamous reputation is a mysterious, evil section where foreigners should not trespass. They have all heard stories like the one Big Butch from the park tells about the time he had to drive into Harlem with his girlfriend on a Saturday night. "I stopped at a light up around 116th and Lenox. I *had* to stop, dig. The light was red. All of a sudden these guys come crawling out of everywhere trying to get in the windows and the doors and even the cracks. They crawled all over that car like big spiders, man. I didn't wait for no green light."

Though it is bright afternoon, the boys walk in a tight bundle down the sidewalk. Pablo Billy flips a coin but DeMont warns him, "You drop a penny in Harlem and foots come out from all over covering that jive."

When we reach St. Nicholas Avenue we run across the street and scramble up the large, rocky hill that separates central Harlem from the western heights. At the top is St. Nicholas Park, and just behind is Mahoney Gymnasium and the City College campus. Inside the gym we sit in the top corner and the Stars quickly begin cheering the pros as they go through a vast assortment of stuff shots.

"Look at Fly! Look at my man!" screams Doodie as Fly tomahawks the ball through the net, leaving particles of lint hovering in the air. The boys stand up in the deserted section of the bleachers and demonstrate each shot to one another with exaggerated swoops and contortions.

When the game starts the Stars go wild with every "face job." They are far more interested in shots "throwed away" than in assists or defense; and only Martin comments on a fast break where Fly passes to a teammate instead of taking it in himself. "I can't believe it. That's like the time I saw Calvin Franks throw three passes in a row!"

When Fly slips in a remarkable left-handed shot from behind the backboard over the hands of 6'9" Larry Kenon, the star New York Nets forward, Doodie stands up and asks Arthur how many points his man Fly could score in a game.

"I don't know. How many?"

"A million, goddamit."

Just before the second quarter a ripple of noise stirs through the audience.

"Hey," says Pablo Billy. "Check it out. Tiny."

Native Harlemite and All-Pro Nate Archibald walks past the

buzzing crowd into the locker room. Within five minutes he is back in the gym dressed in his uniform. He goes straight into the game and soon has the crowd roaring over his incredible passes and lightning moves. For a while the Subway Stars forget about Fly and stare slack-jawed at the man who looks no bigger or older than they as he takes control of the tempo of the game, running through and around the larger players.

Turning back to look at Fly, Mark nudges Martin. "Fly doesn't seem to have his shit together like Nate the Skate."

"Yeh, I know," says Martin. "When he threw those nice passes and the men missed the shots, he sorta gave up. Archibald doesn't do that. His men missed too."

Late in the fourth quarter Ollie Taylor of the New York squad breaks away for a meaningless lay-up. From far back Fly comes running up to give him a midair shove that sends Taylor flying off the court, sprawling beyond the padded pole, narrowly missing a chair and several spectators.

Fly fouls out shortly after that and instead of sitting on the bench walks disgustedly towards the locker room. "Nobody else but me will play defense," he snarls to a reporter. The crowd that had cheered his whirlybirds and fancy dribbling has suddenly reversed its mood. Sporadic boos follow the bowlegged, angry young man as he stomps away.

Out on the street after the game, Doodie and Pablo Billy engage in some one-on-one, using a paper cup and a garbage can as props. I ask the Stars what they thought of the contest. Opinion is pretty evenly divided about almost all the players. Larry Kenon deserved his MVP award, they agree, though Washington didn't have any good big men to check him. Talk quickly turns to the fleet of new moves and shots they must work on back at the park.

Vance, however, stands quietly off to the side, frowning at something. "I don't understand why Fly did that," he says, shaking his head. "I don't get it at all."

Mac, the park supervisor, can recall eleven Foster Park regulars who died from drug overdoses in the past six years. They never shot up right in the park, he says, but they often hung around during the day, sleeping, drinking beer, sometimes playing a little softball. All of them were white.

In the evening, as I stand by the fence near the handball courts, a black man in his mid-twenties shuffles loosely by. He is wearing beads and his eyes are partially closed. "I'm so fine . . . doo-lang, doo-lang, doo-lang . . ." he sings. He reaches up and haphazardly scratches his neck, his ear, his chin. Not long ago Mario saw him sitting by a court, his head dropping almost to the ground before he slowly straightened up—the unmistakable nod of a junkie.

There have never been any black junkies in Foster Park and the appearance of even one is in itself a major sign. The white Flatbush addicts were outcasts who were avoided by all, finding friendship only in a small, highly visible clique. But when a black neighborhood "turns junk" the plague frequently races like fire through the area, sucking in waves of youth.

Rodney, who is leaning against the fence, watches the man go by and makes no comment. He scarcely notices at all, so caught up is he in his own thoughts. He is gloomy and cynical because he is questioning the future of his operations.

"I've almost ruined myself with problem kids," he says. "I made a mistake with Fly and Albert, put in so much time, stayed away from my family. Now coaches tell players to stay away from me and kids give me grief. That's my reward."

He notices the junkie.

"Look at that," he says with a wave, watching the man stroll away. "Myra's been bugging me about moving away from here to a nicer place. She says it isn't safe for the kids. All this feedback I get. People blaming me for failures. With Fly now, if he fails, I'll get blamed."

Rodney has had problems before helping athletes. Two years ago he hustled a 6'4" teen-ager named Derrick Rucker off the streets and sent him to a prep school in Maine along with Derrick Melvin. One day, while the two youths were playing one-on-one at the school, Derrick Rucker had a heart attack in midair.

"They said he was dead before he hit the ground," says

Rodney now. "He would have been a great one, too. He was intelligent and serious and he was going to make it.

"Not long after that a kid came into the park and said, 'You're the guy who killed my man Derrick,' What could I say? I felt responsible because I sent the boy to school. People said if I'd left him in Brooklyn he'd be alive today. He probably would be, too. And then the funeral came along and I couldn't bring myself to go. I felt like nothing. Everybody was there—friends, coaches, teachers—everybody but me.

"Now all I can think is suppose Derrick Melvin gets killed in a car wreck or Danny-O dies in a plane crash on the way to school—where will they point the finger?"

Rodney looks as low as I've ever seen him. I quietly slip away, being unable to help. I'm a reporter, I remind myself. Get the facts and move on.

It is nearly dark now in the park. A cool evening breeze is blowing. On one bench DeMont sits bare-chested, shivering, playing with a small silver wrench which he twirls around each finger in a slow, bored succession. I sit down a few feet from him.

"Hey, ballboy, you look like you're cold."

"I ain't," he says.

He shifts the wrench from pinkie to ring finger to middle finger to index. His face is twisted into the scowl he wears too often, a bothersome, unnatural expression coming from a boy so small, so young.

"You were wearing your Subway Stars T-shirt today, weren't you?"

He says nothing.

"Sure you were, I remember it. Where'd that go?"

"I sold it."

"How much did you get?"

"Two dollars."

"Don't you like being a Subway Star?"

"I ain't a Subway Star. I don't play, I just ride around holding balls. 'Sides, I needed money."

He begins to toss the wrench into the air, still shivering, a tiny, defenseless boy acting like a man.

"What'd you need money for?"

"Joey stole my knives and I needed money."

"What knives?"

"My mom's got these knives in a case and I had 'em out and when I was walking across the street Joey came up and took 'em and said he'd kill me if I tried to get 'em back. He stole 'em."

I ask him why he had the knives out.

"I don't know. Sometimes I get to take 'em out and I can play with 'em. I don't do nothing with 'em. I just like to line 'em up and make little circles and stuff. I can close one eye and the sun shines through the red and yellow things on the handles and I can just see different stuff. . . . Aw, you don't understand . . ."

He stands up and starts to walk slowly toward the exit on Farragut Place.

"Where're you going?"

"Out. Somewhere."

He shuffles away, his head down.

I wander out of the park in the other direction, wondering about DeMont. Does anyone care when he comes home? Does he have a father, a mother? Does he have anyone who cares about him, and him only, who says, "I love you, son. You are my flesh and blood. You are my heart." I wonder about many things all of a sudden, and I feel a cloud descending upon me, the cloud I have been fighting all along, the one I can't let reach me . . .

I walk and walk.

On the corner of Foster and Nostrand I see Lloyd Hill standing, staring furtively at the dark courts.

Lloyd has not been back to the park since the Dwight Morrow High School debacle. He felt so humiliated by his performance that he has stayed home, or if he has gone out at all it has been to the barber shop to cut hair with Cleanhead.

He watches me as I approach. We stand around together for a few moments, saying nothing.

"It's not good when people yell at you," he says finally. "Sometimes I look stupid, awkward, but I try to work hard."

I don't say anything, but I can't recall anyone criticizing Lloyd for his performance.

"You don't always be telling a guy he stinks," Lloyd says, looking at the ground. "He knows he smells. The shit's on him."

Craig, Mario, Possum, and Eddie Campbell have finished playing ball and are relaxing now in the dim park, rubbing their knees and rehashing the action. They have bought some Ripple wine and are starting to feel good. Talk turns to the three-week-old Foster age-group basketball tournament run by Mario and Craig.

"It's pretty bad," admits Mario. "But we didn't get much time to organize."

"Next year I'd like to run the whole thing," says Craig. "I'd have it be really nice, something people could be proud of. Lots of teams, publicity, T-shirts, all that stuff. Yeh, I'd like to manage the whole show."

The young men nod in agreement. The wine bottle is passed along the line, then back. Possum whistles a tune and spreads his arms out along the back of the bench.

"Haven't felt this good in a long time," says Eddie.

From far off a siren starts up, then another one, and another, followed by a series of harsh, honking noises as a row of fire trucks passes through an intersection on its way to a distant emergency. Two alley cats behind the Jamal Food Center cry like forlorn human babies; a car accelerates wildly then screeches to a stop in less than one block, its straight manifold chugging like an outboard motor. Dogs howl after the sirens. A semi on New York Avenue winds slowly through its gears. In the street light the Vanderveer Homes look indestructible, like thick walls erected to keep out invading hordes.

"They've been promising us new baskets and that for years," says Mario. "It's only gonna get worse. Remember when this used to be all Jews and flowers and stuff? Wasn't but five years ago."

"This used to be the meanest court right here," says Possum.

"Yeh, people sitting on the benches and all. But that basket hasn't been up for two years."

"Those other ones been gone for more than three years, except for the one come down just this summer," adds Craig.

The players talk about having serious words with Mac, about getting things on the stick.

"But it isn't his fault," says Possum. And everyone sits quietly. Despite their evening enthusiasm they know this is true, that the blame never rests squarely on anyone.

"Yeh, but maybe we could get some paint and have somebody fix new lines up. Make it just look nicer."

"No money."

"Well, why couldnt we do the work ourselves," asks Eddie, straining with energy. They mull this over and it sounds good on the surface. But they can all feel that there must be more to it than that.

A pair of girls walk by the bench and Eddie perks up again. "Hey, girls, you're looking fine," he shouts. The players laugh because this isn't Eddie's usual style.

Eddie and Possum go over to talk to the pair, sauntering proudly, bolstered by each other's presence. They quickly return to the bench. "Well," says Eddie, "some bitches just aren't friendly."

The players become silent again, passing the bottle until it is drained. When the conversation starts once more they are content to let it drift where it may.

"New York isn't so bad," tosses out Possum.

"Yeh, you know, when you go someplace else a lot of people just want to hear you talk about it."

"That's true. They think, well, he knows what it's about, he's lived."

"My roommate at St. Francis was from Chicago," says Mario. "And he thought he was a gangster. He'd say, 'Don't fuck wit me.' I had to kick his ass about three times before he calmed down. From DuSable High School. That dude thought Chicago was the baddest place in the world.

The young men laugh and the evening passes on.

EARLY AUGUST

A few days ago Fly was playing in a game at The Hole, the battered court across from his project. The referees made several bad calls and things quickly got out of control. When a foul was called on Fly, one that he considered unfair, he flew into a rage. He stampeded around the court, yelling that he was being persecuted. Then he ran to the sideline and grabbed the game ball and, spotting one other ball, snatched it, too. He looked at the crowd and screamed, "It shall be continued," and ran out of the park.

Country James who had been playing in the game was disgusted by his friend's behavior. "It was a bad call and Fly knew it, and he knew the crowd knew it. So that's always when he comes down the hardest, because he feels like . . . well . . . like he *has* to. I got mad and said the hell with him and walked out. Fly came by later and asked me to come back to the tournament. I said, 'You play. You're the big basketball player.'"

Country James is closer to Fly than perhaps anyone else and so is allowed to criticize him. Indeed, Fly looks up to the older man as a sort of ghetto hero. At seventeen James was the warlord of a Brownsville gang called the "Jon-Quells," a position requiring him to keep the gang's roof stocked with bricks and to be "first in line all the time." Since then he has made his living through ghetto enterprise—hustling, gambling, at one time even pushing drugs.

"I could whip Fly's ass," says James, sitting in his apartment near Foster Park. "I'm thirty-two now and when I was sixteen I could squat under a slate pool table and lift it up. But I don't do anything except try to calm him down because I know when he was coming up he got his ass beat all the time. In fact, the first time I met him this big guy named Frank had him on the ground. Sometimes, though, when I try to talk to him he's too far gone, too defensive. He's against the world. He'll be yelling, 'You're with them! I know you're with them!'"

One of the reasons Fly was picked on so much as a boy, James explains, was because he had no older brothers to protect him. (This, technically, isn't true, though Fly's two older brothers were never around. Fly once told John Pulos that both of them were in Attica.)

"See, Jocko who grew up right there always had family to help him out. But Fly, when somebody got mad at him they just beat the crap out of his ass. There was never no help. And now, especially in Brownsville, he's trying to get back. He'll keep trying, too."

The reason that Fly gets away with his antics, Country James claims, is because with his superior talent people allow him to.

"Everybody babies him. His mother did, the high school coaches did, Lake Kelly did. And most of all Rodney does. I cursed Rodney out just the other day because he was coming around and asking me to please tell Fly this and that. I said, 'Rodney, you know how Fly is. Don't soften him up, no violins. If you want to tell him he's a shithead, then tell him he's a shithead.' Nobody ever gets down on Fly now that they're so afraid of him."

John Pulos of Glen Springs agrees with that viewpoint. "Practices at Glen Springs were ridiculously undisciplined," says the headmaster. "Our head coach used to ask scouts, 'Well, what do you want to see, a 2–1–2? Just name it.' If he told Fly to go out on a shooter, Fly would say, 'No, I have to rebound.' And then at Austin Peay they catered to him totally. Once Fly cut in the lunch line and yelled at a lady while Coach Kelly and these state officials watched. Lake was so embarrassed, but nothing came of it.

"At this one game I saw, Fly took fifty shots and had 30-some points. When they took him out, the crowd gave him a standing ovation, but he went to the end of the bench, sulked, threw towels, wouldn't shake hands. After the game the coach told me Fly was just down on himself. I said, 'Bull.' I knew Fly. They lied to me down there all year."

Today Rodney has discovered that what he feared all along has come true. Joe Jeffries-El has given Fly a car, a new Cougar, and is now his official negotiating agent.

Lew Schaffel had called Fly after finding out he was playing in more summer leagues and told the youth he was making it impossible to represent him. "There's got to be some trust involved here," Lew said. "I can't read the papers to find out what you're doing." Fly had denied any wrongdoing and promised to cooperate.

"He said, 'Okay, I understand, blah, blah, blah . . .'" Schaffel explained afterwards. "And then later when Leonard Hamilton, the assistant coach from Peay and now at Kentucky, told me Fly was with Joe El I called Fly again. 'Naw, that guy Hamilton bullshits,' he says. But I found out it was true; he had the car and all. So that was that."

For Rodney the bridge that had been crumbling has now caved in. "He's been bought with a car. A goddam leased car. What does Joe El know about pro contracts? Fly's gonna be out in the streets, that's what's gonna happen."

Though Rodney saw it as a simple betrayal, even claiming that "Fly is not responsible for his acts," Country James saw it in a different light; that despite all Rodney had done for Fly, Fly simply could not respect the man.

"You see, Joe is like a businessman, where Rodney's all buddy-buddy. Fly knew he could just tell Rodney anything at all. In a funny way, Rodney and Fly are just too much alike."

Lionel rides by in the evening and says that after talking to the Fairfield University coach, he is convinced Fairfield is the school for him. "They got all big men and they need guards, so I'll be set. It's only an hour and fifteen minutes from Brooklyn, and I'll be there with Danny-O and we'll be playing in the Garden five times a year."

Even more enthused than Lionel is Possum who has just been

informed by Rodney that if his Erasmus transcripts are satisfac-
tory Trenton State will give him a scholarship.

"I'll do everything to represent Rodney well," says the
eighteen-year-old who has had each shoulder dislocated several
times and has yet to play a minute of varsity basketball. "I won't
let the man down."

One of the white kids who hangs out on the corner of Farragut
and Nostrand near Doyle's Bar comes over to the bench and tells
a couple of the players about three of his buddies who just got
arrested. One of them, Red, had spent most of this summer
sitting behind the baseball fence drinking quart beers.

"He was nuts, you know," says the boy. "Red sniffed so much
glue he couldn't even take a crap. His insides were too sticky, so
he got some pills or something. The doctor said he only had nine
months to live. Now they got him in the crazy bin after they
robbed the judge's house. Jesus, was that dumb. The cops caught
'em on the way out. One guy had a color TV, the other had a
stereo and Red had a ham sandwich."

Derrick Melvin is playing some low-key half-court ball down
on the middle court, but he decides it would be best to go back
to his neighborhood in Bedford-Stuyvesant and work out alone
for a while. In the ghetto, finding an empty basket in a park is a
rare thing, shooting alone being a more suburban privilege.

Some ghetto players solve the problem by going to less-
crowded white neighborhoods or, as Jocko Jackson does, by
playing at four or five A.M. A lucky few will find hidden,
deserted courts right in the ghetto, a spot like the one Derrick
calls his "secret place."

He asks me if I'd like to come along, and after borrowing a
bike I follow him out onto the street. We pedal down New York
Avenue to Empire Boulevard, then over to Utica Avenue, and
finally into the Brevoort project where Derrick nods at the rows
of unsmiling men in front of his building. They watch him go by,
saying nothing.

"People think in the ghetto everybody is cheering you on to
be a success," says Derrick as we pass by. "But that's not how it

is. Like those guys, winos and junkies. They'll say, 'You're just a nothing 5'8" dude and I can whip your ass on the court.' A lot of 'em can, too, and they don't like to see me getting anywhere because they remember how they got screwed over. The real pressure on you is *not* to make it."

Pedaling around the corner from the projects, Derrick stops a couple of blocks away at a small debris-strewn park overgrown with weeds and bushes. The basketball court is wedged between some trees and the Crispus Attucks Grammer School. Just on the other side of the half-court line an area of pavement the size of a station wagon is sunken in nearly three feet. Grass sprouts from the cracks, giving the impression that years ago a meteorite must have landed here and disintegrated with age.

On the walls of the school several "Flys" have been spray-painted in hasty scrawls, rivulets of color dripping from the bottom of each letter. "Just since he came home from school there's been a lot of new writing on the wall," says Derrick, beginning to shoot at the rusty basket.

There is just enough room before the trench for Derrick to dribble and maneuver with relative ease. Over on a shaded bench a bleary-eyed man raises his head to focus on the mysterious noise, then drops back into a drug stupor. Other junkies stir but do not look.

"Missing that plane to Murray State was a mistake," says Derrick working around the key. "But I'm not making mistakes anymore. I made enough in high school. I'm finished being a boy; I'm a man now and this is a job. No more attitudes, no more hotheads. Every day I grade myself. I say: Did I hustle? Did I talk? Did I showboat? Except for the plane, I think I got an A-plus going for the summer."

In high school Derrick made the Erasmus squad as a sophomore but his cocky attitude eventually got him thrown off the team. After his senior year, without a diploma or a job, he knew he was in trouble. "I'm not saying I would have been an armed robber or dope fiend, but, yeh, I might have . . ."

In a last-ditch effort Derrick went to Rodney. "I'd ignored him before when he came around; now I was on my knees, begging. He saw that I was for real. He saved me."

The sound of a basketball on this seldom-used pavement brings a few heads peeking around corners and out of windows. A small young man approaches and asks Derrick if he'd mind playing a little one-on-one.

"Sure, brother," says Derrick. "I don't get many chances to run somebody smaller than me."

They play and Derrick is far too quick for his opponent, scoring at will on jump shots and lay-ups. "I'm a football player. This is just for fun," says the shorter man.

After the game they sit down, sweating profusely. The stranger offers to get some beer at the corner store and Derrick gives him fifty cents.

"Listen, man," he says to me, "let me borrow your ride."

Since I've borrowed the bike from Craig Martin I tell him I'd like to, but I really can't.

He turns to Derrick. "How about yours, brother?"

Derrick looks at the player and then nods. The player leaves on the white ten-speed and Derrick says, "See, he's too small to steal the bike."

Derrick gets up and begins shooting once again. Every so often he glances down the sidewalk, then continues with his work.

Fifteen minutes go by. Then a half hour. Derrick walks to the street and stares in the direction the rider went. He comes back.

"I don't know that dude, but I'll remember his face," he says. "I'll see him again."

The pick-up team from Lower Manhattan that humiliated the Subway Stars has made a show of good faith and come to Foster Park for a rematch.

The Stars are now 5–5, having badly pounded a few weak teams and lost all the close games. Team unity is little improved, but individual skills have climbed. Vance can now dunk occasionally; Doodie has learned at least the meaning of defense. They have yet to overcome their simple frustrations or their tendency to fold under pressure, but they look forward to each game as maybe "the one."

I asked Martin a few days ago why he thought the Subway

Stars had such trouble playing together even though they were good friends. "I don't know," he said. "But if the ghetto didn't do something to black people, there wouldn't be much use for white folks in basketball, would there?"

Today Lloyd Hill returns to the park after a long absence and, setting up a table and a timer in the shade of a tree, announces himself official scorer. He places a six-pack of malt liquor and two reefers before him and orders the game to get underway.

This time instead of the Subway Stars trying to adjust to the court, the Manhattan players are forced to acclimate to the park idiosyncrasies. The basket at one end is three inches higher than the other one. The far rim is completely "dead". Shots can be rammed home but only the Stars know how. In places the out-of-bounds lines are worn away, and there are jagged cracks in the pavement.

The crowd of locals is heavily pro-Subway Stars. One spectator approaches me and asks if I want to "make sure" the other team doesn't win. He smacks one fist into his open palm and smiles. I thank him but decline the offer.

In the far corner Lloyd Hill drinks, smokes, and shouts out directions to the Stars. He refuses to bring his table out to half court and therefore he is shielded from much of the action by spectators. Most of his shouting goes unnoticed.

After Sgt. Rock nearly decapitates a player at the far end, Lloyd, seeing him get slightly jostled at the near end, screams, "Rock, you gonna let him do like that on you?" In his fervor Lloyd forgets about the clock and suddenly yells, "Quarter! Quarter! Time-out!"

Lloyd has also forgotten the score, and a huge consultation takes place before it is decided the Stars are up by two. The Manhattan players holler in protest but Lloyd bangs his fist on the table. "Play ball," he roars.

The game starts again, and even with Lloyd keeping score the visitors gradually begin to pull ahead. From everywhere shouts are directed at the Subway Stars, demanding an incredible variety of strategies.

With chaos around them the Stars begin to falter, coming to me with their grievances.

"Pablo's chucking again," says Mark.

"You're too ugly," retorts Pablo Billy.

The boys raise their fists, but the other players separate them.

With little time left in the game the Stars, apparently without premeditation, begin a rally, the first time such a thing has happened. Slowly at first, with a few key shots falling in, they whittle the lead until with two minutes left they are down by only three baskets. Pablo Billy makes a steal and hits Martin for a short jumper, and then Arthur, so frail and agile, spins his man around completely and scores unmolested to bring the Stars within one basket.

The Manhattan players decide to hold the ball and simply wait for the clock to run out since only seconds remain. They look down at Lloyd and he stares back at them.

"Well, give us the time, blood!" yells their guard, a small Latino in cut-off jeans.

The crowd is screaming and the Stars are charging around, their eyes and mouths wide open. Lloyd stares up in the air. Time goes by and nothing happens. In frustration the player tries a shot and Vance grabs the rebound and calls time-out immediately.

"There is ten seconds left," yells Lloyd.

The Manhattan players race over to the scorer's table.

"You minutes as long as goddamn days!" cries a visitor. "You full a shit!"

"I just may be," says Lloyd. "But I *is* the fucking timekeeper and you in my park and that *is* the time."

The Stars bring the ball inbounds and Mark pots a twelve-foot jump shot to tie the score.

"Time!" screams Lloyd. And for the first time ever the Subway Stars leap on each other and holler congratulations. Pontiac Carr lights a Kool and shakes my hand as the squad gathers together for the overtime strategy.

The first overtime begins slowly and ends with the teams tied once more. Lloyd again is accused of tampering with the clock. "See this table," he replies. "Now if it be a butcher's block I'd be a butcher. But it's a timekeeper's table and I'm behind it so I guess I'm the timekeeper who keep the time and you can play on that time or *pack it on outa here.*"

At the start of the second overtime, Sgt. Rock elbows the big razor-scarred man in the throat on a rebound and the man goes down. "Rock killed a dude," says Pontiac Carr clutching my arm.

When the man is finally revived, the Manhattan squad is fired up. Sick of being abused, they proceed to score point after point, putting the tired, undermanned Stars hopelessly out of reach.

I find myself wishing there was some way we could tactfully bow out of the game right now. This is the best and most selflessly I've seen the boys play, and further humiliation can only erode what little pride they've developed.

Still, I find it hard to believe when, as if with Hollywood timing, an enormous blast of thunder rolls across the court, echoing and re-echoing through the Vanderveer Homes. A few random drops of rain, big as thimbles, fall on the court, sending up hairs of steam. There is a tense silence and then the sound of beating comes down the street like a fleet of street cleaners.

"It's the cavalry!" bellows a spectator. A curtain of torrential rain moves in so quickly there is no sensation of it even falling, just of instant wetness.

People scatter in all directions. Somebody swoops in and grabs the game ball. Lloyd dives under his table. The Stars stand for a moment, getting drenched, looking around in confusion. Some of the Manhattan players are already across the street, running full-bore towards the subway.

Lightning bolts rip across the sky and within five minutes the entire park is empty.

MID-AUGUST

"**L**ook what DeMont done!" one of the smaller boys shouts at me as I walk into the park after an absence of several days.

Last Tuesday I had returned to Illinois and then driven up into Michigan to do some camping, feeling I could use the break. Returning to Brooklyn I was inundated with new sensations. There was so much more noise than I remembered, and litter, and people. I felt absurd with my suntan and mosquito bites. Back home I had been a bit out of touch, too. "Why do you wear your pants so high?" one of my friends had asked. I didn't know at first, but of course it was because that was the style at Foster Park.

"What'd he do?" I ask.

"Look," says the boy grabbing DeMont's wrist and ceremoniously rolling up the sleeve past his elbow. A "D" the size of a silver dollar is formed on his forearm, a homemade tattoo.

I study the welt.

DeMont looks up at me, studying my face for approval. Seeing that I am smiling, he jerks the sleeve down over his wrist and buttons it roughly, a tough-guy look forming on his face.

I tell him I think it is a nice job and ask him how he did it.

"There's nothing to it," he says, the mean look melting away to be replaced by a helpful one. "Just rub your skin with a pencil eraser till it turns pink. Then you can use a pen or a magic marker. It ain't nothing. I'll give you one if you want."

I decline, telling him I'm not sure I'd want an "R" on my arm a few years from now.

"Man, what kind of stuff is that to think about," he frowns.

Music Smith, who has been circulating through the park, now walks over to show me a book he "finally" received in the mail. It is a thick one entitled *The Psychology of Consciousness.* Music dropped out of high school five years ago but he says he's "getting into psychology some" now.

He shows the fine-printed volume to a friend on the bench and they determine that consciousness is probably similar to "getting knocked out and coming to" and that the psychology of it will have to do with being brave and sleeping.

Franks comes by and explains that the school was not in Ohio or Iowa, but Idaho. "I knew it was one of those. They want me solid."

At 3:00 P.M. Fly drives up in his Cougar and gets out to socialize. Rodney spots him and begins digging at him for being bought by Joe El.

"Oh, man," hollers Fly. "You know I'm the one pays your rent. You got money from the Peay for two years."

Rodney says that's a lie.

"Man, the only reason you get over at all is because of me. You wouldn't be nothing without me. You'll always just be here in your park shooting for quarters."

It's a cruel remark and Rodney winces with its sting.

Fly begins to chuckle and asks Rodney for ten dollars to pay a traffic fine. Rodney says he wouldn't give Fly a dime. Once again Fly chases Rodney and after catching him throws him on the ground. Calvin Franks walks over, and while Fly pounds on Rodney's legs Franks tries to dig into Rodney's pocket for his wallet.

Rodney squirms like a huge catepillar and manages to protect his money. When the two finally tire and let Rodney up, he dusts himself off and leaves the park.

Today, being a Friday, the park is filled with more people than usual. The weekend ballplayers have come out, the older men and less-skilled youngsters, as have the socializers—the West Indians in their shirts and ties, the old ladies with Bibles, the young wives with babies. The atmosphere is congenial, filled with traces of celebration over the clear skies, the paychecks and liquor, the weekend to come. Some good ballplayers from other sections of Brooklyn have come to the park, as well. Foster has its reputation as a basketball proving ground and sooner or later every serious city athlete must try his hand.

Eric Short, a fifteen-year-old friend of Albert King's, has stopped by to play in the Foster Park age-group tournament. He played ball with Albert just a few days ago and claims that Albert hasn't changed. "I don't think he's got an attitude," says Eric. "If he does he hides it real well."

While he is talking there is a sudden commotion on the sidewalk. The park quickly empties, crowding around three men rolling in the glass-speckled gutter between two parked cars. One of the fighters is Country James and the other two wear the green T-shirts of one of the senior tournament teams. A third green-shirted team member rests against a tree several feet away, his nose bleeding, his legs wobbly.

James is backing off slowly, his hands held in front of him in readiness.

As the fighters rolled on the street James sliced his finger and leg on some glass and the blood is now dripping off, spotting his white track shoes.

"You're off!" screams the man with the cut eye.

James continues to back up slowly, the excited crowd parting to let the group move with him. A fourth man charges up to him.

"You snuck the man, motherfucker," he shouts. "You're a punk. Take me now."

"All right, we can do that, too," says James. "We can make it four."

But two policemen have arrived and they block the paths of the two factions. "This is so stupid," mutters Country James. "All this over a damn parking spot. I just live down there. I could have parked in my garage."

One of the bloody fighters walks off and climbs in his car pointing his finger at James. The little boys in the crowd dance up and down. "He going to get the guns! He going to get the guns!"

But the man doesn't return for ten minutes and the tension begins to subside. Then suddenly, in his new green Cougar, Fly Williams drives cheerfully up to the scene. He climbs out of the car, wearing shorts and his red D.C. Pros jersey. He looks confusedly around at the policemen, the people, the fighters. "Oh, shit," says DeMont, jumping up and down with excitement. Fly spots James off to one side, sees blood and the rag around his finger, and realization floods into his face. His eyes darken and his expression changes instantly from curiosity to rage; he runs over to his friend and asks who did it.

"Nothing. Nobody," says James grabbing Fly by the arm. "Let's go."

Fly sees the other fighters and he attempts to break away.

Country James pulls him into Fly's car and orders him to drive off. Fly tries to get up but James pulls him down and they slowly move off.

"We'll get Brownsville over here!" screams Fly through the window. "We'll have the ghetto, man, we'll . . ." But his voice trails off as the car moves down the street.

Upon rising Rodney gets a call from Fred Barakat, the head coach at Fairfield. He has watched both Danny and Lionel play and wants to thank Rodney for steering them his way.

"Hey, Danny's a nice kid, he'll fit right in. Boy, he looks like an octopus out there some times. He can go in fast and lay the ball up soft. And Worrell is so unselfish. He sees the whole game and man, is he strong inside."

Rodney is pleased. He knows Danny will never give anyone a hard time, and it's good to hear at least one of his players from this predominantly scrawny group called "strong."

Moments after Rodney hangs up, the phone rings again. It is the coach at the Pennsylvania high school. He is despondent. In today's paper Albert King has been named the MVP of the United States Youth Games. The honor is like salt in the man's recruiting wounds.

"I'm so discouraged. When he was here he said 'I'll do whatever Rodney says.' But now he's with those other people, like you said."

The man's voice is whining and sad, like a child who has been sent to his room unfairly.

"You know how people say whites are always using blacks? Well, if he comes here he'll get treated better than anybody else, better than anything anybody could offer him.

"What's he get now—$100, $200 a month? Chicken feed, Rodney. We're getting together a lot of professional people to help. We can do what it takes. But I'd hate to have to buy the kid, I mean I'm sincere. I'm down in the dumps but I'll fight it to the end."

Rodney hangs up the phone. He sighs deeply, then shakes his head, putting Albert King aside for now.

"Lloyd Hill, Lloyd Hill," he murmurs. "All his friends are going to school so he doesn't want to get left out. Yeh, when Lenny Wilkens and my friends were going away I wanted to go, too. But Lloyd won't take that equivalency exam. I don't think he can write."

Rodney calls a friend who used to do promotional work for a high school all-star game, a man on the periphery of basketball who knows names.

"Listen," says Rodney, "I need junior colleges or something for three players. Can you help."

"Are they good kids?" asks the man. "Not on drugs and all that?"

"Don't worry about them."

"I'll see what I can locate. What's their names?"

"Eddie Campbell, Calvin Franks, and Lloyd Hill. Oh, yeh, and the last guy doesn't have his diploma."

"Hell, a twelve-year-old can pass the equivalency. I'll check around."

At midnight Rodney goes out of the apartment and down to the street where Possum, Eddie, and several other ballplayers are draped like giant snails over the roofs and hoods of two parked cars.

The Sunday night garbage is out, lying in a stinking mound of brown bags next to the fire hydrant. Cockroaches lope across the sidewalk, diving into cracks, then suddenly reappearing and scurrying another few feet before hiding again from the greenish light of the street lamps.

Tonight Rodney is unhappy with the moodiness of Mario Donawa. Normally Mario is one of his prized examples, a young man who talks always of bettering himself, about going to law school, about being the breadwinner for his impoverished mother and three brothers. But today he came to Rodney asking for five hundred dollars to buy a new stereo, saying he would sign over his entire check for working the Foster Summer Tournament when he got it. Rodney refused and Mario had turned and walked away muttering "Later for you, then."

Whenever there are several ballplayers sitting in one place, Rodney, if he has the chance, will lecture them on his vision of the "real world" and his infallible methods of getting ahead. Seeing the boys lying prone on the cars now, he walks over to them and begins to talk. Normally in these affairs he uses Mario's and Danny's names as examples; tonight, though, he substitutes Lionel for Mario.

"With Fly it's all show," he tells the players. "Basketball isn't like diving where you get ten points for a perfect dive or nothing for a belly flop. It's always two. Watch Danny or even Lionel, it's the basics that make them solid."

But this is rhetoric, and the players yawn and stretch.

Standing with his elbows on the hood, little Ernie listens in silence. He doesn't really belong with this crowd, but occasionally he will smoke some grass with them or share a beer. He has several groups he floats between, one even as far away as Bedford-Stuyvesant. But in all of them he is something less than a full member.

"And that's another thing," says Rodney. "I don't like you guys smoking dope. You ain't supermen. It hurts your games."

"No it don't," says one of the players.

"It sure as hell does."

"You got to remember, Rod, you're dealing with black people."

The players lean back and look at the night sky.

"All right, I'll handle white kids."

No one pays attention to this for they know it is an idle threat. Without his boys to eat his food, borrow his money, and cause him continual problems Rodney would be lost.

Seeing their cavalier attitudes, Rodney throws his arms up in disgust and walks off.

Yesterday shortly after noon another violent August rainstorm hit Brooklyn, and Foster Park quickly emptied. Rodney and his boys escaped to the luncheonette across the street where they sat eating hamburgers he paid for and staring vacantly out through the greasy window.

Franks, who had already ordered two hamburgers and a shake, ordered two more.

"Why'd you do that?" Rodney asked angrily.

"I wanted 'em."

Rodney shook his head and walked outside to stand underneath the resonating awning. "Damn rain," he said pacing back and forth.

He began to read the comic section of the *Daily News* but stopped and put the paper under his arm. "I've never read a book in my life," he said, as if that were relevant to whatever he was thinking. "You know who my favorite author is? The guy who writes 'Dick Tracy.'"

He looked in at the players, then paced some more.

"I can't judge these guys. I'm no psychologist. I should try to understand, not judge . . ."

The paper had fallen from his arm onto the wet pavement, turning deep gray as it absorbed water. Rodney made no effort to pick it up.

"Did you hear about Fly?" he asked.

I had, from several people.

Earlier Fly had been out in front of his apartment building washing his car with the aid of a long hose hooked to an outdoor faucet. A project security guard had noticed the hose and brusquely informed Fly that it was illegal to use project water for private purposes. Fly had yelled at the guard, saying he wanted to see the sergeant. "You see me," said the guard.

Fly continued to argue, going into what Country James calls

his "defensive berserk thing." The guard arrested Fly, and after Fly had been bailed out, Joe Jeffries-El claimed that the whole thing came about because the Housing Authority Police "had a hard-on for him."

"Maybe they don't like the guy," Rodney said, holding his hand out to test the velocity of the rain. "So what. Wouldn't a normal suburban kid have said, 'Okay, I'm sorry' and turned the water off?"

Joe Jeffries-El, Fly's new agent, is finding out that his client is not a particularly easy product to sell. "Brother Joseph," as Joe prefers to be called, owing to the fact he is an ordained Islamic minister as well as a wealthy businessman, had always felt Fly was simply mishandled by Rodney. Now, his tone has changed.

"Whew, I've never seen a guy with so many problems," Joe states from behind his desk at his fire-prevention equipment company. "His back is to the wall, he doesn't have many friends, he goes to court at the end of the month. This is a hard nut."

In his search through the ABA Joe El has been getting the identical responses Rodney and Lew had gotten. One pro coach had told Rodney that he wouldn't touch Fly with radar. When Joe spoke with Kevin Loughery of the New York Nets saying, "Let's discuss Fly," the coach had snapped, "Let's not." As Country James put it, Fly was indeed on "the deep shit list."

"Well," says Joe El straightening the sleeves of his three-piece suit, "with Fly it's now a question of bringing him to normalcy. What worries me is that if he doesn't make pro ball he'll have to turn to the streets, to hustling and crime, to live the way he wants.

"But I feel he could be the Muhammad Ali of basketball. He's controversial, mouthy, arrogant, and the seats are filled when he plays. He just has one problem: he is forced to live in two worlds. He is programmed for the ghetto—anything he does there is understood—but the same actions in the other world, the marketplace, appear obscene."

Indeed, Fly's heroic stature in a place like Foster Park is a sharp counterpoint to his notoriety elsewhere. Boys in the playgrounds appreciate his flash, mimicking his moves and court

style, worshipful displays not lost on Fly. "Little keeids," he said
the other day. "I take time to talk to 'em. Jocko and I had a camp
at The Hole for two years for kids. No pay or nothing. When I
was coming up nobody cared what you did."

But there are times when Fly's ghetto behavior is misunderstood even by his best fans. On such occasions his defensive
posture crumbles. Several days after the ball-swiping incident
Fly and James had been walking down the sidewalk. Seeing
them, a little boy had grabbed his buddy and whispered, "Oh
man, that's Fly Williams. He crazy."

"I looked at Fly's face to see if there's any kind of expression,"
said James afterwards. "But he, like, turned away so I couldn't
see his eyes. It hurt bad though. I mean here's a kid, maybe eight
or nine, saying Fly's crazy. And even Fly can't say anything back
to an eight-year-old."

Late in the afternoon Joe El gets a call from the director of
operations of the newly formed St. Louis Spirits ABA team. The
man tells Joe that they are one of the few teams who understand
Fly's problems and are willing to deal with them.

"Yes," says Joe El, "I'm very concerned about changing his
image. Uh-huh. Yes. I believe he's a great asset to the game."

The offer given Joe El is this: Fly can come to St. Louis on
Tuesday for a two-day rookie camp with fifteen other hopefuls. The coaches will be watching, and if things work out
satisfactorily they will decide whether or not to offer Fly a
contract. Even if they offer one it won't be a big one. Joe accepts
eagerly.

"He's got to do it," says Joe, hanging up. "It's his big chance."

It has been decided by the players that if the Subway Stars are
to become a solid unit their name must become known in the
neighborhood. A sign, perhaps two, should be painted on
something permanent. Besides being illegal, graffiti is not my
idea of permanence, but I bend to the team mood.

After several hours of riding through the neighborhood
Pontiac Carr has found the sites. Safety has been a major

prerequisite. "They're mean around here," Pontiac had said. "They caught this guy I knew who was doing his name and made him clean a whole subway station. By the end he was crying. He don't even doodle in class no more."

But too much caution could undermine the whole project, Pontiac had added. A balance had to be struck. "It's got to be *seen,* right?"

Now he feels he's got the spots: one in an open ramp to a no-longer-used Vanderveer garage, the other on a wide brick wall behind the Nostrand Avenue A & P.

"I gotta get my artist," he says, riding off to one of the side courts at Foster Park where he whistles to a small, shifty-eyed boy playing twenty-one. The youth nods his head. Together they leave the park and a half-block away begin rummaging through a trash can. After several moments Pontiac pulls forth a hidden shopping bag filled with black and orange spray-paint cans. He tests one and then quickly slides it back into the bag.

The two boys act nonchalant as they move down the sidewalk. Most ghetto hardware stores will not sell spray paint to young blacks; to get caught even carrying a bag of the stuff can mean juvenile court. For this project I had to supply the materials.

"I'm kinda rusty," says Pontiac. "I haven't done this since sixth grade."

"Yeh, I feel out of tune," answers the other boy whose name is Jackson.

"If the cops see us after it's done I'm gonna tell them, 'Subway Stars? I thought it was a newspaper.'"

A squad car drives slowly down an adjacent street and the boys walk in silence for half a block. I walk several steps behind them, far enough so it looks as though I'm not involved but close enough so I can hear their conversation.

"Last time I painted, this friend swiped fourteen cans and we went wild for two nights," Pontiac comments. "When the new blue buses came out everybody went nuts. One guy I knew got twenty-three in a day. Remember that? It was bad."

Jackson nods without enthusiasm. He was never a part of that scurrying, scrawling horde content to merely slash its mark and run. He was, rather, a serious devotee of the craft as practiced by an earnest few.

Before lifting his first can of spray he spent days studying the subway cars returning to Brooklyn from Harlem and the Lower East Side and the South Bronx. They rolled into the stations carrying the best techniques of the whole city, the Paris of graffiti. Jackson began practicing the styles—the balloons, the clouds, the arrows and blocks and script—until he found his own technique.

With an apprentice he began riding the subways then, paying thirty-five cents to cover hundreds of underground miles to add his touch to the moving canvases. Rodney Parker, a great subway art aficionado, claims to have once seen a farm scene covering an entire train at the Queens turnaround. "The guy used about ten colors. There were chickens and barns and tractors. It was incredible."

Above all, Jackson the artist was serious. To make a lasting mark of his own, with style and skill and bravery, seemed very important. Rather than hide out in eerily-lit station yards, he rode the trains themselves, hopping out at each stop for a few quick spurts, then darting back as the doors closed. His apprentices' job was to hold the bag and watch for Transit Police while Jackson worked. In this fashion Jackson's pieces became representative of the entire city; a design started in Flatbush might be colored at Atlantic Avenue, outlined in the Village, highlighted in Harlem and signed and underlined at 242nd Street in the Bronx.

After several months of painting and three or four near-clashes with the law, Jackson retired from the practice. He was fourteen. He says now that the experience left him with contrary feelings of accomplishment and futility. "I did some nice things," he says. "But you know how they're always scrubbing the cars and guys painting over things. Now I hardly ever see my stuff go by."

Pontiac Carr has enlisted him for this project because of his past reputation, but Jackson wants it known that if his best work is behind him, his pride isn't. "People remember you by what you paint," he says as the boys reach the first spot.

Descending into the driveway Jackson surveys the wall and the escape routes. He rubs the cement and crouches down by some debris to check the perspective.

"You stay up there, Carr," he says. "I only want one can down here at a time. If the cops come I'll toss it up and pretend I'm peeing."

He begins his project, doing a rough outline first, then standing back to analyze the symmetry, then filling in and evening out. His style is puffed blocks running into each adjacent letter, closest in technique to the bloated signature popular in the Bronx.

At one point a lady in the nearby building opens her sixth-floor window and peers out. Pontiac whistles, an orange can comes flying up, and Jackson runs to a corner pulling down his zipper as he moves. The lady disappears and Pontiac tosses the can back down. "Better hurry now," he whispers. "She may be calling somebody."

Jackson does not like to rush and a scowl comes over his face, but he finishes the work quickly. He moves back to get a better look and then applies a few more bursts at the corners. The painting is nearly fifteen feet long and reads, "SUBWAY STARS #1." Underneath the letters is a slender arrow like a devil's tail, curled around at one end to point at a basketball.

"That's mean," says Pontiac, hanging over the wall.

The boys jog out of the area and then walk to the next spot in the alley between the A & P and the western most Vanderveer buildings. Here there is an exit in either direction, as well as a hole in the back fence, and Jackson settles down for a leisurely project. He sketches out the letters again, but this time he makes them so tall he has to use a milk crate to reach the peaks.

Pontiac helps him with this painting, taking directions and doing bit pieces like a worker on a Chagall mural.

"I've seen Mani and Mico's stuff," says Jackson as he moves about, speaking of Brooklyn's two most prolific writers. "No style. I've seen Mani painting his straight lines on buses, just a little nervous guy, taking hemorrhoid signs down off the insides, always in a hurry. You gotta do more than just cover things."

The work moves along steadily although night is falling and the orange is beginning to lose itself in the red of the bricks. Pontiac's can starts to sputter, then whistles and stops. "Damn," says Jackson, realizing there won't be enough paint for proper detail. He economizes what he has left, but in the upper circle of the "B" his can goes dry. He says something to Pontiac.

"Hey, Rick," says Pontiac turning around, "can you get us some more black?"

I look at the painting and decide that it looks good enough. There are some mistakes, particularly one of the basketballs with a nearly illegible "31" in it. I painted that one after deciding there was nothing to this craft. Still, I'm not wild about buying more paint and I tell them so.

Both the boys walk back a few paces and squint to appraise the work. It is almost identical to the other drawing except larger, perhaps twenty feet long and four or five feet high. Around the outside the boys have added smaller basketballs with each player's number inset. For emphasis, Jackson has drawn a subway train coming out of the "1".

"Well," says Jackson. "At least it's big."

Pontiac Carr throws the empty cans into a littered corner and dusts his hands together.

"Yeh, people gonna know now."

"Dig this," says Rodney sweeping his arms around in front of him, "my old neighborhood."

He has taken the day off from scalping, deciding instead to take me on a tour of the area around Pitkin and Sutter Avenues where he grew up. This is the center of the East New York district, located at the northeast tip of Brooklyn just to the left of Brownsville and Bedford-Stuyvesant, roughly four miles from Flatbush. Spread before us is a scene of filthy, wreckage-strewn decay. It is a sobering vision, for people say Flatbush will soon be like East New York.

"This is where I shined shoes," Rodney states. Up and down

the street houses are scarred and unpainted, stores are boarded up with splintering plywood, apartment buildings are gutted, their shattered windows glaring like jagged teeth in old skulls. Dogs snoop in the gutters and papers twirl in the occasional whirlwinds. There are very few people about, which seems fitting, for this reminds one of nothing so much as a war zone.

Rodney trots down the street checking out places he used to know. He climbs into an abandoned building, and peering out through a second-floor window waves a salute to the world. At an aimlessly spraying fire hydrant he stops and gets a drink of water.

"We used to live above the liquor store over there," he points. "I remember going to sleep with the light flashing on and off."

On the sidewalk in front of the store a few wasted people wander, their faces hard, their eyes darting, a wariness to them like cattle who have lived too close to snakes and electric fences.

At the corner Rodney suddenly makes a left and heads down Sutter to Berriman Street where he knocks on the door of a ground-floor apartment. Anthony Harris, 6'8", 230 pounds, comes out wearing jeans and a Fairfield T-shirt like the other ones Rodney has distributed among his boys.

"It's the Mystery Man!" laughs Anthony, slapping Rodney's hand.

"How's things?"

Anthony settles down on the steps, taking the question seriously.

"I'll tell you, Rod," he says, "this is a crazy neighborhood. Last night I was sitting on the stoop, right here, and this guy walks by and says, 'What'd you say?' And I said, 'I didn't say nothing,' which I hadn't. He leaves and then about five minutes later I see him on the corner with his arm out straight, aiming down a gun at me. This girl I was sitting with went upstairs and got her .38, but I came inside, man."

Anthony spent last year at St. Francis College with Mario Donawa, and for a long time he couldn't adjust to the peace and quiet.

"It was like a big woods in the mountains where you just take a patch out and put a school there," he says. But recently the school has informed Anthony they don't want him back, even after his successful term at summer school. His attitude during the season hadn't been the best and then there was the business of his friend Mario abruptly transferring. Anthony is worried now.

Last summer at Foster Park Fly and some of the other players had been talking about junkies in their respective neighborhoods. Anthony had commented that heroin wasn't a problem where he lived. "All the junkies have been shot," he said. But this year is another story.

"See that Puerto Rican family on the porch over there," he asks. "The mom and dad and the kids? Every one of them's a junkie and every one of 'em's a dealer."

Rodney eases the young man's mind by telling him he's gotten a place for him at Paducah Junior College. "See? The man always takes care of you."

Anthony smiles and asks Rodney where the school is.

"I don't know, somewhere out there in Kentucky or whatever. Listen, I gotta go, man. Gotta finish my tour."

Rodney gets up and with his stubby legs churning once more, zips down the sidewalk, looking into old buildings and alleys.

Coming around the corner of Jerome and Belmont he proclaims, "Here's Jim McMillian's house."

He laughs because the entire block is missing, being nothing but a great brown field filled with craters and rusting, demolished things. McMillian himself had laughed, sadly, about the old neighborhood. "I went by to take a look at my old house," he told me, "and I had to check out the street signs to make sure I was in the right place. It was like after a bombing."

"Right there by that old car," says Rodney. "That's where he grew up."

Only a block away on Barbey Street Rodney comes to the apartment building where he lived with Myra from just after their marriage until they moved to Flatbush. He has no trouble spotting the location because "425 B" is whitewashed on one of the barricaded front windows. Graffiti covers the building, and the front door has been jimmied open.

We walk in and climb the littered stairways. Walls have caved in and chunks of plaster lie in the third-floor hallway directly below gaping holes in the roof. Rodney enters his old apartment and urinates on the floor of what used to be the bathroom. In his daughter Suzette's room a "shooting gallery" has been set up. There is a ratty mattress in the corner, a couple of chairs, empty matchbooks and beer cans strewn about, a broken hypodermic needle on the floor. Rodney looks in and then goes over to inspect the door jamb that leads to the main hallway.

"It's still here," he remarks, rubbing his hand along a crack in the wood. "The place where the first break-in happened. All they got was twenty bucks. The second time they got more."

Back on Pitkin Avenue Rodney stops at a sidewalk snack bar that is nothing more than a window opening on the street. The man working the grill is white, a prisoner from the old days, unable to sell his tiny business and not wealthy enough to move away.

"Hey, Rod," he cries. "How ya doing? Say, it's been a long time. Boy, I'll tell you I don't understand this game anymore. Remember when the parks used to be filled until ten at night? Now the baskets are all gone, they're all stolen. It's crazy. The world is crazy. They tried to rob me by coming through the roof the other night . . ."

The iron bars that close in front of the snack shop window are gouged and twisted as though they've stopped several runaway cars. "Just people trying to get in," says the man.

As Rodney and I walk back towards the subway line a young man decked out in flashy apparel and carrying a rectangular board filled with cheap earrings runs up to us. He seems very excited and Rodney's first response is to tell him he doesn't want to buy anything. Mine is to run.

"No, man," the young man says, his forehead glistening. "It's cool. See, uh, it's going around the neighborhood that there's like this dude, like, I mean are you the basketball scout that's going around?"

Rodney, flattered, says yeh, that must be him.

"Well, listen," the stranger says. "Here, I wanta—just a second, let me, you know, get rid of this. Don't go away."

He disappears up the block and comes running back without the board.

"See, I heard this scout was around who was hip to ball, and I was wondering, uh, can you just come down over here, man? The other dude, too."

The man leads us along the sidewalk, sweating profusely, making short, quick gestures of explanation. "I went out and got these guys, younger kids, you know, but they play ball. One of them's name is, uh, Eddie Johnson and he's nice—somebody ought to hook the dude up, see . . ."

We walk around a corner. Sitting on the curb and the trunk of a car are six or seven teen-agers. On the lefthand side of the street is a netless rim and plywood backboard nailed to a telephone pole. The boys stare up silently as the man points in their direction.

"That one in the blue shirt, that's Eddie," he says, gesturing for the boy to come over. "This is the scout, his name's uh . . . Rodney, yeh. How old are you, Eddie? Sixteen, okay. Hey, Rodney, help this kid. I mean he can definitely play . . ."

The sweating young jewelry salesman turns to the youth standing silently at attention. "Listen, man, don't stand here, get those guys up and do it."

Eddie Johnson, a dark, chiseled-featured youth with perfect white teeth, sprints back to the car, and immediately he and three other youths are locked in a fierce two-on-two battle.

Rodney sizes up the 5'11" teen-ager. He shows good quickness and a nice soft shot, but most important he displays a full-tilt hustle that frequently sends him flying over the treacherous curb into the walls of the building in pursuit of loose balls.

After the competition Rodney gives Eddie directions to Foster Park. The teen-ager nods his head solemnly over and over. "Stop by this Sunday around two o'clock," says Rodney. "And bring a couple friends." He hands the youth a dollar for subway fare.

Before leaving Rodney thanks the street peddler for setting up the exhibition.

"No man, dig, it ain't nothing," he says. "I see these guys, you know, out in the street and all, and I figure they can use a hook-up so I just keep my eyes open. Around here you can play ball and uh, just disappear. It's nothing. . . . Later, man. . . ." And he runs off.

On the way back we walk past the Liberty Avenue Park. Inside there is row after row of trim, deserted courts, a mysterious contrast to the crowded street corner baskets we've passed. It is hard for me to believe that boys would not use such elegant surroundings if they had the choice. I walk up and down the courts, but only after intense scrutiny do I realize why they are empty: there are no rims on any of the backboards. They get stolen as soon as they're put up, Rodney says.

LATE AUGUST

The Subway Stars have accepted a challenge to play an undefeated team of fifteen- and sixteen-year-olds coached by George Murden of the Bedford-Stuyvesant Restoration League. George is the man I met on the Fourth of July at Manhattan Beach. We had discussed the possibility of a game between his team and mine, and two days ago he had called me to confirm the plan. The game is set for one-thirty at a playground on Halsey Street in Bedford-Stuyvesant.

At eleven-thirty the Stars hold a brief meeting under the maple tree at Foster Park.

"Rick, I know George Murden," says Vance, "and that mother hates to lose."

"He'll be cheating," adds Pablo Billy. "Man, you know we gots to load up."

I look around at our ranks.

"Where's Champagne?" I ask.

"Oh, yeh," says Pontiac Carr. "I went over by his place this morning and he's gone. His whole family split."

"What do you mean?" I ask.

Pontiac shrugs.

"Rick," says Martin, noticing my concern, "around here with the way family situations are a lot of people just sorta come and go."

"So check this out," says Pablo Billy, "we better do some fast recruitin'."

All the players nod. They stare out at the courts and the sidewalk. Little Ernie is sitting on a bench not far away. I suggest maybe we pick him up—his stitches were removed and he has been able to play for several weeks.

The players shake their heads. "No, man," says Martin. "He can't help us. We need big men, forwards and centers." Ernie looks indifferent anyway, almost sleepy as he relaxes in the morning sun.

Martin snaps his fingers. "Ivory! We can get Ivory if he's not working at the shoe store."

Mark runs off to check. The Stars come up with two other players—Skeemo and a boy known as Captain Crunch. With Ivory, who arrives shortly, they feel they've got a powerhouse.

"If George asks," says Vance to the newcomers, "you all just sixteen." The players nod.

On the ride over the Subway Stars take up the last third of a city bus, singing and playing the dozens and pounding good-naturedly on DeMont, whose tattoo has taken on a deep purplish hue. As we walk towards the playground, however, silence prevails. In a halfhearted attempt at humor, the players form a "V" and tell me to walk inside it. "When they come after you," says Martin, "we'll go down fighting."

In formation we march past crumbling brownstones and garbage cans so full of trash that the containers are invisible under peaked mountains of debris. Still, some of the buildings are well-kept, evoking by their hard-earned stateliness a bygone era of respectability.

At the park itself the decay is manifest. Three of six rims are missing, the fences are bowed, garbage litters the area like leaves in a forest. The main court is so coated with glass fragments that it sparkles in the sun like a beach. All around the edges sit the locals, and as the Stars approach they begin their catcalls.

Everyone at the park seems angry, it appears to me, with sneers and frowns and evil looks creasing their dark faces. What they are angry at, I can't tell.

Nobody notices me. I feel as though I am invisible, the way I have felt on most of our ghetto trips. The Stars told me this is because people believe any white man crazy enough to come into the neighborhood must have things under control and therefore is of no concern to them. "See, you don't look like no cop," said Music Smith. "And you don't look like no social worker. So you gotta be a basketball coach. And that's cool."

After the Stars fumble around for a half hour, not quite knowing how to defend themselves from the heckling, George Murden arrives with a referee and a broom. After the sweeping I have the team begin lay-ups as we wait for the Restoration team. The first few players to come out of the adjacent school building look regal in their powder blue double-knit uniforms. But they are small, apparently only fifteen and sixteen years old as George said they would be, and the Stars grow confident. Sgt. Rock points a finger at the players and raises one fist. Ivory dunks the ball. Then Vance does, and Skeemo, and the others take fancy shots.

But then two more Restoration players trot around the corner, followed by four more. These boys are tall, agile, and solemn-looking and when they reach the court all twelve players begin a rhythmic hand-clapping and a patterned, muscular assault on the basket. One man stuffs the ball and then the next does, and the next, one after the other until the four shortest players run in and slap the backboard high above the rim.

Doodie has stopped shooting and stares slack-jawed at the other team. He grabs my arm. "Rick," he whispers, "that's some flying niggers."

The other Subway Stars are nearly as unsettled as Doodie. I'm not in much better shape. I wonder to myself it this is how coaches through the years have felt before playing the Boston Celtics or UCLA, whether they really believe it's "an honor to play the best" or whether they'd prefer a forfeit.

Before the game starts the Stars calm down. "If we screen the dudes out it don't matter how high they can jump," says Vance. All hands come into the circle and we give a cheer: "Do it!"

It becomes apparent from the opening tip, however, that the game will be no contest. The Restoration team is stronger, they have plays and discipline, there is no backtalk, they are taller, better coached—everything, as Martin points out, but older. At halftime the Stars are down by eighteen.

In the second half the lead widens, although the Stars make a few surges and provoke loud taunts from the hoodlums ringing the court. At the quarter I tell the Stars not to listen to the birds under the baskets.

"'Birds,'" says Martin. "I like that, Rick. Gimme five."

In the final minutes Pablo Billy angrily calls a time-out. On the sidelines he points at Doodie.

"This chump out there laughing," he shouts. "He takes a shot that don't even pull iron and then he's giggling down the court."

I ask what's going on.

"Well, this one dude's funny," says Doodie starting to laugh again, his big head and crossed eyes resembling a poorly carved pumpkin. "He hollered, 'Boo!' just when I'm letting fly with the ball and I sorta jerked and the ball goes over the rim. When I come down he say, 'Okay, wipe yourself now.'"

The game goes from a runaway to a slaughter and I begin to feel embarrassed, feeling as though people are watching me now and saying what's a honky doing around here if he can't coach any better than this.

I watch George Murden's style—berating his players, pushing them on, demanding silence, obedience—his eyes carrying always the threat of violence. He must be laughing at me, for the absurd looseness of my reign, for believing that anything but total control can come first. And it bothered me that as his players work and sweat and succeed they fill up with pride, the angry furrows disappear, and they become a unit molded from common suffering.

We had talked about our players, George and I, that day at the beach. I told him about all the problems I thought my kids had. He nodded and then told me he had players whose mothers were prostitutes, players who had been thieves, who had been beaten and battered as children, who were gang members, who lived in any household that would take them in. He told me how his wife came to games to serve as surrogate mother for boys who in their whole lives had never had a relative watch them play.

I watch his players as he scolds them during a break, see the respect that comes from being important enough to be scolded, and while I'm watching, the game ends.

On the bus ride home Vance complains that Pablo Billy never looks up when he dribbles.

"No goddam excuses!" I yell.

The players look at me oddly for a few moments. Nobody says anything the rest of the way home.

On Thursday Lionel Worrell had been talking about his season at the University of Michigan. "You know, man, in the Big Ten it's all politics. I should have started ahead of Grote, the white freshman guard. I had 14 points against UCLA in only ten minutes, but then they sat me down. Now though, it's gonna be just Danny-O and me up at Fairfield."

Shortly after that statement Lionel and some of the other players went to Manhattan with Rodney and played a pickup game watched by agent Lew Schaffel. The agent had been mightily impressed by Worrell and had sat down with him afterwards to discuss his career. At the end of the session Worrell had decided, on Lew's advice, to go not to Fairfield but to Oral Roberts University in Tulsa, Oklahoma.

Today Lionel is adamant about his new choice.

"See, Oral Roberts is more national exposure. They got this assistant coach, Draf Young, who's a guard specialist. He was with the Kansas City Kings and the Cincinnati Royals and he's worked with Norm Van Lier, Jimmy Walker, Archibald, the Big O. See, all I want is pro ball; college is just a stepping stone. I just want to get in the spotlight for a year and then get six figures. Even though I got to sit out a year Draf Young will be working with me and man, like Lew says, I'm a definite first-round pick once I show my stuff."

One of the players asks whether Oral Roberts isn't some kind of religious school.

"Well, yeh, you gotta wear a tie," says Lionel, "but it can be a bow tie. And you go to chapel twice a week but you ain't gotta pray. People, like, do homework and that. The alumni, they say, all have money and they take care of you for life, and there's never an empty seat in the gym."

Lionel, I feel, has been sold a bill of goods, but as I talk to him there's no shaking his conviction.

"Oral Roberts," he says again and again. "It's big time."

Yesterday Mario and Derrick Melvin became the first of the Foster Park players to leave for school. Their departure is a solid indication that summer is ending, and, to the many hopefuls in Foster Park, that it is getting desperately late.

A week ago Lloyd Hill had been swaggering through the park after hearing that Rodney was actually searching for a college for him. He pulled a hat down low over his eyes, stuck one arm down straight at his side, and bent the other in front of him with the palm loose, one finger pointing straight ahead, and strutted like a streetcorner slick. "Bring me them college entrance tests," he crowed. "I can't sign my name but I can pass them mothers. I'll lay my John Hancock down and it'll be nothing but a big damn X. Y'all can start calling me Lloyd of the campus."

But seeing Derrick and Mario leave, and with no more reports from Rodney, Lloyd's confidence has vanished. Though he doesn't like to talk about it, he has made no preparation for the exam or the reality of college life.

"Maybe I'll go home for a while," he says. "I haven't been feeling too good lately. I think I need to clean out for a while. I'm just a little sick. Too full of weed and wine. I'll be okay in a while."

Though few players know it, the departure of Mario and Derrick had not been the spectacular farewell most of them envisioned. Once again Mario had called Rodney from the airport.

"I don't know where Derrick is," he said. "And the plane's about ready to go."

Rodney flew into a lengthy rage that finally ended with him telling Mario simply to get on board and forget about Derrick. Moments later Rodney got a call from Derrick who mumbled something about making a wrong turn on the way to the airport. Rodney screamed at him, calling him everything vile and ungrateful he could think of.

Derrick listened to it all and then once again waited all day at the airport and caught a late plane to Tennessee.

Today Fly is returning from his tryout with the St. Louis Spirits. In a call late last night he had asked Country James to bring his car out to La Guardia around four o'clock.

At noon James stops at Foster Park and asks me if I'd like to go along with him. I accept, hoping that at the airport I perhaps can get Fly's first impressions of the disciplines of a pro camp.

On the way over to the Interboro Parkway James takes a leisurely detour through the Brownsville district of Brooklyn. The day is hot and sunny and the streets are crowded. When we stop to get some sodas people come up to James and call out, "Hey, James," "How you been, James," "It's everything, James," their tones filled with deference and respect.

James is a heavily muscled man with strong, ominous features, a presence that demands respect—something I can sense from my own feeling of safety as I walk by his side. But, the recent fight notwithstanding, he is an affable person, not prone to intimidation. His sense of humor and self-irony is well developed, a point which has helped cement his friendship with Fly; for Fly, when not wrapped in a defensive posture, is also a very funny man.

James first came to Brownsville at sixteen, after he and a friend had robbed an unlocked cigarette truck in South Carolina and then fled for the paradise of New York City.

"There was twelve hundred dollars in that bag," James chuckles, thinking back. "In *change*, man. We put it in a trunk and every time that Greyhound bus went around a corner, me and my friend liked to died. Lord, the racket!"

Like most other blacks up from the South, James went straight to Harlem where he'd heard there was magic in the air. He bought himself some new clothes and tried to imitate the dandies, but the veneer was transparent.

"Let's see, I got me a three-quarter length shirt and some sharkskin pants and some blue suede shoes—I swear to God, some real blue suede shoes with buckles on the sides. Elvis Presley was the thing then, man, and he had that song about not stepping on anybody's blue suede shoes and when some dude stepped on my shoes in the subway, I flattened him. I did, man. One of my first deeds in New York City.

"So then I wandered around thinking I'm city slick but everybody could see I'm a country bumpkin. I went to a pool hall somewhere around 116th Street, playing nine-ball, and got hustled so bad a blind man woulda died. I lost a thousand dollars in one night. My buddy panicked and took the next bus back to South Carolina."

Destitute and alone, James drifted finally to Brownsville where he began to make a living by his wits, gambling, selling marijuana, driving trucks, gradually rising in stature until he became a figure of success to the street corner population. He lived in the same project as Fly until 1971 when he moved to Flatbush. "The junkies had about closed the place down by then," he says.

We turn a corner and walk past an empty and locked sporting goods store. Through the window I can see that the right wall is still covered with an oil painting of Fly Williams, number 35, in his red and white Austin Peay uniform. The picture shows Fly as he rises beyond several hapless defenders en route to what will certainly be a rim-shattering stuff shot. A year ago I had seen this same store crowded with boys appraising the merchandise and the picture.

"Just after the owner got the place going, he got busted for pushing drugs," says James. "He's doing five to ten now."

Across the street I can see the raised mound that encloses The Hole. Above it stand several rows of shade trees laid out parallel to the court. Playing on the sunken basketball surface gives one the feeling of playing in a pit—hence the name.

But The Hole has other meanings: graffiti is scrawled over its entirety and filth lines its boundaries. Players there frequently find their palms bleeding from dribbling basketballs that have picked up too much glass. And it is not uncommon for games to be interrupted because of knife fights between players. At night the area often becomes the scene of shootings and gang fights.

Country James has played many games there with Fly and he shakes his head thinking back on them.

"You know, I have never seen Fly play what I would actually call 'good' in The Hole. He really goes off in Brownsville, goes wild. It's because he's still just a kid and he's into getting back and making guys look stupid. Like me, I grew up at sixteen, but Fly's twenty-one and maybe he won't grow up til he's twenty-five, maybe thirty. That may sound funny coming from a dude like me but it's true. It's that damn immature temper of his."

John Pulos used to call the difference between Fly on court and off "the difference of Jekyll and Hyde." Perhaps the most illustrative incident occurred at an away-game in prep school when Fly suddenly challenged the entire gymnasium to battle.

"He jumped on the scorer's table and starting swinging a chair around his head," recalls Pulos. "There were only about fifty of us and two thousand of them. Thank God my father leaped out of the stands and held him."

The reason for the excesses on court, James feels, is that basketball and its rewards mean everything to Fly. "It's like the *one thing* he knows how to do."

Ironically, the ghetto that spawned Fly's game plays an ambivalent role, for despite Fly's obsessively dramatic talk about its survival-of-the-fittest benefits, his rages point at a profound hatred of the ghetto world—a hatred sprung from fear.

At Glen Springs Fly played a decidedly tough-guy role. But John Pulos saw chinks in the armor. "There were little things," he says. "All the boys used to go to the cemetery at night and see who'd be the last one scared. Big brave Fly didn't last too long, though. He was afraid of the dark."

Another sign of some apparently deep-rooted fear is Fly's tendency to become almost uncontrollable when he senses imminent danger. Once in the dorm at Glen Springs he was horsing around with a fellow student when the boy playfully pulled out a knife. Fly backed up, his eyes became huge, his face turned ashen. "He just pointed and yelled 'Look at the knife!'" says Pulos. "Over and over. 'Look at the knife! Look at the knife! Look at the knife!'"

Country James at first was amazed that Fly, so obviously the city type, could be content at rural Austin Peay. Even Mrs. Williams was dumbfounded. "Two years in the South?" she marvelled. "He was born and raised in Brownsville but when I ask him he say 'Mama, I just like it.'"

"He not only liked it, he loved it," says James as we climb back into Fly's car and start off for the airport. "He loved that Tennessee atmosphere. If he gets some money, you know what he wants to do? He wants to buy a farm down there. He's always talking about it."

James turns on the air conditioner and rolls down the windows, the way he likes to travel.

"I'll tell you," he continues. "No matter what Fly has done, one thing is always there—he *loves* basketball. He'll play for nothing, all night long. I mean, I remember him with this sprained ankle, the doctor told him not to play for a week. But we're playing in The Hole and the action's good. He can't be still—he's mumbling and walking up and down the sideline. So I go for some water and when I come back he's out there playing. I had to physically drag him off.

"I've seen Fly so engrossed in games he doesn't know anything else is happening. It's like the time I saw Bill Bradley of the Knicks standing ten feet from Red Holzman and Holzman's yelling his head off for a time-out but Bradley can't hear a thing. He might as well been a million miles away. After nights when Fly gets like that he can barely walk off the court and go to bed."

James leans into the center of the car, gangster-style, and turns the radio up a few notches.

"One problem is he's got too much talent. Before games he'll check and see who's playing and then he'll set a goal for himself. Like he'll tell me, 'I'm getting thirty tonight,' or 'I'm getting forty,' and when he gets to thirty or forty or whatever, the rest is all showboat, he's done for the evening.

"Once for kicks I said, 'I'll bet you twenty dollars you can't score sixty points.' He worked like a dog and you know how many he got? Sixty-two. Another time, in the Rucker, he was playing this guy named Bubba Garrett who's like a superstar over there in Harlem. People told Fly, he'll score all over you because you can't play defense. Fly held him to twelve points."

John Pulos used to say that Fly did everything "a little bit harder" than any of the other boys. Once some of the Glen Springs students turned out the hall lights in the dorm and knocked on the head coach's door. When he came out they threw empty cans at his feet. But Fly threw a door knob that hit the coach in the head.

One other time Fly risked his neck by jumping from one third-floor window to another to take some beers off the coach's sill. "He denied doing it," Pulos recalled. "But we didn't even have to ask. We knew nobody else could have done it."

We pull into the La Guardia parking lot and go into the terminal to wait for Fly.

"The money really isn't important to Fly," says James lighting a cigarette. "I mean he just kicked that big bonus from Denver right in the ass. And the only reason he took his name out of the NBA draft was so he could set all the records at Austin Peay's new gym. He told me, real serious, he said, 'James, I want standing room only to see the Fly.' To him, that was *it*."

When Fly's flight comes in and he doesn't appear, James calls Mrs. Williams to see if something's wrong. Fly had called her long distance and he mentioned something about his bags going to La Guardia and him going to Kennedy or vice versa. But then he also said he might take another later flight or not come today at all.

James hangs up and smokes another cigarette, then he motions me back to the parking lot.

"The hell with him. He can take a cab."

On Tuesday morning Rodney talks to Leonard Hamilton, formerly on the staff at Austin Peay and now an assistant coach at Kentucky. Together they manage to scrape up three possible college scholarship offers to small schools. One will go for Doug Tollefson, a boy Rodney has been sporadically helping from another part of Brooklyn, one goes for Calvin Franks, and the third Rodney leaves tentatively open.

"I told one of the coaches everything about Franks except that he's crazy," says Rodney after the call. "He said he'd get in touch with Franks today. Maybe Franks can pull it off, who knows?"

Immediately after the last series of calls the phone rings again. This time it is the University of Michigan and they are hopping mad, having just learned that Lionel Worrell does not plan to return to school. They have called Rodney because they know his influence over the youth. A coach will be coming out, possibly tomorrow, to straighten things out.

"My God, do they want him back," screams Rodney as he heads out of the apartment to the park.

Just as the door is about to slam, the phone rings again and he darts back inside. This time it is Mario and Derrick calling from Murray State to tell Rodney how fantastic the school is.

"It's paradise," says Mario. "Air conditioning, carpets, good food, never mind the stereo." Derrick gets on and with great humility tries to express his gratitude. "Rodney," he says, "the situation is me."

Listening to the conversation I have to wonder what college really is like for these Brooklyn youths. Away from neighborhood confines for the first extended period of time, thrown into university environments dominated by whites with little comprehension of street behavior, the players must find themselves in strange land. Perhaps their whole personality changes to fit the surroundings; perhaps they return to smaller groups of similarly displaced blacks. At the larger, more cosmopolitan schools the change probably is not so dramatic. But at the Austin Peays and Murray States and St. Francises and Fairfields, where Rodney sends most of his players, the social climate occasionally must be so at odds with the experiences of ghetto life as to seem totally bizarre, if not incomprehensible.

A lot of the players Rodney helps return home quickly, burned out. Some like Mark Harris, who went to the school in Michigan, are unable even to explain their disenchantment. Others, like one 6′8″ forward Rodney helped to a scholarship, find that the unnatural atmosphere only makes ghetto vices more tempting. That particular player became a junkie.

But the ones who remain even for a year are changed. They are stronger and more mature, with outlooks tempered by perspective. Even Fly Williams mellowed during his career, though his status as superstar separated his experience from the others. And the magic of the college experience, with its dreams and possibilities of advancement, is passed on quietly to the younger boys by those who have returned. Indeed, all the pep talks in the world mean nothing compared to the subtle and powerful vibrations emanating from one player who has made it.

When Rodney finally arrives at the park, Henry Kinsey, another of his protéges and a junior in college, is waiting for him on the bench. He asks Rodney for forty dollars for plane fare to get back to school.

"See that," cries Rodney digging into his pocket, "these cheap-assed schools don't even give their players routine expenses."

He hands Henry forty dollars in crinkled ones and fives. He gives him a few words of advice and then makes a blessing over the youth's head.

Action like this makes Rodney wild, staccato, filled with blabbering enthusiasm. He charges around the park now with his hands clasped behind him, his head down, his jaw thrust forward.

"Who wants to go to college?" he yells. "Who's ready? Where's the talent? A strong finish. I'm losing my voice. The phone never stops ringing, coaches, high schools, prep schools, colleges. I'm closing like a motherfucker!"

Rodney scurries back into his apartment to call some players for a game he has organized at Billy Cunningham's Basketball Camp near New Brunswick, New Jersey. He calls Winston because he'll need a driver.

"Winston wants me to find him a lawyer because he says they're trying to deport him," says Rodney. "I can't be bothered with that stuff now. Winston's got no jump shot."

Around noon one of the coaches Rodney has contacted calls Calvin Franks at a friend's house. He talks with Franks about his SAT entrance exam test scores. Franks replies that he got 1500 on the test. The coach asks a few more questions and then says he needs to discuss some things with some other people. If he's still interested, he says, he'll call back right away.

The afternoon goes by and no call comes. In the early evening Rodney is gathering his group which includes Possum, Craig Martin, Anthony Harris, Eddie Campbell, Eddie Johnson, a player named Tyrone Davis from Boys High, and Rodney's most recent discovery, a visiting twenty-three-year-old Panamanian named Carlos Blackwood whom he spotted in the park. Franks rides by on a tiny girl's bicycle. "Ding ding," he says. "Taxi service. All aboard."

Rodney shakes his head. "He told the coach he had a 1500 on the SAT. My God, sixteen hundred's perfect! I could get him into Harvard Medical School with a 1500."

Franks rides by again, "Ding, ding. Aaaaaahh . . ."

"Well, I tried," says Rodney walking to Winston's car, making motions of washing his hands. "He can't get in anywhere, right? I'm finished."

Rodney whistles to Eddie Johnson who climbs in the back seat of the car. Eddie is nervous and excited, having been waiting in the park for several hours already.

He came to Foster Park last Saturday equally excited, bringing with him four other East New York teen-agers as Rodney had requested. Rodney had then demanded that I gather the Subway Stars for a game, which I did, reluctantly.

The Stars had not been planning on the game and so they played halfheartedly, sloppily. The East New York players, other than Eddie, were not very talented and very little could be gauged from the display.

Midway through the second quarter, however, Sgt. Rock and his tall, light-skinned opponent had words. Another minute went by and Sgt. Rock began to pummel the boy. Rodney rushed in.

"What's the matter with you," he yelled at Sgt. Rock. "What are you always fighting for? Are you sick or something?"

Sgt. Rock played grimly for the rest of the game, but as soon as it ended he once again attacked the player, cursing him and driving him from the park.

This time I ran in to find out what was going on.

Sgt. Rock turned to me angrily.

"What am I supposed to do when some Puerto Rican from another park comes in here and acts like that?"

"Like what?"

"Boning me all the time, and I live here."

"But the guy wasn't Puerto Rican."

"Rodney said, 'After the game you fight.' So I did. Nobody comes into the park and does that. Nobody tells me what to do."

Eddie Johnson had merely watched, saying nothing. He was a quiet kid, a hard worker, and I knew Rodney would have big plans for him in the future.

At the New Jersey game, however, in which All-Pro Billy Cunningham himself plays center for the other team, Rodney forgets about Eddie and screams praises for his other recent discovery, Carlos Blackwood.

"Carlos!" Rodney yells at the 6′4″, 200-pound forward after he rips a rebound out of the air, "You're an animal! You're killing them!"

On the ride back Rodney can speak of nothing else but the way Carlos has developed since he first started playing on the Foster Park West Indian court a few months ago. When the ride is about half over Rodney looks back at Eddie Johnson who has been forced to sit on the hump in the middle of the back seat. His knees are up around his chin and there is an anguished expression on his face.

"Wanna stretch your legs out on the console?" asks Rodney.

The boy beams; as he unfolds each knee a loud crack follows. I can't help wincing, knowing the pain of inflamed tendons and ligaments that comes from playing on pavement all summer. Eddie smiles now and, closing his eyes, rests his head by the back speaker and quietly hums himself to sleep.

In the other car containing Carlos, Possum, Anthony Harris, and Raymond, a park regular who came along just to watch, things don't go as well. A state patrol car follows them for ten minutes, then pulls the car over. One of the policemen rushes to the front, pulls his pistol, and tells Raymond to get out and hand over his driver's license. The other policeman guards the proceedings from the rear, his pistol also drawn.

Raymond, who has his hands in the air, says, "All right, I am going to lower my right hand and reach into my pants for my wallet. That's where my license is. I'll do it real slow. I don't want to be in no *accident*."

The troopers check Raymond thoroughly, and the other

players and the car. When they are finished one of them issues a
minor speeding ticket, and the patrol car drives off.

As Raymond heads back to Brooklyn he sighs. "It ain't
nothing unusual. Just some cops stopping some suspicious-
looking niggers on the New Jersey Turnpike."

At 8:30 A.M. Rodney nearly tears his front door off the
hinges, dashing out of the elevator and running two blocks to a
small apartment building on the south side of Foster Avenue.

Before he is a hundred feet away he is yelling, "Carlos! Carlos!
Come on out!" At the doorway Rodney pounds on the buzzer.
Sleepy-eyed, Carlos Blackwood pokes his head out of a screen-
less second-floor window.

"What is it? What's going on?" he asks.

"How long have you been in America?"

"About three months, I guess."

"Are you a citizen?"

"No."

"I don't care. Do you want to go to college?"

"Yeh, sure I do."

"Ever been to Waco, Texas?"

"Where?"

"Never mind. I got you a full ride to a school down there. You
got about fifteen minutes to catch the plane."

Carlos looks at Rodney and smiles, his gold front tooth
shining in the morning sun. Then he tilts his head and closes
one eye, staring as hard as he can at the man below him. He
leaves the window and dashes downstairs.

"Rodney, you're just slinging it. I can tell."

"Would I be playing jokes at this hour? You got about fourteen
minutes now."

Carlos stares at Rodney for another instant then sprints back
up to his room. While he is packing Rodney asks him if he has a
high school diploma. Carlos says, "Yeh, sort of," and throws out
a faded piece of paper resembling a photocopy of a cafeteria
menu.

"What the hell is this?" Rodney says. "It's in Hebrew or
something."

He shows the paper to the two boys who have followed him up from the park.

One of the boys looks at the piece of paper. "Something about . . . refer . . . refer-ation . . . well, I'd say maybe refrigerators. It's got his name in the middle, though."

"Carlos," hollers Rodney. "What's this about refrigerators?"

Carlos comes to the window. "It's 'refrigeration.' I was going to be an air-conditioner repairman in Panama."

On the way to the bus stop Rodney tells Carlos that the citizenship business will be taken care of in Texas. Then he asks him if he ever thought he'd go to college.

"No," says Carlos. "I just came here to visit for the summer. My parents were terrified of me being in New York. My mother told me never to sit in the window at night with the blinds open."

On his walk back to the park Rodney is filled with the magnitude of his power.

"I changed the guy's life. It's that simple. Think if he'd gone to a park a mile away. Next year coaches from everywhere will be begging me for players. I'll outfit the whole ghetto in T-shirts . . ."

When Rodney arrives at the park, however, a sobering vision is there. Jim Dutcher, the assistant coach at Michigan, and none too happy about circumstances concerning Lionel Worrell, stands nervously by the swings. As far as the Michigan people knew, Lionel left school in the spring with no animosity and no intentions of transferring. Something, they and Dutcher suspect, has happened since he left Ann Arbor.

"Rodney," says the coach with a dark, meaningful look, "I can't believe he didn't change his mind this summer. I don't know who's to blame but I'll tell you, Lionel belongs at Michigan. He had about as good a freshman year as anyone could have—sixth man on a Big Ten championship team, good grades, good student. Even after two o'clock road trips, he'd make his eight o'clock classes."

Coach Dutcher looks at Rodney, who paces back and forth in a small rectangle.

"Okay, he feels he should have played more," continues the

coach. "Hell, Grote, the kid he played behind, made Second Team All-Conference, he had three 22-plus games, against Indiana he had eleven rebounds. Rodney he's *good*. It's not that he's white. He's gonna be a pro, I mean there were days when he beat the crap out of Worrell."

The coach halts abruptly, fearing perhaps he has laid it on too thick.

"Don't get me wrong, Lionel figures big in our plans. He keeps talking about the Notre Dame game when Grote didn't play well. Okay, maybe he should have seen more action that game. It's over. This is a new year, I don't know who's going to start. A coach isn't going to hurt himself, is he?"

Rodney and Coach Dutcher argue about who has been influencing Lionel.

"Coach, I'll tell you straight," says Rodney. "He came to me and he said he was absolutely not going back to Michigan. Absolutely. So I helped him find alternatives."

"Well, Rodney," says Dutcher. "This is the freshman syndrome, never being satisfied. Transferring schools is just transferring problems."

In the midst of their debate Lionel himself rides into the park. He is wearing the same easy smile as always. Dutcher now is plainly distraught. He shakes hands with the young man, and Lionel's fingers nearly reach the coach's wrist.

"Lionel, what about my family, my job," he says in a weak attempt at humor, his smile disintegrating almost immediately. "You just made us the fifth best team in the conference."

Lionel explains that he's thought about the whole affair for a long time. "See, coach, I like you but Johnny Orr and I don't see eye to eye. It might be different if you was head coach. Oral Roberts is a better situation. I'm looking to the future."

"Who knows what the future will be," pleads the coach. "Maybe I will be head coach, maybe I'll be gone. At Oral Roberts lightning may strike the good man himself."

But there is no dissuading Lionel, and the coach, sensing this, prepares to leave. He stops in front of Rodney again; this time his words are bitter, rancorous.

"How long's that school been around? Four years? We've been

in existence a hundred and fifty-seven. Rodney, I don't want to see this kid back here in the park after two years."

He stares at Rodney, spins on his heel, and leaves.

In the evening I decide to take some time off and catch a movie. I walk down Flatbush Avenue to the theater across from Erasmus High School where *The Education of Sonny Carson* is playing.

As I move slowly down the darkened aisle I hear a "Yo, Rick," from one of the rows. Squinting my eyes I can see that it is Danny Odums, and next to him little Ernie. I step into the row and take a seat next to the players.

"Is this supposed to be a good flick?" I whisper.

"Yeh," says Ernie. "It's for real."

As I look at him slouched low in his seat, small as a twelve-year-old, it occurs to me that he has stopped bothering Rodney to send him to prep school. He seems to have made some realization, to have become less aggressive, perhaps more realistic about his potential. In the park he sits on the bench, looking vacant, his face unlined, seemingly without care or hope. The ebullience of the Subway Stars seems to mock him, though, and when he sees the team preparing to leave for a game he walks far away from the shouting and horseplay.

Last night I had noticed him sitting on a car hood reading a basketball preview magazine. I walked over to him and asked if I could see the magazine when he finished.

After a long time he gave it to me and I started thumbing through the pages. But something seemed wrong; all the players looked younger than they should have, and the information seemed incorrect. I looked at the date on the cover. The magazine was almost three years old.

"Damn, Ernie, did you see how old this thing is?"

"I know," he said, yawning and closing his eyes. "It don't matter."

The Sonny Carson movie plot is based on the real life adventures of Brooklyn criminal-gang-member-activist Sonny Carson, and its material covers places and things well known to all in the black audience. The big rumble scene takes place in

Prospect Park where Pablo Billy, Arthur, and Martin sometimes go to run. The desolate ghetto scenes are lifted unretouched from Brownsville and Bedford-Stuyvesant. The Jolly Stompers, Tomahawks, and Black Spades who receive thanks for their cooperation in the filming are quite real off screen as well.

Several times during the action Ernie sits up to yell, "There's Punky! There's Leroy! There's a couple of dudes I seen at the park!"

At the end of the movie Sonny Carson is released from prison, and returning home he finds his friends, his gang members, even his girlfriend wasting away on drugs. The people shuffle up to him, specter-like, grinning, scratching, spineless, begging for enough money to score.

Little Ernie sits low in his seat, smoking a cigarette. "That's a true story," he says. "Everything man, it's the truth. Ain't that the truth, Danny?"

Young Moses Malone is in the morning papers again today, this time making the front page of the *Daily News*. In a large photograph he stands with his arm outstretched next to portly, slick-haired Jim Collier, president of the Utah Stars of the ABA. Collier is expressing amazement over Moses' reach. Moses himself looks bewildered, with the sort of dazed uncertainly one sees frequently in the eyes of grand champion heifers.

Just a few weeks ago he had announced he would be going to the University of Maryland in the fall; today he has opted for a $1 million-plus contract with the Stars. Al McGuire, the head coach at Marquette, has stated that if someone could get an hour alone with Malone they could convince him he'd be the first black astronaut on the moon.

In the early afternoon Albert King, long absent from the Foster Park scene, calls Winston at work. Albert knows Moses from the Kutscher's All-Star game, and the thought of Moses being manipulated has him worried, has in fact touched on his own situation.

"I'm not going to do what Moses did," he says. "I'm not, Winston. I'm going to get good grades and then go to college. I'm not gonna be like that."

Over at the Noble Drew Ali Apartments in Brownsville, a low-income housing complex he developed himself, Joseph Jeffries-El stands in the parking lot next to his sepia Mercedes. His three-piece white suit and tan sunglasses give him the look of a model from the pages of *Ebony*. He holds his palm out and catches a few of the first drops of rain and then, motioning to Nathan Militzok, the white attorney who is helping with Fly's negotiations, he leads the way to a covered archway between two buildings.

Fly had stopped by twenty minutes ago and had talked for a while with Ruben Collins, Jocko Jackson, and a few of the other players who were waiting to go to a Moorish American League practice game in Queens. He stayed long enough to proclaim that if "Joe El says do something, I'll do it," but then he had left in his car saying he'd be right back.

"Make sure you hurry," said Joe El. "We have to get out to the game soon."

Now Joe El has told the other players to leave. As he waits, Nathan Militzok becomes restless. He is an intense, humorless man with a quick frown and a businessman's respect for punctuality. Earlier he had appraised Fly's situation: "There's no tomorrow, nobody's knocking on his door anymore. And I think he understands."

But as twenty minutes drags into a half hour and then forty minutes the attorney frowns more pointedly. "I'll tell you," he says, "some of these damn kids are in the toilet, ready to pull the chain."

Fly is off somewhere, cruising in his Cougar, the biggest symbol of status he has ever had. "He likes to pull up to stop lights and just look around," says Rodney. Even though Fly has no driver's license he has further car plans. Danny Odums, who just returned from a quick trip to Austin Peay, talked to a friend of Fly's at a local garage in Clarksville. "He was supposed to send Fly four new tires for his Cougar, but while I was there Fly called and said he didn't need them. He's got a Continental ordered."

Militzok paces back and forth and looks at his watch. He and Joe decide to leave without Fly in five minutes. The time goes painfully by. They wait another five minutes.

"I'm used to dealing with college players," says the attorney. "I mean guys who went four years, who are mature, who know what's up . . . I think these ghetto kids are afraid of failure, and that's why they subconsciously screw up.

"Take Joe Hammond over in Harlem, the big hero in the tradition of Herman the Helicopter, Manigault and the others. He had so many pro camps to show up at. But he never did. Why? Because if he didn't make it how could he go home? He wouldn't have the street rep in Harlem and the satisfied ego. And what else have these kids got besides their egos?

"I can trace it back to this great city shooter named Rabbit Walthour. He played in the old American League for a while, and everybody said he was the greatest guard ever. Then he tried out for the Boston Celtics and didn't make it. From there it was all downhill. He was in an institution for a while. He still turns up at a bar around 139th and Lenox, but he must weigh 270 pounds."

Joe El takes another look down the street and then, shaking his head, he and Nathan Militzok climb into the Mercedes and leave.

Shortly after the rain lets up the awards ceremony for the age-group basketball league is held at Foster Park. A small platform has been erected, and the presentations are made over a fuzzy p.a. system. A sizeable crowd has turned out and the air fills with applause and shouts of "all right" as the winners of each division are announced.

All goes well until the program reaches the final bracket, a division that featured two undefeated teams whose championship contest was repeatedly rained out. The players learn now that the one team that did not show up at the last rained-out contest is ruled the loser by forfeit. At first the losers only scream in protest. Then, one after another, they hold aloft their second-place trophies and smash them to the ground. For a long moment nobody does anything; only the angry players shout and move about.

Then a small boy dashes out and picks up the top half of a

shattered metal basketball player, looking at it for a moment before darting away.

Immediately another boy runs over to the wreckage; and soon the entire area is filled with children scrambling over one another for pieces of the broken awards. They quarrel and trade heads for bases and arms for basketballs, and when the asphalt is picked clean they dance around in triumph.

EARLY SEPTEMBER

For many of the Foster Park regulars the end of summer is a time to assess accomplishments, to measure against marks on hallway doors, to step on scales, to check opposition for the coming school year. But for others, such as Music Smith, it is a time like any other—cooler perhaps, but heralding no real changes, no new possibilities, no unique sensations.

Day after day Music sits on the bench and watches and talks. He reports to me anything he thinks is worth noticing, and from time to time we share a few beers. He comes early and leaves late. He plays in a few games and never seems to be far from any of the major park events. He chats with the younger kids and raps with the older ones, and he says that when it gets uncomfortable under the tree he'll probably try to find a job stocking shelves or something. The park for him is not a place to develop but somewhere to be.

Rodney, in one of his peak moments of enthusiasm, had asked Music if he wanted to go to college. Music had shaken his head bashfully. No, he didn't want to.

"Why? You're 6′4″. You can jump, you can shoot. I don't care if you only weigh 130 pounds."

Music had just shaken his head back and forth, thanking Rodney profusely, embarrassment in his eyes. College was the type of challenge Music had long ago deemed beyond his sphere, and like many others he now wants it to remain that way.

Having grown up in Brownsville his eye has always been more

on the street life, though the world of academia at times made a pleasant enough fantasy. He stopped carrying his *Psychology of Consciousness* book soon after the initial impression was made and now is careful not to mention academic advancement again for fear someone might take him seriously.

Today, as he sits in the near-deserted park, the canopy of the maple tree protecting him from the drizzle, he talks about what he knows best, the things he observes firsthand.

"There's things going down around here, man, that aren't so good. Things, like, that I don't figure you even notice. But see, there's something funny about the way certain dudes walk or talk or just are. A guy doesn't have to be bent all over in a deep nod for me to spot him, you know. I can tell a junkie from a hundred yards away. Lloyd can, too."

He says it so matter-of-factly that I don't even question him.

"Joey and some of those kids who go superfly, they're on it. Maybe not shooting, but snorting. Lloyd knows, he's seen it like me. And that guy Andre is one. You know him, the dude always laughin' and shufflin'. But the thing that surprised even me was the time about two weeks ago, yeh, it was a day almost like this, raining and nobody around, and me and little Ernie and this dude I'd never seen before were sitting on the bench.

"Well, this guy goes into the trash and gets a bottle cap and right away I figured something was up. Then he got a bottle and filled it with water and walked into the toilet over there. After a bit Ernie goes in, too. And then Ernie comes out rubbing his arm. He sits down and I ask him how he got so mellow. 'We did some dynamite weed,' he says. But no weed can make you like that.

"One time after that I started to talk to him about it and he said, 'Mind you own fucking business.' I haven't seen him around too much lately. I could be wrong but I don't think so, these dudes who keep their arms covered, it's happening, man. I'm here at nine o'clock in the morning until late at night and I just, like, see the stuff going down."

We sit and say nothing. I try to pretend as though I knew it all along.

* * *

Calvin Franks' mother has returned from New Orleans where she has been living for nearly a year. For the first time in a long while Calvin has a place to stay. The boys at the park joke to each other about Mooch not sleeping on doorsteps any more or gobbling down cockroaches.

But early in the morning Mrs. Franks calls Rodney, a desperate tone in her voice.

"Rodney, I been gone a while now and Lord, a change has come over Calvin. I seen him and I said, 'Calvin, what's happened to my boy?' I know he had a bad thing here with his stepfather. He's a rough man. But I can't understand why he turned so strange. He always was a quiet boy. Now he don't express himself like he should. I mean he brags and mouths off like he's trying to be brave. Do you know how I mean, Rodney? And he talks about you and college all the time but he's on the edge a doing nothin'. If he don't go this year he can sack it in. And you're the only man what can help."

Rodney explains how ungrateful Calvin has acted, how he didn't pay for his transcripts last year when he had a scholarship, how he won't get a job, how he has alienated all the coaches and scouts Rodney has tried to interest in the youth.

"He's thrown everything back in my face," says Rodney.

"Oh, I know, I know. But he sees everybody going to school, and Rodney, I can't help him no more. I got no money. I didn't have any for the transcripts last year. And Calvin can't stay here with me much longer."

Mrs. Franks pauses for a moment, as if trying to come up with a few answers, to her life perhaps, or to Calvin's. She asks a question instead.

"Why is it, Rodney? He used to have friends, lots of 'em, and they looked up to him. But it seems he just never grew into a man. I wish somebody could do something for him, Rodney. I'm gonna pray for Calvin."

At Foster Park the rain has made several of the courts unusable. On the streets, people's faces are becoming tighter and less filled with light. The pre-Labor Day block parties that have started up lack enthusiasm, and what frivolity there is seems forced.

In the morning Mac the park supervisor comes over to me bubbling with uncharacteristic enthusiasm. "Look at that," he says proudly. He points to the front number two court where a new rim has suddenly appeared on an empty blue backboard.

We both stare at the orange iron ring for several minutes, admiring it as though it were a just-unveiled sculpture. Beyond it I notice that the once clean handball walls are now covered with black, artistically uninspired graffiti. The clean handball walls had always been a source of pride to Mac. Now, as I point them out, Mac's cheerful expression fades. "Yeh, I know," he says sadly. "And I don't think the city will paint over those walls again."

Little Ernie has not been seen around the park for several days, and rumor of his involvement in something strange has begun circulating.

"He had another group he started hanging with," says Lloyd Hill. "Guys into purse snatching and other sick shit."

Most are aware it has something to do with drugs. During the last two days a pair of evil-looking men has come into the park carrying long, carved walking sticks which they impatiently beat against their legs as they slowly walk past the courts, looking in all directions. Music says they are drug dealers from another part of Brooklyn.

Yesterday Lloyd Hill played in his first game in nearly two weeks. He seemed to have little of his usual pep, depression obviously riding him like a stone. Most of the college players have gone and Lloyd's dream of following in their footsteps is returning to its old place in the dust at the back of his mind. "What's Rodney doing?" he asked one of the boys during a break. Nobody knew.

After the game Lloyd sat down, his face gloomy. "My body just hurts," he said. "My legs and my chest are all achy." He called one of the players over. "Am I just getting old? Maybe I'm just getting old and hurt."

Today Lloyd plays a game of taps with two little boys, his eyes darting off to scan the sidewalk after every half-hearted shot, searching for Rodney. He looks pathetic, surrounded by children half his age. After a time he wanders off to the diamond and watches some girls retrieve fly balls.

"I guess it'd all been better if I'd knew this was how it was gonna be," he says. "The diploma, well . . ."

Last week Rodney had commented that in Lloyd's entire family there probably weren't enough years for a high school diploma. Nor is there any chance now of taking the exam to receive an equivalency diploma. "He'll have to go to Coney Island and buy one," Rodney said.

"I thought somehow it would all be cool," says Lloyd, watching a girl pound one past third. "I guess I wanted it to be cool. Yeh, I guess I'm stupid."

He wanders back by the courts and then over to the deserted benches across from the swings. Some young boys are swinging so high they reach an angle parallel with the ground, like beams. On the upswing they slide from their seats and soar over the chain-line fence onto the piled-up rubber mats.

"I got to get out of the city," says Lloyd, suddenly looking afraid. "Winter's coming and I'll be doing the same damn thing, playing in centers during the day and getting messed up at night. Then pretty soon I'll start getting messed up in the day, too. But I know I got to get on my jump shot. I can't be standing and shooting my feets on the floor and all. Lionel showed me that; good players take my standing jump shot and throw it away. But in games around here nobody wants to check me and I do what I want.

"What'll happen is I'll probably get down with one of these bitches a few times and then she'll be getting all fat and pregnant like they do, real slick and all, saying, 'Oh, I didn't know it was going to happen.' Then what can I do? I can't say. 'Well, let's kill the little asshole.' And now winter is coming down. I'm looking around and I'm thinking where the hell is everybody? . . ."

* * *

Eddie Johnson returns to Foster Park today, but he leaves behind the tall, skinny "Puerto Rican" Sgt. Rock beat up after the last game. The group has come simply to play ball, not to fight, and they shoot around at a basket waiting for Rodney to set up the game.

Rodney, who looks tired with bags forming under his eyes and a slight stiffness in his gait, asks me to round up the Subway Stars. I relay the message to Pontiac Carr and he jogs out of the park. Rodney then takes a few of his patented thirty-footers, the same shot he built his mediocre playground career around over two decades ago. He watches four shots in a row go through, shakes his head. "I shoulda been a surgeon" he says, then walks over to the bench next to me and sits down.

He relaxes now, stretching in the sun and squinting his eyes to catch the action at every court. Boys come up to him and ask if he can get them in schools somewhere. "Yeh, yeh, quit bugging me. I'll ship this whole park off to college before I'm done."

Rodney has said that his payment is having coaches tell him he sent them a great one or seeing a boy like Danny Odums warming up in the smoke-filled light of Madison Square Garden. But this is also his reward; the local small fry pulling at his arms, pleading, showing through their subservience that he is a man of power and respect. "Rodney thrives on helping people he doesn't know," says Winston. "He'll give a bum a dollar before he'll give it to his wife."

The Subway Stars begin to drift into the park, coming from various directions, indicating by the haphazard pattern of arrival the route Pontiac Carr took.

I watch them change into their red shirts. Vance, growing stronger, taller, almost 6'4" now; Arthur, slender, the most agile of the boys, smiling more since his braces have come off; Martin and Pablo Billy, short and talkative; Sgt. Rock, barrel-chested, resembling a boxer more than a forward; Doodie, getting taller, skinnier and probably more stupid; Mark and the new kid Freddy, a smooth sixteen-year-old, both with long arms and untapped potential. I study the group, trying to envision what they will look like next summer after another year of growth.

"Eddie," says Rodney, "we'll have to find your team a fifth man so you can play these bums."

The Stars yell angrily at the insult but Rodney ignores them, bending over to tie a shoelace. He shuts his eyes and tilts his face into the warm, late summer rays. "This is ticket-scalping weather," he says fondly. "A man could do all right on a day like today, over at Shea, selling three-dollar grandstands for six bucks."

After a few minutes Rodney gets up to find Eddie's team a fifth player, somebody, preferably, that he will enjoy seeing in action. He scans all the courts, then looks out toward the park entrance.

He shades his eyes and leans forward. His mouth opens with the intensity of his gaze. His jaw goes slack. He shakes his head once and jumps to his feet. He sees Winston leaning against the fence. But next to Winston he sees a tall, angular figure wearing long pants and a light blue jacket. Rodney dashes ahead several yards and observes the circular Youth Games patch on the jacket, not even looking at the unmistakable features of the long, dark face now turning in his direction.

"The King . . ." he starts to yell but stops midway, trying hard to maintain the composure he has ordered for himself.

Albert King has been in the park for several minutes now, chatting with Winston who had a hunch the youth might show up after his unexpected phone call last week. Albert claimed he'd just had "nothing else to do today," but his cheerfulness hints at more.

I walk up to him, rather cautiously, and say hello. I tell him I hope he doesn't hold the incident at the agent's office against me.

"The thing at Schaffel's," he says, "I don't even known what it was about. I just forgot the whole thing. Let's not even bring it up."

Albert carries with him a huge AM-FM radio he bought with his earnings this summer, and when a favorite tune comes on he turns the volume to a roar and dances in place. "Rock-a the boat," he sings. "Don't tip the boat over. . . ."

The main reason Albert feels at ease is because, for the

moment at least, the recruiting war is over. Not knowing which of the dozens of fast-talking high-school scouts to believe, he trusted none of them. He enrolled instead at Fort Hamilton High School in the far southeast Bay Ridge section of Brooklyn. Located in a white neighborhood, the school is mediocre athletically, old, with poor facilities, and little sports interest. But it is where Albert's two older brothers went and it is soothingly low key. "Fort Hamilton accepted me, not a basketball player," says Albert. "I had to apply like a normal person. They didn't offer me nothing."

Now, with Rodney bouncing towards him Albert can joke about the old man's waddle and slap his open palm.

"Come on, Big Al," says Rodney. "I got a run all waiting for you."

The Subway Stars have been watching quietly from where they are warming up. Seeing that Albert King is going to play, they decide to hold a team meeting.

As I walk into the huddle I can't help recalling that just two weeks ago we had reached what I felt was perhaps our lowest point of the summer.

We had taken the subway to Central Park for a game, but finding no ready competition we were faced with the prospect of going home or playing an intrasquad game. Instead, I suggested we hold shooting contests and the winner of each contest would get a quarter, which I would provide. But the money element had unsettled the boys, and before the contests were half done, name-calling and fights broke out.

Then on the way back to the subway we stopped into a store on 85th Street, and despite my warnings the team went into their shoplifting routine. As I was walking out the door I happened to look back to see the owner holding a gun on Pablo Billy, Mark, and Doodie. Only through some very smooth talking were we able to get out with only having to pay for the stolen goods.

As the circle closes now, Vance looks at each of the players.

"Rodney's the man on our asses all year," he says, "and that's two of his favorite boys gonna be out there."

"He wants to put us down good," says Pablo Billy. "He thinks we're punks."

Martin steps in. "We been together for a whole summer now. This is our chance to show we learned something."

The boys all look at me.

My pre-game speeches haven't varied much all summer, and I can see no reason to change now. I tell them to play hard on defense and to pass the ball and to block out. But then I add a few lines, making this by far the longest speech of my career.

"You guys are right—this is a chance to show Rodney and Albert and Eddie Johnson and everybody else what you've learned. You can play as a team or you can play as a bunch of individuals, arguing and bitching at everybody else's mistakes. You guys are friends and teamwork is the greatest way to show friendship. That's why you should stick together, because each guy on this team is your buddy. And having buddies is what it's all about."

The players bring their hands in solemnly on top of mine to form a pile. We holler, "Do it!" and the first five take their places on court. The game will be to eighty by twos—fouls will be called and free throws will be shot.

After the opening tip the team with Eddie Johnson, Albert, and the East New York players moves to a quick lead, Albert clearing the boards and Eddie hitting from outside. Rodney, who acts as referee, can no longer suppress his glee. "Super move!" he cries. "The greatest! Albert the King!"

But the Subway Stars come right back, and Albert, for one, can see the intensity in their eyes and feel the seriousness in their elbows. He, personally, has nothing to prove out here, and he allows himself to be jostled more than he should. Vance and Sgt. Rock team up to screen him away from the basket while Pablo Billy and Martin harass him whenever he puts the ball on the ground. When Albert turns and sinks a long jump shot, Vance turns to him and yells, "That's your last free one!"

The Subway Stars race up and down, swarming and scrapping and passing like they never have. For the first time they don't lose their tempers or yell at each other after mistakes, directing their anger instead into the fundamentals of the game. They completely overwhelm Eddie Johnson who can do little but go repeatedly to Albert. For once the Stars make their opponents look disorganized.

I've had little to do with it. I'm not a coach; I know that completely now. I got over my anger after the George Murden game soon enough by reminding myself I'm really just an observer. Still, I can't help feeling a coach's pride as the Subway Stars come into the half leading 40-38.

We meet again in the tight circle. "We ain't gonna talk about it," says Vance. "We gonna do it."

As the second half starts and Vance drops in a fall-away over the flailing Albert, Rodney gives him a modest, "Good shot." When Arthur and then Mark throw some perfect assists, Rodney says, "Nice pass." Even when the much-despised Sgt. Rock pulls down a rebound in the middle of a leaping pack Rodney forces out a "Nice sky."

The Stars battle without let-up, coming to the sideline for substitution only when they are too exhausted to run. Doodie comes off the bench, Freddie does, and the pace stays the same. In the midst of the chaos Albert remains silent, ignoring the malfunctions of his team and simply ducking his head to sprint from one end to another. It's an attitude that can only be marveled at in a fourteen-year-old.

Soon Albert gets caught up in the energy transmitted from the Stars and begins attacking the boards, tapping in rebounds and throwing rifle outlet passes to Eddie Johnson. The confrontation between him and Vance brings old men to the fences. Vance is no longer a pushover, something I have witnessed personally. At the start of the summer I could handle him easily in one-on-one situations. But the last time I practiced against Vance he made me look like an old white fool, blocking my shots and leaping far above me for rebounds.

With the Stars leading 78-73, Albert takes a high pass from Eddie Johnson and whirls, catlike, to lay it in. One of his teammates hits a basket and the Subway Stars' lead has been cut to one, 78-77.

After a missed shot Albert gets the ball again in the lane. The only criticism observant coaches have made about his game is the same one they've made about his brother's—that occasionally he moves too fast for his defender, faking once, then again while the opponent is still reacting to the initial move. This is what happens now as Albert turns once, then spins back into Vance who, though off-balance, forces Albert to take a poor shot which hits the rim, bounces to the backboard, then out.

Mark snatches the rebound and outlets to Pablo Billy who passes to Martin. Martin dribbles to the baseline, then heads back out, stops, and hits a ten-footer to win the game, 80-77.

I sit on the ground on the sideline as the Stars go wild around me. "We showed that old man!" cries Sgt. Rock. The boys leap about like puppies, slapping each other and yelping. Rodney has quietly walked off the court to get a drink of water.

"Let's go spit in his face," says Pablo Billy, and the players all yell agreement. But as they continue to dance about, savoring the taste of victory, they begin to realize just how well they played, and why. And the vengeful looks slowly fade on their faces.

"No," says Martin finally. "No, let's just be cool and say nothing. He knows what happened. He saw it."

The Stars think this over and one by one nod their assent.

And as we leave the park for sodas, aside from some high-pitched jungle noises from Sgt. Rock, nobody says a word to Rodney.

Apprehensively, Lionel Worrell left for the University of Michigan two days ago. It was still in the athletic department's power to deny his request to leave and if that happened Lionel would be a man without a team; he had vowed he would not play at Michigan again.

Though no one at Foster Park heard from him, yesterday's edition of the *Michigan Daily* newspaper told the story.

The train has pulled out of town. Lionel "Main Train" Worrell, one of the more popular players ever to set foot in Crisler Arena, is transferring to Oral Roberts University in Tulsa, Oklahoma.

Wearing the blue beret that has become his trademark, Main Train paid one last visit to Ann Arbor yesterday to obtain his release and pick up his transcripts. It is unlikely that he will miss Ann Arbor very much.

"I just didn't like it here," Worrell said as he waited for his transcripts to be handed over to him. "The situation here—it just wasn't me. Ann Arbor is a difficult town to adjust to, particularly if you are from New York."

But Lew Schaffel, who along with Rodney had arranged the transfer, could have told them that the school and the place really were of no importance compared to Lionel's peace of mind.

"There was no way in the world he would have gone back," said Lew after Lionel had left Brooklyn. "Because he felt embarrassed there. He *knew* he had more talent than the other players. In fact, Campy Russell, their All-American center, used to say he was the second best player on the team. But he wasn't starting, and in the ghetto it's always the guy with the most talent who plays.

"Lionel sees his whole life, his whole future, in basketball. You could never explain to a ghetto kid like him that another player, particularly a white one, plays because of intangibles— 'because he follows the game plan, because he makes the team click.'"

Head Coach Johnny Orr, according to the paper, accepted Worrell's decision "with good grace."

I won't say whether he made the right decision or not. Only time will tell. If he gets his degree and plays regularly, he has made a wise move. But I'll tell you, to my mind, moving from Michigan to Oral Roberts is not sound judgement. But when you're young you make mistakes. You make 'em even when you're old.

Rodney walks down the sidewalk without his characteristic flair this morning, without the usual energy that seems to make his striding more than simply a way to get somewhere but an event in itself. He looks tired, haggard, almost grim. His bloodshot eyes point at too little sleep. His weary motion indicates a battle recently fought, more than likely over the telephone to places far away.

He turns the corner on East 26th Street and walks up to a decrepit three-story house, ringing the doorbell and standing motionless on the stoop. An elderly woman comes to the door.

"Is Lloyd here?" asks Rodney.

"I think he's still in bed, just a minute."

Rodney steps into the front room and within seconds Lloyd Hill stumbles down the stairs. He is wearing only a pair of Jockey shorts and his face is stupid with sleep. Seeing Rodney, Lloyd slows down, then proceeds very cautiously to the bottom step and onto the floor. Rodney has never been in his house before.

They confront each other and a look of near-terror fills Lloyd's eyes.

"No," says Lloyd. "Not me."

Rodney shakes his head slowly. Lloyd feels his way over a table and a lamp to the sofa, where he sits down. Incomprehension fills his face.

Rodney moves toward the steps and leans against the banister. Lloyd watches him the way a dog watches its master.

"A j.c. in Texas. I don't know if it's near Carlos. School's starting. Get your stuff."

Lloyd slowly rises from his seat and very cautiously climbs the stairs. He stops and looks back several times before he disappears.

It hadn't been easy. The task in its energy-depletion and challenge to pure, no-holds-barred salesmanship had equalled anything Rodney had ever done. School after school had asked about grades, diplomas, entrance scores, age, background, playing record—any of which meant a strikeout. Rodney began weeding out the obvious impossibilities—the big schools, the conference schools, the cautious schools, the worried, the disciplined, the high-budget, the local, the suspicious. He called friends everywhere for names of little-known, distant junior colleges. Many coaches he talked to said they'd be interested but it was too late. Most wanted at least a sketchy idea of Lloyd's scholastic career.

Finally late at night he got a coach with a thick Texas accent. The connection was poor, crackling and buzzing, but Rodney gave his story one more time.

"I've got this unbelievable 6'4", wiry, strong, quick leaper who can develop into a great one. He's mature because he's been out of school for a while. He's learned the ropes in park competition. He's a city ballplayer, but he loves the country, flowers and horses and everything. In fact, he plans to settle in a small town some day, possibly own a store or run a barber shop."

The coach asked about Lloyd's skills. "Where'd yuh say the boy played his ball?"

"In New York City. In the playgrounds and city leagues against the best competition in the world. Fly Williams, Lenny Wilkens, Jim McMillian, Albert King—he's played them all, he's done it to pros and All-Americans in Brooklyn, Queens, Harlem, the Bronx; he destroys people wherever he goes. He can dribble like a Globetrotter. The kid can rest his chin on the rim. They call him Highrise because he can dunk with his elbows . . ."

There had been silence for a moment followed by several buzzes and faint sounds of bells ringing.

"Hello? Yuh still there?" said the man.

"Yeh, coach."

"Uh, we've been lookin' for a good reboundin' forward and New Yo-wark's a nice place to get a boy from. Ah believe we'll take him. And you know grades aren't a real problem out here."

Rodney had made the necessary travel arrangements and then hung up, too tired to congratulate himself.

Just before he left for Murray State, Mario had shaken his head over Lloyd's plight. "How can he go to college? The way he is, the life he knows?"

Now as Lloyd moves through the house collecting his things, he speaks not a word. The magnitude of it all has silenced him. There is no mention by Rodney or him about the school or the circumstances. Everything is understood. This is Lloyd's one chance.

Rodney leaves and comes back an hour later. By this time Lloyd is sitting on the Hills' stained couch in his red shirt and green pants with the clear vinyl belt. Next to him are two shopping bags.

Rodney leads the way to the subway, giving the tight-lipped young man directions to the airport and instructions on where to pick up his prepaid ticket, where to transfer, what bus to take, who to look for in Texas. The farthest west Lloyd has ever been is Jersey City. They walk down into the station.

Rodney buys a token and slides it into the turnstile for Lloyd.

"You know?" Rodney says. And Lloyd looks at him with wide, innocent, streetwise, uncomprehending, yellowish eyes and nods. Rodney hands him twenty dollars and pushes him through the gate.

The train comes and Lloyd climbs on and looks out through the sliding doors. Rodney laughs out loud and raises his fist.

"Do it, baby!" he screams as the train pulls away from the platform. "Do it Lloyd! Tear 'em a new asshole!"

MID-SEPTEMBER

The park is virtually deserted. School started yesterday, and even the slicks and the dropouts have vanished, having relocated at pool halls and street corners where the action will continue regardless of class schedules.

The first tints of yellow have come to the big maple tree above the main bench. In the bright sun the change is almost imperceptible, but the leaves make a drier, clattering sound in the breeze, and someone who could remember the moist ripple of June would notice. The whole park seems bleached of its bright colors; the courts are disturbingly still without their usual crowd. Except for a few mothers with babies, some boys already playing hooky and a few old men, the park is empty.

I sit alone, thinking, among other things, about Albert King's return. Yesterday Albert had called Winston again and the two had laughed about their old recruiting trip to Pennsylvania. But after a few stories Albert had suddenly grown quiet.

"What's up?" Winston asked.

"Winston, I'm sorry."

"For what?"

"For what you won't get because of me, because I didn't go there."

Albert then told Winston that all summer people kept telling him Rodney was getting money for players and would try to sell him if he could. Albert didn't really believe it then and he doesn't believe it now, but he was just too confused for a long time.

Personally, I was never convinced that Rodney was not actually selling his players in the fashion of the traditional flesh peddlers—dangling out talent to see which hungry scout, coach, or alumni group would pay the most. But a recent visit to agent Lew Schaffel's had shown me otherwise.

The talk around the playgrounds had been that when Fly blew the reputed $1 million no-cut Denver contract he lost Rodney at least $100,000.

"We-ell," said Lew. "Realistically, I think if Fly had done things right he could have gotten more like a no-cut $500,000, and if Rodney had signed a split-deal with an agent he could have gotten half of ten percent or about $25,000. But here we didn't offer him a thing. Nothing. Oh, we might have given him a little something as a thank you when it was all over, but he didn't even ask for money."

What was it then that Rodney wanted?

"He wanted to be Fly's friend," said Lew.

In a small blurb in one of the New York papers today it says that Fly Williams signed with the St. Louis Spirits of the American Basketball League for $250,000.

In his plush office at his fire protection implement company Joseph Jeffries-El laughs loudly. His voice is filled with relief and playfulness.

"Oh, yes, Fly is going to take St. Louis by storm! Then next year we ask for the huge multimillion-dollar no-cut contract and Fly plays forever. I told him, 'Fly, you've got charisma. It's time to cut a record. If Joe Frazier and The Knockouts can do it, why can't you?"

Joe laughs again as though a great burden has been lifted from his soul.

"The paper said a quarter of a million?" he asks, smiling. "Well, you know how they like to excite the public. That's a real impressive figure."

Joe twiddles his fingers and then forms a cup on his desk. His smile lessens a bit in intensity.

"The truth of the matter is the guy is starving and barely has enough money to get to St. Louis. But he took his trunk with him so I think he plans to stay a while. Oh yes, about the Continental he had ordered. I told him to stick with the Cougar for now."

Before he left, Fly had been subdued, but not quite solemn. It was still unclear if the facts had really sunken in with force. There were lingering overtones of Fly against the world. "Yeh, I'll show them I'm worth more at the gate," he said. "I'll do it the hard way, the way I been doing it all my life."

A coach recently said of problem player Larry Fogle, the number one collegiate scorer in the nation last year, that during his whole career nobody ever told him how to act. Fly and Larry grew up within blocks of each other. But Fly has been told now, and in that respect there is nothing else anyone can do for him. He has even confronted the possibility of not making it.

"I'd be able to live somehow. In the ghetto there's a lot of people don't know where they're gonna get their next meal. A lot of people live day by day."

The day is shortly underway when the park maintenance man, a gimp-legged fellow who has worked at Foster almost as long as Mac, is out with his bag and poker cleaning the previous day's refuse. By 8:00 A.M. he has things reasonably shipshape, though kids on their way to school are already throwing out new litter.

One group comes by and a boy runs out in front of them. He holds a candy wrapper in his hand and spinning around as though dribbling, shouts. "Who'm I?"

"Earl the Pearl!" the boys cry.

Then he holds the wrapper over his head and rotates his arm like a cowboy twirling a rope, before throwing the paper to the ground.

"Who?"

"The Doctor! Doctor J!"

Next he holds the wrapper gently in his palm and lofts a slow hook shot towards an imaginary basket no higher than his head.

"Jabbar! Jabbar!" the boys shout, jumping in the air.

Then he does a double pirouette and rolls the candy wrapper off his outstretched fingertips like a coin.

"The Fly, man! The Fly!" And the whole group chatters and laughs, disappearing down the street.

After a while several old ladies make their way slowly into the park, trailing empty two-wheeled shopping carts. They rest near the wading pool, then gradually drift on towards the stores on Nostrand Avenue.

Just before 11:00 A.M. Rodney comes zipping down the sidewalk, moving in his bowlegged semi-jog that indicates business is at hand. He peers into the park, looking for anything of interest, sees me, waves, continues on.

I lounge back in my seat, watching Foster Park progress through a day, sifting memories and trying to store them away.

Mac the supervisor sits relaxing on a bench not far from me. Though there are no fields and few enough trees in the vicinity, this is still the start of Indian summer, and the once oppressive heat of the sun has become a comfort. Mac rubs his arm and looks at the freckles and deep, weather-beaten tan. In his nearly two decades of city employment he has accumulated forty-six weeks of unused paid-vacation time.

"Hell, I used to spend my off days out here," he says. "The kids aren't the same. Nothin's the same, but I still love this park."

Not until school lets out does the playground really begin to fill, and not until dinner time are there any high-level basketball games underway.

Around 6:30 P.M. members of the Subway Stars start to wander in. They come out of habit but also because they have designated tonight as their last official meeting. In all, six different high schools are represented by the team and it will be hard for the Stars to keep in touch during the school year. It is also my last night in Brooklyn and the boys had mentioned they'd sort of like to say good-bye.

They mill about and eventually meander onto a court since it is much easier to shoot baskets than to sit still. They don't have a ball at first, but Sgt. Rock solves that by taking one away from some smaller boys. When they scream in protest, Sgt. Rock thrusts out his chest and tells them he'll break their arms if they don't keep quiet.

The Stars chatter aimlessly since they have nothing specific to say, having come together not so much to do anything as to honor the vague feeling of unity that has surfaced since the Albert King game.

While they are on court the old German in the green hat makes his usual appearance. He walks over to his place on the bench by the park house and sits down backwards so he can watch the games going on two fences away from him. Fiddling with his radio, he sets it to a classical station and, finally pleased with the swarm of violins and resonating bassoons, begins to study the action. After a while he nods his head.

"This isn't bad but I like it best when those teams come from other parts of the city and they have challenge games. That's when you see them looking so graceful, so good to the eye."

He reaches over and readjusts his radio which has gone too treble.

"Well, I'll go soon. Next month to Florida. I'm hoping it's good there. I'm hoping also they have basketball down there. But why should they? There is so much grass in Florida."

The Subway Stars gravitate once again to the bench. Pontiac Carr walks over to me and makes an announcement.

"We've decided this should be kind of a party for you, Rick, you going away and all. And like, we have even decided this party needs some booze."

I mention that that's nice but that none of the players are near the legal age.

Pontiac dismisses this with a wave of his hand. "Hell, you know nobody cares around here."

He sits down next to me and there is a momentary pause. He leans in a little closer.

"Uh, the guys are a little short of cash. . . ."

I pull three dollars from my wallet and hand it to him, and he runs out of the park. Though Pontiac is smaller and younger-looking than everyone on the team except ballboy DeMont, he soon comes racing back to the bench with two six-packs of Miller High Life.

While he is passing the cans out to the team, two unsmiling men with wicked-looking clubs walk past our bench, eyeing the group closely. There is a darkness to them, an aura of evil that frightens the boys to silence.

"There go Ernie's men," whispers Vance.

The players watch the men move slowly among the courts, searching the faces of all they pass. They circle over to the baseball diamond before walking out through the far gate.

"Man, that little Ernie is stupid," says Sgt. Rock, when the men are gone. "Shooting dope and trying to be *it*. And we thought he wanted to be a ballplayer."

There is harsh irony in his words, an irony that hurts me by its accidental truth. I had liked Ernie just as I had liked almost everyone I had met in the park this summer. And now I can only wonder what would have happened if I'd been a bit more perceptive, if I'd let Ernie join the Subway Stars way back in June despite our eight-man quota or the fact that at five feet tall he probably couldn't have helped us. That such a small thing could be so important here in the ghetto is one of the most difficult realizations I have made.

"Sometimes he didn't play all that bad," says Martin, his tone almost one of eulogy.

The players ponder this briefly.

"Well, it doesn't matter because he'll die now," says Sgt. Rock.

"Yeh, if they find him they'll at least break his legs," says Pablo Billy.

The boys have lost their hesitancy over the beer and begin grappling for the last swallows in the remaining cans.

Music Smith has joined us, and with his radio blaring out soul music from WBLS the celebration takes a positive step forward. I send Pontiac Carr for more beer and when he returns the boys are discussing the merits of their respective high schools.

Doodie, who will be a sophomore, has enrolled at a school called Food and Maritime in Manhattan and tells everyone he's learning how to bake bread and measure ships. "Man, we go out in the Hudson River in dinghies. And our jerseys got a baker's hat in the middle. I had to get in a special reading class, too. I read good but I don't read fast."

At Erasmus only Vance and Mark got into the special basketball p.e. classes. Sgt. Rock didn't but he isn't upset.

"Rodney asked me to play on his team the other day and we didn't lose for two hours. He kept saying, 'Super move!' to me. Ever since we beat his boys he's biting on us. He even said he could maybe get some of us in a college."

Suddenly DeMont comes roaring down the pavement, his sneakers nearly touching the seat of his pants. He skids to a stop and makes a big show of wiping away sweat and looking around him as though being pursued by Satan's hounds. Two little friends pull up beside him.

"Wow, Rick, we just hit a man in the head with a rock," DeMont gasps. "Now we're gonna watch Joey and them roll that old wino going down the sidewalk. Come on, guys!"

And the trio tears out of the park.

The Subway Stars work on their second and third beers and do some free-lance dancing to the beat of The Stylistics and Kool and The Gang. Suddenly Sgt. Rock walks over to where Music Smith is sitting.

"Gimme that box," he says. He picks up the radio and walks over to me. "Rick, since this is your party we're gonna give you a present. We're gonna listen to some white music."

He thrusts the radio into my lap. I look around at the other players and see that they are all more or less in agreement. I spin the dial until I hear the Beatles finishing off "Hey, Jude." A few of the Stars wince but Sgt. Rock takes the radio and places it on the bench so all can hear.

Pontiac Carr's eyes are rapidly closing, and when he stands up to do some slow dancing he does a flurry of pirouettes instead.

"Next year, man," he proclaims, "you're going to see 'Subway Stars' on the walls of Brooklyn. By the season I'll have me a black doctor's bag loaded with a fifth of White Label. Rick, I'll keep these suckers *well*."

"And next year we all play twice as hard," adds Sgt. Rock.

"No more giving each other shit." He looks menacingly up and down the bench.

The boys nod and Doodie's head wobbles precariously on its stalk-like neck.

"I'm seeing purple cows," he says.

"That's great," says Pontiac, draining his beer.

"I'll tell you who's great and that's Martin Luther King," replies Doodie, looking around to gauge the impact of his statement. "He wanted the world to be like a big merry-go-round. He had a dream about it."

Martin falls off the bench, spilling his beer and spitting foam from his mouth.

"It's true," says Doodie, swiveling his head like a big doorknob. "And so was Robert Kennedy. He got black people into Central Park."

"So what," says Pontiac Carr.

"You can laugh, but you'd have been there, too. They was giving out free franks."

Martin climbs over the back of the bench and runs out ten yards. He slowly walks back, quaking with laughter.

"I'll tell you what I remember about Robert Kennedy," Martin says. "I was a kid visiting my aunt on 112th Street in Harlem and Kennedy and his crowd were marching by. I looked in the street and saw this pile of dog shit and when they walked past, that dog shit was gone. Because it was all over Kennedy's shoes."

Martin reaches out and slaps a few palms.

"Well," says Doodie, his face screwed up in thought, "if we had a president who liked sports more, maybe we'd have more basketball leagues.

On the sidewalk several giggling girls go clopping past in their four-inch platform heels.

"It's nights like this make you think about women," comments Pablo Billy abstractly.

"Yeh, I got a friend who says pussy taste just like spinach," adds Doodie.

Martin falls to the ground in a paroxysm of howls. "Oh, my God, somebody shut him up!"

"Doodie, you talk almost as crazy as Fly," says Vance.

Doodie tilts his head in confusion and shrugs, taking a sip of beer. The boys begin to get up and wander around, bumping into the fences.

One by one the players come over to me to shake my hand; we do the shake, clasp, squeeze soul grip that they taught me. Some of the boys are too bashful to say much. Arthur hangs his head. Pablo Billy winks.

Sgt. Rock comes up, looking slightly distraught. "Rick," he says. "That white music, it's so *sad*."

Then Doodie shakes my hand with great formality, and Pontiac Carr spins and slaps five.

When Martin comes up I start to reach out with the soul grip but he shakes his head. "Rick, you're our coach. But man, I gotta save some things for the black folks."

We shake like two businessmen, and I tell him I hope the Subway Stars keep going even though I won't be around.

"We're together," he says. "Count on it."

It is after 11:00 P.M. and the players start to leave the park in twos and threes, their arms around each other, noisy and full of intense camaraderie. I sit on the bench with Music Smith who remains behind. He is drunk, bent over his blasting radio which has secretively been switched back to soul, soundly asleep.

After a time I wander off to Rodney's apartment where he is relaxing in front of the television. He worked hard at the ballet today and the scalping action has worn him out. Calvin Franks rang the doorbell an hour ago but Myra Parker told him to go away and leave everyone alone.

On the table today's newspaper lies open to a column stating that Jim McMillian, Rodney's old neighbor and friend, has been voted the new captain of the Buffalo Braves of the NBA.

On the back of the apartment's front door is a red bumper sticker with a picture of Fly stuffing the ball. It reads "Fly With the Gov's." Next to that is a blue sticker that says simply, "Basketball—It's A Way of Life."

Rodney looks at Winston sitting in the chair beside him. He chuckles.

"Relax, Win, nobody's going to deport you. Don't I always solve everything? Hey, look at your shoes! Don't move."

Rodney disappears into his bedroom and after crashing about for a few minutes emerges with a small, trapezoidal box that appears to have been gnawed by beavers. It is stuffed with rags and bottles and trash, and on the top sits a tilted metal plate. Winston watches as Rodney digs into his twenty-five-year-old shoeshine box and pulls out some ancient polish.

"Put your foot out," orders Rodney. "My God, look at the condition of your shoe."

He slaps on some cleaner, then some paste and starts an old rag cracking. From reflex he snaps his thumb against the sole of Winston's shoe when he's done and quickly moves on to the next. He winces from a pain in his back but he throws the brush from hand to hand with the same razzle-dazzle that earned many a tip in East New York.

"I was good this summer, wasn't I, Winston?" he asks.

"Naw, you didn't do nothing."

Rodney isn't listening, and after putting the final sparkle on Winston's toe he stands up and puts his antique box away.

"I mean there's so much basketball," he says coming back and gazing at the TV. "So many kids. It's like there's no end. You know what I mean? Like it's all beginning, just one big beginning."

Nobody in the room is listening. Rodney stretches out again on the couch. His daughter Suzette comes up to him holding a piece of paper. "What about this?" she pouts. "You promised, Daddy."

The paper is a contract she wrote out and made Rodney sign, saying he would take the three children and Myra out for an evening of fun last Monday, no basketball games allowed. Monday night came and Rodney was down in the park watching games.

"Yeh, Suzette, we'll go out. Don't worry," he says. "We'll go to Coney Island or something. I promise."

Out in the hall the elevator opens with a clatter and three people get off, talking loudly, entering the apartment two doors from Rodney's. As I start to get in the elevator the light briefly illuminates a figure sitting in the shadows by the stairs. I walk over for a closer look.

The youth is staring straight ahead and is wearing a pair of badly scratched sunglasses pulled down low on his nose. I look closer and see he is talking softly to himself. Clutched in one hand he holds a battered, imitation-leather briefcase from which he occasionally draws a piece of paper which he scans and then carefully replaces. Calvin Franks is waiting to talk to Rodney about colleges.

There is nothing I can do now. Nothing left for me to do but to leave, to catch a plane home. I take the elevator down, step out past the broken apartment doors onto the street and head up to the park. I nod to everyone I pass, thinking that I know them all.

The basketball courts are deserted, though a few children are wandering near the baseball diamond, whispering to each other and lighting cigarettes. In the gutter a basketball half lies between two cars, staring up like an orange Cyclops eye, dribbled to death.

Music Smith is where I left him, slumped over his blaring radio, his mouth slightly ajar, a strand of saliva hanging like thread from his lip.

I don't know what to do so I just look at him. I look around. I pat Music on the shoulder. Then I walk away, the rhythm section behind me like a million basketballs whack-whacking on pavement.

EPILOGUE

I t would be a year before I had the chance to return to Foster Park. It was a hot late summer afternoon, the streets were crowded and nothing seemed to have changed. One of the first people I spotted was DeMont, a tiny figure walking up the sidewalk, his eyes on the pavement.

"Hey kid, watch where you're going," I muttered, stepping out of my way to bump into him. He balled his fists, took a step back and looked up in defiance. Then he squinted.

"Aw Rick," he said. "Aw Rick. I was wondering where the hell you were."

I had to come back. I had to see everybody, see what time had done.

DeMont and I headed over to the playground and even before we got in the gate I could see Rodney Parker refereeing a fast-paced game on the number one court. The players were good-sized, quick and hard-running. It took me several minutes to realize that one of the teams was comprised entirely of Subway Stars.

When the game ended they came over and greeted me. They looked older than I remembered and for some reason this astounded me. I caught myself starting to say stupid, grand-fatherly things about maturing and nutrition.

Pablo Billy and Martin were still about the same size but Mark had grown another inch and Doodie was at least 6'2" now, though no heavier. Vance's face was thinner, his shoulders broader, and he had skyrocketed to 6'5". I'd seen him in the game batting away shots and tearing down rebounds in heavy traffic. He was going to be a prize.

I asked the Stars where the rest of the team was. Arthur, they explained, had gotten a full ride to a junior college and had left only two days ago. Rodney had gotten him the scholarship. Pontiac Carr had moved out somewhere near Coney Island and nobody saw him much anymore. I asked about Sgt. Rock.

Hearing the name, Rodney came scuttling over to the bench. "Rock is the best player I've ever seen!" he cried. "He is super! He passes, he shoots, he rebounds, he hits the open man. He kills people in games, I mean he *kills* people." Rodney's eyes were squeezed shut from the force of his smile. The last I recalled he and Sgt. Rock were close to mortal enemies.

"I sent him to a j.c. down south. The coach absolutely loves the kid, says he's the strongest rebounder he's ever seen. Rock worked so hard this summer it was unbelievable. He really wanted school."

Rodney's other players were showing mixed results in their careers. Danny Odums had done well at Fairfield. Lionel Worrell had lost eight pounds at Oral Roberts in the first two weeks but had held on through the rest of the year even though he could not play because of his transfer status.

Derrick Melvin did all right at Murray State though Mario Donawa, despite his lofty ambitions, had dropped out. Carlos Blackwood was thriving at his college in Texas and had gotten his residency papers taken care of by some concerned fans.

As for himself Rodney Parker was still scalping tickets, still scouting basketball. One day at Shea Stadium I saw him receive a summons for scalping before a Jets game. As the cop wrote up the citation other policemen greeted Rodney by name, and one asked him to please see if he couldn't get his kid into college somewhere. "He's growing, Rod," said the man, pleading.

At the store across the street I bought everybody sodas. Music Smith came along and got a beer. The Subway Stars told me then that they had recently won the championship in the Senior Boys Division of the Foster Park Tournament. They had stuck together and worked out their problems and, as friends, had become successful. They felt bad, Pablo Billy admitted, because they didn't have a trophy to give to me.

I asked about Fly but nobody was sure what exactly had happened. I knew he had played sporadically for the St. Louis Spirits, riding the bench for long periods of time, then occasionally scoring 20 or more points in quick bursts of action. I also knew he was through in the big leagues, that he had been released, ostensibly for committing "too many turnovers," and that no one had picked him up. Some of the boys said they saw Fly in the neighborhood from time to time, usually riding in the Rolls with Country James.

Calvin Franks had vanished from the scene, and nobody seemed too concerned to find out where he had gone.

Lloyd Hill had lasted several months at school, but in the end the transition had been too much. His motivation deteriorated and he had returned to Foster Park and the pick-up games. His play had improved a notch or so, however, and people now mentioned that Lloyd had, after all, "played on a college team."

I didn't have to come to Brooklyn to learn of Albert King's success. One day in the Chicago papers I read that he had become the first sophomore since Lew Alcindor to be named a High School All-American. His brother, Bernard, a freshman at Tennessee, had led the Southeastern Conference in scoring the same season, and articles about him invariably mentioned his little brother Albert as being the best in the family. The pros, word had it, would be after Albert before he turned eighteen.

Little Ernie, a foot-and-a-half shorter than Albert and light years away in potential, had not reappeared in the neighborhood. I had hoped, for his sake, and, I realized more than a little, for my own personal comfort, that he might show up, scarred but better adjusted to the realities of this world. Around Foster Park, however, nobody expected to see him again.

POSTSCRIPT

Time passes. The way I see it sometimes is as a colorful scroll mounted on a wall that stretches into the distance. I walk swiftly along in a crowd next to the wall, watching as the patterns on the scroll change, fading in front of us and behind. People jabber. Memory and anticipation grapple with the things I see and hear at the moment, but there's no stopping to sort it out. Because we never stop.

It has been almost fourteen years since I spent my summer at Foster Park. *Heaven Is a Playground* is out of my hands now, a book complete and freestanding, a tiny section of the scroll. All the guys—myself included—are locked in our summer actions, all the shots falling the way they fell, all the raps and jive and fights and laughs and heartbreaks happening just the way they happened. But of course, we all have moved along as well.

Here I am, for instance, middle-aged, struggling to stay in shape, with three little daughters, a mortgage, a garage that needs painting, and all the rest. I play basketball whenever I can, but my knees and ankles are against it, and someday they are going to rebel completely. Basketball is an increasingly risky sport for an aging gym rat like me, but I don't care. I never worried whether the game was healthy or not. Pete Maravich was only a year older than I am right now when his heart gave out in a pickup game, so I know the risks. I have told my wife and friends not to mourn if I should die on court, but to hoist a glass and know I went out doing something that made me happy, particularly if I was pounding the boards and nailing the gimmes at the end. (It would be too much to ask that my j. was dropping, too.)

I think back on those days at Foster Park and I know now that they were among the happiest in my life. To wake up each morning and break out the paraphernalia for this book—tape recorder, notebooks, pens, subway tokens, sunglasses, basketball garb—and then just to go to the park and play all day long—God, what a gift!

How I still love the game. Even at a time when basketball is dominated almost prohibitively by great young black athletes, I see my niche in the sport. In fact, more than ever I say the hell with those solitary or country-club sports—jogging, tennis, racquetball, swimming, golf, aerobics; give me the thrill of three, four or five men working together like threads in a close weave. The sweat, the recurring decision to pass, shoot, dribble or simply freeze, the jumping, the necessary touching of other men—when it all blends I get carried to another place, transported beyond.

Since *Heaven* was first published, the two questions I get asked most often by readers are Where did I sleep that summer? and What happened to Fly Williams? To answer the first, I slept on a sleeping bag on the hardwood floor of Winston Karim's living room. Winston had a bed in his bedroom, but he had no other furniture. He'd get to it someday, he said. I put the seat down on the toilet and sat there to read the newspaper or write in my notebooks, and I stood up in the kitchen to eat cereal in the morning. I can't remember if I paid Winston anything for rent; probably not, because Winston is just a nice guy and because I had no money anyway. My advance against royalties on *Heaven* was $2,250, and I lived on that for most of the year.

I should note also that Winston still lives in that same apartment not far from Foster Park and is still a gracious host. Rodney Parker visits him often—Rodney has relocated to Los Angeles—as does Albert King when he is back from his NBA tours. Of course, when Rodney visits, Rodney sleeps in the bed and Winston takes a place out on the floor. "You know Rodney," Winston says. Certainly I do.

Fly Williams is another matter. He played for a while in the Eastern semipro leagues that offer vague hope to NBA pretenders and then, as everyone anticipated, he rapidly fell out. Last summer he was shotgunned on a Queens street by an off-duty court officer and charged with attempted robbery, unlawful imprisonment, criminal possession of a weapon, and menacing. He almost died in the hospital, but survived, with scars. Fly is a sports legend now—beyond me, beyond us all, a hero of failure—and his message will not be complete until he leaves this earth.

Little Ernie, the earnest little man, has already left us. He was killed in a drug-related deal. Using the phrase "drug-related" to describe a ghetto crime is almost a redundancy now, for there are virtually nothing but drug-related crimes these days. I recently wrote a long piece for *Sports Illustrated* on prison sports, visiting state and federal penitentiaries around the United States, and most prison officials estimated that over 75 percent of their inmate populations are doing time for drug-related offenses. That is, either they were buying, selling, using, or financing drugs during their crime, or else they were sending a "message" to others in the trade. Ernie was given the ultimate message. None of this makes his death any less tragic. For several years afterward the young men of Foster Park held an annual benefit tournament for Ernie; they printed up jackets and T-shirts with his name on them and ran boisterous full-court games to show their understanding of all that rips one from the flock.

Music Smith also is gone. He was stabbed to death by angry drug dudes. Indeed, the rumor is that his head was cut off in the mayhem.

Drugs—cocaine and its derivatives, particularly—have changed the structure of urban American society. They also have changed the city game. At its highest levels, basketball is still the black man's game—22 out of the 25 players in last February's NBA All-Star Game were black—but it is more and more the suburban and small-town game as well. In that recent All-Star Game only 8 athletes came from large cities, while 17 came from towns such as Leeds, Alabama, Summerfield, Louisiana, and French Lick, Indiana. Six players came from the rural Carolinas, while only prehistoric Kareem Abdul-Jabbar represented the very cradle of the city game, New York City. Two reasons for this change are that TV and collegiate integration have finally opened the game to all regardless of geography or race. Another is that drugs have changed many city playgrounds from battle zones to dead zones. Foster Park survives, but barely.

Just barely.

All is not gloomy with the original *Heaven* cast, however. Albert King, for one, is doing quite well. He is in his seventh NBA season—not a star, certainly, but productive—playing now for the Philadelphia 76ers. I talked with him recently in Milwaukee before a game with the Bucks and he laughed, noting that he was now older than I was when I wrote *Heaven*. "Fly?" he said, pondering that name for a moment. "A lot of people were like that in the ghetto. You have to see that there are other things to life than the environment you're in. Myself, I grew up pretty fast, with all the older people around me, but my home life was very old-fashioned. Playgrounds, homework, home life—that was my whole existence."

I noted that he and his brother, Bernard, once impoverished kids, now bring in over a million dollars a year between them.

"Money, it doesn't mean that much to me," he replied. "I never had any, so I didn't crave it. You know, my parents still live in the same neighborhood, same apartment in Fort Greene. They have roots there. They won't leave."

And was he happy, even though he had not become the superstar everyone said he would?

"I'm very happy. I have a lovely wife, been married four years. No kids yet, but one of these days. I am very much at peace."

It was time for him to get dressed, and we stood up and shook hands. "You were this size when you were fourteen, weren't you?" I said, wondering instinctively if I could box him out now, stop him in any way, maybe with a stiff elbow to the ribs. He smiled. "I'm a little heavier."

I turned to go.

"Hey, Rick," Albert said. He was smiling wide. "Remember 'Rock the Boat,' my song?"

I said I did.

He nodded, and I could see once again the shy, wide-eyed kid sweating in the August heat. "I still play it."

The Subway Stars have scattered the way young men will. DeMont is in prison for something or other, and Vance has had a hard time adjusting to life without basketball. But Martin, the leader, graduated from Brooklyn College, earned a master's degree at the University of North Carolina, and is now a community-planning analyst for the city of Portsmouth, Virginia. He's still in shape and at thirty plays in an employees' league in Portsmouth. "I don't have a gut, Rick," he told me proudly over the phone. "I'm five foot eight and three-quarters, but I love basketball."

I asked him to think back to that summer in Brooklyn, his sixteenth, and he said it was something he often did, though he steadfastly refused to dwell in the past. "Sometimes I think that, yeh, that's me—Martin—I beat Albert King on my jump shot. I underlined that in red. But I can attribute only so much to that summer, to making me what I am today. I had a family. Being on the Subway Stars sweetened the pot for me, is what it did."

And now that we could talk man to man—now that we were, in fact, communicating for the first time as two men—what had the Subway Stars really thought of me back then? "Honestly, Rick, we respected you. You didn't let us do a lot of punk stuff, and that meant a lot to us. We never said anything behind your back. Any bad vibes came from other guys who wanted to be in on a good thing. We defended you. And as far as we knew, there never was going to be a book, so that wasn't an issue. Now that there is a book, well, that's our legacy."

Old Martin. Thoughtful and clever. Meticulous. Bright. He gave me hell that summer, constantly made me confront my own failings. Pride is what he had. Self-esteem. He was a perfect gadfly.

"Rick," he said after a while. "I destroyed my Subway Stars shirts a while ago. I tore them up and shined my shoes with them. And last summer, I threw out my trophies. I don't want to be too philosophical about this, but I am no longer a child; I have grown. You know what I mean?"

I do. Of course I do. As time passes, I see the futility of clinging to old pieces of the scroll. All the people are here anyway, forever. All of us. And I think of Red Auerbach, the basketball wizard, who wants his epitaph to read, "He didn't come to play—he came to win."

That's nice, and it'll work for that crafty old curmudgeon. But I did come to play, I think. Heaven is a playground. So I'll go with the words chiseled into urban novelist Nelson Algren's tombstone: "The end is nothing. The road is all." On and on until it circles back. Like the game itself.

Rick Telander
CHICAGO, 1988